JUDAISM'S ENCOUNTER WITH AMERICAN SPORTS

THE MODERN JEWISH EXPERIENCE

PAULA HYMAN AND DEBORAH DASH MOORE, EDITORS

JUDAISM'S ENCOUNTER WITH AMERICAN SPORTS

Jeffrey S. Gurock

Indiana University Press
Bloomington & Indianapolis

This book is a publication of

Indiana University Press
601 North Morton Street
Bloomington, IN 47404-3797 USA

http://iupress.indiana.edu

Telephone orders   800-842-6796
Fax orders   812-855-7931
Orders by e-mail   IUORDER@INDIANA.EDU

The paper used in this publication meets the minimum requirements of American
National Standard for Information Sciences — Permanence of Paper for Printed
Library Materials, ANSI Z39.48-1984.

Manufactured in the United States of America

Library of Congress Cataloging-in-Publication Data

Gurock, Jeffrey S.
Judaism's encounter with American sports / Jeffrey S. Gurock.
p. cm. — (The modern Jewish experience)
Includes bibliographical references and index.
ISBN 0-253-34700-9 (cloth : alk. paper) 1. Jews — Sports — United States — History.
2. Jewish athletes — United States — History. 3. Jews — United States — Social life
and customs. 4. Judaism — United States — History. I. Title. II. Modern Jewish
experience (Bloomington, Ind.)
GV709.6.G87 2005
796'.089'924'073 — dc22
2005003012
1   2   3   4   5   10   09   08   07   06   05

FOR AUDREY SOFIA AND MIRA ABIGAIL

CONTENTS

ACKNOWLEDGMENTS

It is a pleasure to thank the many people who encouraged and assisted me in the writing of this book. Foremost among my academic colleagues, Professor Deborah Dash Moore started insisting, more than twenty years ago, that I had an important contribution to make to American Jewish history through a serious study of Judaism and sports. It is fitting that this book should appear now in a series on the modern Jewish experience that she edits so ably. I am also thankful that Janet Rabinowitch and her associates at Indiana University Press share Deborah's enthusiasm and belief in this subject. Early in my career, Professor David Berger also saw much merit in my topic and convinced the Memorial Foundation for Jewish Culture to grant me a research fellowship to begin my labors. I thank the foundation for its patience as I have finally brought this project to fruition. More recently, in 2001, Professor Jack Kugelmass's invitation to speak at his conference on "Jews, Sports and the Rites of Citizenship" spurred my efforts. A small portion of my research on Orthodox Jews and sports appears in his conference volume. Along the way, as my book took shape, Professors Stephen Whitfield, Riv-Ellen Prell, and Joanne Jacobson were uncommonly kind intellectual and emotional supporters. At my home institution, Yeshiva University, over the past few years, its distinguished Chancellor Dr. Norman Lamm patiently listened to my ideas. This scholar's untempered interest helped convince me that my work would intrigue students of all fields of Jewish studies. I also thank Yeshiva for awarding me its Murray and Madeline Baumel Faculty Incentive Grant in support of this study. Within my circle of personal friends outside of the academy, Mrs. Miriam Pfifferling and my City College of New York lacrosse alumni teammates stand out among those who share in the joy of this completed endeavor.

Several librarians and archivists have extended themselves in helping me uncover the resources necessary to research this book. At Yeshiva University's library and archive, Shulamith Berger, Zalman Alpert, Zvi Erenyi, and

Mary Ann Linahan were especially helpful. Norman Goldberg and Peter Robertson of the university's public affairs office helped out enormously with the photographs that appear in this book. Their colleague, Hedy Shulman, director of media relations, gave worthy advice and support in developing this study's themes. Lynne Slome of the Library of the American Jewish Historical Society, Steven Siegel of the 92nd Street Y's Library, Ruth Dancyger of Temple Tifereth Israel Archives (Cleveland, Ohio), Susan M. Melnick of the Rauh Jewish Archives Historical Society of Western Pennsylvania and Holly Teasdle, Rabbi Leo M. Franklin Archives, Temple Beth El (Detroit, Michigan), made important sources available from their institutional depositories. I am also grateful to my friend, David Vyorst, producer and director of the documentary film "The First Basket," for letting me use interview material from the rough cut of his film. I should also acknowledge the many individuals who readily agreed to be interviewed for this book. Their names appear in the endnotes, and the tapes of our discussions are on deposit in Yeshiva University's archive. Thanks also to Nachum Segal for facilitating my work in this area.

A scholar is fortunate when colleagues readily respond to questions in their areas of expertise and read sections of a work-in-progress. I am grateful that Professors Steven Fine, Gershon Hundert, David Fishman, Markus Wenninger, Mark Cohen, Yaakov Elman, and Ephraim Kanarfogel took time out from their own important research to improve my work. I am also privileged to have had Professors Benjamin Gampel, Riv-Ellen Prell, and Marc Lee Raphael review a penultimate draft. All these scholars' comments were, hopefully, incorporated correctly in this final version. All errors of fact or interpretation are mine alone.

Since the publication of my last book, several wonderful changes have taken place in my life. Sheri married Eli. Rosie and Michael have become adults and will be avid readers of this book. Audrey Sofia and Mira Abigail were born. Although neither is quite ready to read this study, I am thrilled to dedicate this book to them anyway. It is my way of telling them how much their presence in my life inspires their grandfather.

As always, Pamela is very happy that another project is completed. She more than any else knows how much this book means to me.

Riverdale, New York
September 2004

JUDAISM'S ENCOUNTER WITH AMERICAN SPORTS

PROLOGUE: A HISTORIAN'S CHALLENGE

My interest in writing a book on sports and Judaism dates back more than thirty years to a locker room incident in Lewisohn Stadium on the campus of the City College of New York. I was then in the midst of an undistinguished career as an attackman on "City's" lacrosse team. At halftime of another less-than-sparkling performance, my coach, George Baron, CCNY's one and only first team All-American lacrosse player and — as significant for this story — of Ukrainian-American extraction, turned to me in exasperation and said, "You know, Gurock, there is this *Encyclopedia of Jews in Sports.* I'm in it and you're never going to be in it." How did Baron make his way into Bernard Postal, Jesse Silver, and Roy Silver's volume? Seemingly, in their zeal to find and lionize every possibly Jewish sports figure identifiable or imaginable, they presumed that a fellow with a Jewish-sounding name who attended that predominantly Jewish school in the late 1940s had to be Jewish.[1]

Back then, I only despaired about my inability to compete with Coach Baron's record, of ever compiling the statistics necessary to play myself on to a celebratory book. I was not yet ready, nor sophisticated enough, to do Baron one better, to write my own sports book and thus find a way of putting myself front and center, if not as the subject, at least as the author of a reliable work on Jews and sports. Indeed, I had a long way to go before I would possess both the academic skills and the personal confidence as a professional historian to produce the book I was destined to author. While I played for Baron, I was just an undergraduate history major with no true sense of the scholarly field. Ironically, my learning what it really meant to be a historian — with all its attendant values and prejudices — deterred me, for many years, from attempting a book about Jews and sports. Early on in my graduate studies at Columbia University, I was made to understand, first of all, that scholars do not associate themselves with celebratory works. That was the province of apologists, ancestor-worshippers, and popularizers. The message was clear. If I, as a promising student of American Jewish history wanted myself or my field to be taken seriously, I had to steer away from any topic that suggested a Jewish cheering section. Too many works on this country's Jewish life — like Postal's and the Silvers' encyclopedia — possessed that unfortunate tone, even when they were not adding Gentiles to the lineup.

What the world of academe might countenance was a social history of an immigrant or ethnic group's adjustment to the American environment as seen through the metaphor of sports. The American culture of sports challenged millennia-old Jewish images, traditions, and values. How Jews in America dealt with ideas, symbols, and circumstances that were largely foreign in their prior historical experience could be a legitimate topic for scholarly exploration.

Yet whatever its intrinsic academic merit, writing about such a topic as a first, or as an early, scholarly endeavor would have been, career-wise, an extremely dicey move. At that time, in the early 1970s, even the best and most imaginative American Jewish historical works ran the risk of being dismissed by intellectually haughty classicists and medievalists as frivolous. In an era where a thoughtful examination of immigrant entrepreneurial endeavor in an outer-borough could be caricatured as a study of "breweries in Brooklyn," I was wary of being tarred through an association with such a lowbrow subject as sports. A dismissive doyen might chair a potential search committee, so I resolved to stay clear of a work that was close to my heart but would probably marginalize me in the academic marketplace. In the quest to be viewed as a serious scholar, I put my sports book on hold.

Besides that, to ensure a place for myself in the world of scholarship, I had another stereotype to overcome. Although I was far from a star athlete at City — George Baron could readily attest to that — at Columbia, among real eggheads, I was considered a jock, primarily since I talked incessantly about my just-completed playing days. I was also then starting my coaching career, working with junior high school basketball players. (I told everyone who might listen that I took that job in order to supplement my income. But those who knew me at all felt I was addressing a much deeper need.) When I was not talking about my college athletic achievements and my present ballclub's performances, I was apt to review, for my less-than-amused and less-than-interested colleagues, my views on the pressing sports topics of the day. Others would spend their lunch or other free hours bemoaning the state of the American short story or the fate of Spinozistic historiography. I preferred to explore and debate the impact of the upcoming National Football League draft on the future of the New York Giants. Finally, whenever I did speak with those around me about the travails of breaking into the world of academe, I resorted invariably to sports metaphors to explain our anxieties and predicaments. I would say, "graduate school is like a horse race on a very wet track. Mudders and not thoroughbreds are the first to make it to the finish line." I proudly, if insecurely, described myself as a mudder.

Such rhetoric led some of my fellow students to incorrectly assume that someone so engrossed with such mundane interests could not be an intellectual. I remember one green-eyed classmate commenting within earshot after I received kudos for a seminar paper on a nineteenth-century British Jewish intellectual, "That Gurock, all he ever talks about is sports. And he ends up writing a first class paper."

Years of personal reflection on comments like that have convinced me that those who raised their eyebrows about my idiosyncratic interests and persona were either intimidated by me or were manifesting a secular attenuation of a deep-seated traditional Jewish fear of physicality and aggressiveness. (We will concern ourselves with these notions in the course of this book.) I still trip over this tendency to make light of the "athletic other" whenever I attend a Jewish scholars' conference or meeting. Cracks and comments about "how all of my teams are doing" may also grow out of the general nastiness or competitiveness of colleagues who seek to probe at a perceived weak point in a competitor's background. It is a form of academic trash talk.

Typically, my rejoinder has been to act as if a serious question really has been posed to me, and I have forced my interlocutors to listen to my latest sports tale. By the 1990s, the sites for these encounters were usually the front lobbies of conference centers, where I, dressed in running clothes as befitting my new interest as a marathon runner, would drip sweat on my questioner as I offered a long-winded answer. Still, my professional ethic has been, until now, to be wary of overstepping my boundaries. I have studiously avoided making a vocation out of an avocation. Nonetheless, almost unconsciously, sports references have always popped up in my scholarship. Most recently, a friendly critic of my work on American Jewish religious life pointed out that no other historian uses as many sports-like terms as I do. For example, when evaluating Orthodox Jewish efforts in the 1950s to "litigate Judaism" against Conservative inroads in American legal courts,

I have argued that the traditionalists "won in places like Mount Clemens, Michigan, lost in areas like Cincinnati and Louisiana and held their opponents to a draw in North Hollywood, California." I know for certain that the easiest historical paragraphs for me to write are about political or interdenominational conflict. Terms like "crushed," "defeated," "margin of victory," "bullpen," "baseline," always pepper my prose.[2]

Meanwhile, as I was busy building a reputation as a scholar of American Judaism, other equally reliable, if obviously more courageous, historians risked their careers and began to develop the study of American Jewish sports as a legitimate field for academic exploration. Not that those celebratory tomes have been driven from the field. Today for example, Robert Slater's *Great Jews in Sports*,[3] written in the spirit of Postal's and the Silvers' well-intentioned encyclopedia, is still a common bar mitzvah gift. A number of Jewish sports halls of fame have been established in Israel and in this country. And board members of the American Jewish Historical Society have established an on-line American Jewish sports archive. To the minds of these sincere, if myopic, amateur historians, such a project would help Jewish youngsters feel a greater sense of pride in their Jewish background. To give them their sympathetic due, their communal objective is laudable, even if Jewish character building is not the job of the professional historian.

What sophisticated scholars have done is to raise American Jewish sports history to a much higher level. When they have done it well, they have used the experience of Jews on and off the field, track, or pool as a lens through which the larger dimensions of that group's life in America can be understood. Indeed, over the past two decades, a group of scholarly pioneers have begun to explore, rather than to extol, what sports have symbolized for Jews.

Two metaphors that others have used, and which have influenced me, immediately come to mind. Marty Glickman's exclusion from running in the Berlin Olympic Games has been drawn upon to effectively personify the sad saga of American Jewish powerlessness and marginality during the 1930s. The object of prejudice and deliberate discrimination, the young Jewish sprinter found he had no one to whom he could turn. Such proved too to be the fate of his people, in forthcoming years, worldwide. Indeed, the willingness of our country's self-appointed Olympic officials to readily kowtow to Nazi demands that they not be embarrassed by the presence of a Jew on the victory stand has been cast as anticipating our government's later, and far more horrible, acquiescence toward Hitler's murderous policies during the Second World War.[4]

Not incidentally, Glickman's lead antagonist, Avery Brundage, who in 1936 was head of the American delegation, eventually became president of the International Olympic Committee and presided over the 1972 Munich Games which witnessed Palestinian terrorists murder eleven Israeli athletes. One need go no further than Brundage's decision that the games continue, after only one day of mourning for the slain Jewish sportsmen, for a sense of how the world community then felt about Israel, in an era when the United Nations equated Zionism with racism.

In another related context, Hank Greenberg and Sandy Koufax's very different experiences with baseball and the Jewish High Holidays have been used to underscore the changing and improving social status of American Jews from the interwar period — Glickman's dark days — to the present. In 1934, in an uncaring if not intolerant America, general society demanded that Greenberg put the needs of his town's team ahead of his faith's commitments. (It is of some moment to me that the Detroit all-star first baseman has been widely extolled for his courage in staying away from the ballpark on Yom Kippur, when in fact, he actually succumbed to local and national pressures to compete during the High Holidays. One dispassionate historian has pointed out that Greenberg was told to play on Rosh Hashanah, when the pennant was still on the line, and he did. The slugger did stay away from the park a week later. But by that time his Tigers had reduced the "magic number" to clinch the flag to three with ten games to play and the pressure to perform was off.[5] That Jews then, and later on, were proud of even that limited statement of ethnic pride is also indicative of how that minority group saw itself and its possibilities within a less-than-fully hospitable world. The only historical note the *New York Times* took of Greenberg's absence was that "it was the first break this season in the ranks of the Detroit infielders, the four regulars having participated in all the 143 games up to today."[6]) In 1965, a far more understanding American society did not question Koufax's decision to stay away from the ballpark on Yom Kippur.[7]

Taking the tolerance metaphor one step, or one additional era, further, by 1986 Jews were so accepted, and so confident in this country, that some of them who were New York Mets fans had the chutzpah to protest to major league baseball officials about the scheduling of division championship games on the holiest day in the Jewish calendar. At that point, there were no Jewish players on the Mets although several of the owners were Jews. Why, they implicitly argued, were the "Lords of Baseball" so insensitive to Jewish religious traditions? Giving voice to the disaffected, sportswriter George Vecsey prophesied, only semi–tongue-in-cheek, that supernatural involvement would undo the sins of hardball's fathers. "It is going to rain," Vecsey predicted, "for 24 solid hours, children. A storm front is blowin' in the wind, untrackable on any human-built radarscope. Television and baseball have defied the fates by scheduling not one but two baseball games with 24 hours in the city that has the most Jewish residents of any city in the world. . . . Public officials are advised to prepare arks."[8]

In the end, the proprietors of the national pastime did not fold to Jewish complaints and it did not rain on October 12–13, 1986. Still, I have to think that this Jewish stance, promoting faith commitments over sports at sacred times during the year, undoubtedly was not lost upon New York's Archbishop. Indeed, in 1999, John Cardinal O'Connor spoke out, within his own community, against the major leagues' playing on Good Friday. Such an act, said his Eminence, "cheapens our culture, no matter how big the box-office receipts."[9]

Clearly, as these comments about Glickman, Greenberg, Koufax, and the Mets indicate, the proper use of legendary sports figures and events has deepened my appreciation of the American Jewish experience. I have learned from this emerging area of research that one cannot even begin to talk effectively about changing immigrant attitudes toward what it means to be a Jewish male or female in America without using sports as a major frame of reference. For example, thoughtful treatments on how masses of Jewish youths — boys and girls — learned the values of sports, recreation, and physical fitness, both in settlement houses and through more informal play in downtown streets, touch deeply on issues of intergenerational conflict. Jewish sports sagas remind us that youngsters acclimated themselves so much quicker than their parents to new cultural symbols and definitions of life, much to the consternation of their elders.

However, even as I have gained much from sports historians, I have remained, until now, largely on the sidelines, basically a non-participant or non-contributor to this field of study. Despite some prodding from friends within and without the academy who have suggested that I have something unique and important to say on this subject, I have, only once, overcome my reticence against merging my scholarly and personal agendas. A small part of my large-scale history of Yeshiva University, published in 1988, pauses to consider the role intercollegiate sports played in the 1950s and 1960s in defining the type of student this Orthodox institution sought to attract and the sort of public image it needed to project. However, I did not then really see myself as engaged in writing sports history.

That portion of *The Men and Women of Yeshiva*[10] acquired a life of its own when Peter Levine, author of *Ellis Island to Ebbets Field: Sport and the American Jewish Experience,* the most comprehensive book to date on our subject, cannibalized my work into his chapter on Jews and sports after the Second World War. Most significantly for me, he not only drew upon my work as a historian to flesh out his study, but he used my recollections and experiences with Yeshiva's basketball team as a quotable source. (By 1980, I had become — to quote Levine — "a history professor and sometimes assistant basketball coach at the institution."[11]) In any event, the exciting part was that my life in sports was now being chronicled; I was getting close to proving George Baron wrong.

It remained, ultimately, for a popular article I wrote several years ago to provide me with the motivation I needed to finally start work on "my book." At that point, I had a lot of fun with an autobiographical piece for a Jewish women's magazine about my experiences in training a young Orthodox woman for her first attempt at running the New York City Marathon. There, through my choice of words and images, I projected long-distance running as a religion with its own rituals, traditions, and sense of community to which devotees are committed. And I showed how my acolyte melded and/or reconciled her own deeply felt Jewish values and the demands of her real faith with her drive to pursue this most secular of activities.[12]

In so doing, I came to realize that there was a larger story for a scholar to tell, not so much about Jews and American sports, but about sports and American Judaism. Although the pioneers in this field have not been totally oblivious to this angle, I felt uniquely qualified to do that job comprehensively. For almost all of my work these past twenty years has examined some aspect of how the Jewish faith and its followers in America—particularly its more traditional elements—have dealt with the American social and cultural influences around them. Those who know my work will attest that I have posited over and over again that most Jewish religious actions in response to the American way of life can be construed or calibrated as within a "resistance vs. accommodation" continuum. I basically built my reputation on that singular observation. The impact of sports on American Judaism clearly falls within those lines.

The Jewish social, cultural, and religious encounter with America's world of teams and games is, thus, one serious topic worthy of all the analytical skills and gravitas a professional historian can bring to its study. And, if in writing this book I have also along the way fulfilled a less-than-stellar athlete's long-standing fantasy of intimate involvement with a sports book, my larger victory is ultimately an intellectual one. I am using my passion, my voice, and my metaphor to tell an important story of a heritage, its teachings, and the adjustment of its way of life to American realities.

INTRODUCTION:
SPORTS AND JUDAISM IN COMPETITION

The right to play on a team — what did we say as kids, the chance to be "chosen in" — is among the surest signs of an individual's or group's acceptance in a society. That is why the story of Glickman in Berlin looms so large in Jewish memory for what it says about a defining moment within an era when Jews were not allowed to participate fully in American life. But with that admission into an open, alternative community of athletes come a variety of strictures, commitments, and obligations that challenge ancestral faith and practice. For sports, in many ways, is a competing, secular religion complete with its own book of rules and holy in its own right. It possesses traditions to be followed, a lifestyle to be adhered to, central historical figures and personalities worthy of emulation, holidays — think of that American civic observance called Super Bowl Sunday — and even a belief system that speaks reverently about personal salvation at the end of days, the quest for immortality through victory at the finish line.

At its best, sports, like religion in its own most welcoming incarnation, have the capacity to unite disparate groups in brotherhood and sisterhood and to bring out love, empathy, and concern for others. My home town, New York City, elevates athletics to these ultimate heights every November when two million people congregate, as one community, in the city's streets and within its diverse ethnic neighborhoods to embrace participants in what has been called a "people's marathon." At the same time, when at its worst, sports' "fan-aticism" can tragically resemble religious extremism. Unconscionable stadium atrocities can occur when hooligans in the stands attack visiting players and their rooters for the sins of believing in, and striving for, a different ultimate result or destiny.

One immigrant Jewish writer expressed some of these very sentiments so well some eighty years ago, when, upon encountering big-time sports, he observed that "it was a highly developed cult, sprung out of the soil and the native spirit, and possessed of all the distinguishing characteristics of its type. It had a hierarchy and a symbolic ritual of its own . . . with all the solemnity and all the fervor and color of a religious service." For this novice, "all this was plainly not a game but a significant national worship, something akin to the high mass and the festival of Dionysus."[1]

The problem for Judaism with this belief system has been that, until very recently, the sports world's clock, calendar, and social group dynamics were highly inimical to the religious sensibilities of many Jews and most certainly their rabbis. When Jews were chosen in, they were admitted at the expense of their religion. Game or practice schedules that clashed with the Sabbath or Jewish holidays were an issue for all that hallowed that day. Meanwhile, for considerable numbers of Jewish minds, hearts, and stomachs, attractive, sumptuous, but patently unkosher training table meals beckoned Jews and undermined a different set of ancient faith obligations. And, for some Jewish ways of thinking, even if these hurdles could be surmounted, the daily time and effort sports required of its devotees to perfect their bodies to achieve success in the physical arena challenged, on an existential level, what Jewish life was supposed to be all about.

But nineteenth- and twentieth-century American rabbis, major protagonists in this book, were far from the first Jewish religious leaders to deal with the problems that the realm of athletics posed for their community. Sports' clashes with Judaism's values and way of life date back more than two millennia to a time when major athletic events, like the ancient Olympics, were far from secular jamborees. They were nothing less than "sacred games, staged in a sacred place and at a sacred festival . . . a religious act in honor of the deity."[2] It was then in Greco-Roman times that Hellenizing Jews used sports as a vehicle for integration, if not assimilation, into the wider culture around them. Here, early on, the enduring question of how one can engage in such activities that countenance neither Jewish religious demands nor teachings initially emerged. It was also before the Common Era that the rabbis first sought solutions to these dilemmas, because from that moment on for a Jew to be a practicing athlete, or even to be intrigued by arena events, called for a degree of personal detachment — and for some it was a statement of profound dissent — from Jewish life. The curbs and remedies that were conceived during this first engagement also anticipated what modern rabbis would say or do.

The clashes inherent in sports disappeared from Jewish concerns during the long Middle Ages, reflecting the impossibility of that group's acceptance within a hostile world. The only difficult decisions medieval rabbis made had to do with determining how much informal recreation they would permit within their religious societies, especially on Judaism's holy days. To borrow a sports phrase, the Middle Ages were a "time-out" for Judaism's problems with sports. But ancient concerns have revived and intensified in the past three or four centuries as modern Jews fought their way toward full acceptance within general society.

Adumbrations of the tensions were already visible in Renaissance Italy as Jewish athletic types, acting as their Gentile neighbors did, crossed over religious boundaries. There, one very early modern rabbi looked for ways to mitigate Judaism's problem with sports. Then, in the centuries that followed, most notably in nineteenth-century Germany, some Jews used their proficiency in, or at least their enthusiasm for, athletic combat to battle resistance against their participation in elite society. Elsewhere, in more comfortable and convenient settings, like England, Jews slowly became involved in the sports scene as part of their sharing the interests of those with whom they were living. In either case, Jews often played their games, fought their bouts, or ran their races at the expense of their traditions and heritages. And what became true in the different European venues was magnified many times over in the United States, where in the past century or so, sports have become extraordinarily meaningful to Jews. Here, more than in any other place, Jews became enamored with sports either as participants or as fans. And with that almost universal popularity have come many dilemmas, all related to Jews finding a place for their traditions as they embraced great American pastimes. The decisions Jews and their religious institutions have made about these problems are at the core of our considerations.

The history of American Jewish athletes playing rather than praying, consuming instead of abstaining, or even dedicating themselves too much to physical attainments, forms a backdrop to this book. However, no less worthy of scrutiny is the question of how Jews who possessed some degree of religious feeling — but not enough to keep them off the diamond on Saturday morning or out of the locker room the rest of the week — worked through their choices with themselves and with those around them who might have disapproved. This pattern of religious non-observance, the phenomenon of "slipping away," is no different from the more commonly chronicled story of Jews who fully immersed themselves in other cultural pursuits to the chagrin of an older generation. The young boxing fan who looked forward to going out Friday night to a prizefight had the same sorts of problems with her temple-going parents as did the adolescent opera buff who was determined to make his eight o'clock curtain. How these youngsters dealt with their elders is an element common to both lifestyles.

The history of the defensive strategies that American Judaism's leaders have employed to defeat these offending tendencies is also crucial to this study. What did rabbis and lay leaders do, through their synagogues and schools, when it became abundantly clear that most of their youngsters would rather be part of their new sports community than remain within their religious group? There is a long and unique history of American Judaism's accommodations to the problems engendered by mass Jewish clamor for sports. No other group of modern Jews went so far down this route. I must also emphasize here my intentional use of the term "accommodations" in the plural. Given their own definitions of the demands and constraints Jewish tradition imposes upon the modern Jew, different brands of Orthodox, Conservative, Reform, and Reconstructionist spokespeople have each harbored unique apprehensions of sports' threat to the faith. Here's the basic lineup: All religious leaders have been perturbed over what sports have done to synagogue attendance and Sabbath observance. But only Conservative and Orthodox rabbis have had issues with the non-kosher training tables. And the dilemma over whether to let boys and girls play ball at all, or to play together, resides solely within the realm of some, but not all, Orthodox Jews.

However, notwithstanding their varying degrees of concern, almost all Jewish religious movements have long agreed that a game plan exists for fighting back against the corrosive spirit of sports. Only the most Orthodox of Jews have not adopted the following strategy. The widespread notion has been to create space for sports within religious institutions in the hope that those who initially came to a shul's gym to play might be convinced to repair to its sanctuary to pray. To use sports to lead athletes toward and not away from Judaism has required that those who would teach the faith have had to be more than just conversant with the world of fun and games. Spiritual leaders have had to be as proficient and respected in the playground as in the pulpit, to counter the clout of secular coaches and managers. They also have had to be able to fight a more subtle battle against those who offered sports programming within nominally Jewish environments, ethnic settings that were largely devoid of religious values. And all the while, these "regular guy" — and today "regular gal" — rabbis would have to answer naysayers who deemed their actions as somehow an unwarranted invasion of the sacred space of the synagogue.

Rabbi Solomon Schechter, the first twentieth-century leader of Conservative Judaism, probably said it best for all such Jewish religious activists when he declared that "unless you can play baseball, you will never get to be a rabbi in America." But he was neither the first, nor ultimately the most important, advocate for the cause. A quarter-century earlier, some American Reform rabbis, concerned that their young people experienced "Judaism" only in a social club, were already integrating sports into the lives of their congregants. Soon after Schechter spoke, the young Jewish Theological Seminary of America graduate Mordecai M. Kaplan promoted the incipient Temple/Jewish Center idea and made it that century's central Jewish institution. In the generation following Kaplan's emergence, American Orthodox rabbis not only made statements comparable to Schechter's, but acted in a way reminiscent of Kaplan as they too sought to reach out to American Jewish youth. For more than fifty years, rabbis trained at Yeshiva University's theological seminary used their knowledge of sports, and their ability to play ball, as a means of proving to themselves and to the world that they were not part of a transplanted eastern European Jewish culture, a turnoff to modern kids. Rather, they were Orthodox all-American boys in step with the times. Ultimately, Yeshiva's rabbi–athlete–sports enthusiasts became invaluable institutional standard-bearers in its mid-century battle against both assimilation and the men of the Jewish Theological Seminary of America for the souls of the acculturated.

This remarkable transformation of the persona and lifestyle of this specific type of American yeshiva student *cum* jock leads immediately to another critical realm of Jewish religion-sports decision making. What are the limits, if any, to Orthodox Jewish countenancing of sports within its community?

In most instances, whenever a member of this small and most traditionally observant segment of American Jews engaged in sports, he — and in more recent days she — did so with the demands of his faith's clock, calendar, and cafeteria clearly in mind. This, of course, set him apart from most other American Jews. Incidentally, I said "in most instances" because there were always renegades within that group who might have slipped away surreptitiously to play ball on the Sabbath and holidays. Indeed, not long ago, a columnist for a local New York Jewish newspaper satirized this long-standing and noticeable phenomenon — for those who might look — among Jews who do their "jogging before shul [while] avoiding the main thoroughfares" or who "slink . . . through [the] lobby on Shabbat afternoon en route to Central Park but loathe to run into a neighbor." These individuals might carbo-load on snacks that promised increased energy and staying power but were not exactingly kosher.[3]

In all events, the very act of playing ball, even under controlled Orthodox auspices and with all due deference to the Jewish legal system (halacha), constituted a break with past mores and a challenge to those who still hallowed the culture of eastern European religious society. For a century ago, sports were totally unheard of in the cloistered yeshiva environment. Even recreational activities and organized physical training were undervalued, as its educational mission was to perfect the minds of its disciples — to produce the rarified talmudic scholar, the *talmid chacham* —with little regard for physical attributes. If it was true that premodern Judaism always hallowed intellectual pursuits at the expense of physical endeavors, it was in eighteenth- and nineteenth-century Russia and Poland that this tradition had its most profound recent incarnation. And yet in America, the reality was that even the "best learning boys" were also American youngsters and found themselves, like all other fellows, caught up in a new world of activity.

Evidently, somewhere along the road, and I will paint that line, a decision was made at Yeshiva University to accept and even to praise the synthesis of sports and Orthodoxy. But the terms of that community's approbation were neither absolute nor unchanging. Most importantly, the rise, and more recently the decline, of the athlete's role as an institutional standard-bearer — and even of coeducational activities — speaks of that school's ongoing encounter with the modern world around it.

This question of limits, of establishing a baseline for the integration of sports into an Orthodox lifestyle, is also pertinent to other religious elements which have not been as open as Yeshiva University came to be — and still basically is — to American culture. A culture of concession evolved within the so-called "yeshiva world" to sports, that irresistible American force stronger than it. Forms of physical training, organized recreation, and even athletic competition became part of much of the twentieth-century history of almost all schools ostensibly founded to recreate, as unchanged as possible, the religious environment of eastern Europe. That by the close of the millennium, some elements within the yeshiva world community, in a shift away from twentieth-century trends, would come to consider not only sporting interests, but even affinities for recreation and physical fitness, as undesirable traits for its members reflects fundamental shifts in a traditional community's attitudes both toward modern culture and the larger Jewish polity.

As another sign of contemporary times within American Judaism, sports became a battleground issue pitting modern Orthodox day schools against Conservative-based Solomon Schechter schools which sought admission into Orthodox-run leagues. Once more, basic American Jewish religious conflicts were played out in the athletic forum. The buzzwords of the present era, "non-recognition," "delegitimization," "deviant movements," and "negative influences," were all expressed in explaining the unwillingness of some Orthodox schools to officially countenance their Conservative counterparts, even in a sports venue. These conflicts and decisions — regarding who would be chosen in — reflect the strains within recent American Jewish religious life.

This examination of what sports has meant to, and said about, American Judaism also includes and concludes with an athlete's-eye view of the challenges of assimilation and the possibilities for sustained religious commitment within the contemporary Jewish community. In a most accepting American society, it is more possible than ever for the sports-minded to drift away and become fully part of America's teams, losing all regard for Jewish group ties. At the same, a very tolerant twenty-first-century America has made it easier than before, for those who are interested, to make it in the sporting world while keeping faith with Jewish traditions. Yom Kippur is a day off for almost any Jewish athlete who wants it. The same can be said, in some exceptional cases, about Sabbath observance. For example, there is a Russian-American Jewish boxer who is keeping the Sabbath while moving up in the welterweight ranks. There is, likewise, a Jewish kid from Worcester, Mass., who in 2002 was applauded by both Jews and Gentiles for absenting himself from a crucial Little League World Series game until sundown Saturday night, the conclusion of the Jewish Sabbath. And then there is hoopster Tamir Goodman, a Baltimore yeshiva student who, beginning in 1999, was touted as so proficient on the hardwood that big-time college basketball was reportedly ready to change the way it did business to make this observant young man feel comfortable within its midst. A fantasy world, not to mention a media frenzy, was created around Goodman's persona and athletic prowess as his story became the subject of intense national Jewish and general public attention. His saga serves, in its own right, as a most useful gauge both of Jewish acceptance within present-day American society and the extent of sports' pervasiveness within so many segments of the Jewish community.

1

FROM ANCIENT STRUGGLES THROUGH
A MEDIEVAL TIME-OUT

The world of sports has always placed the physical and aggressive competitor on its highest pedestal. Judaism has never honored the athlete as its quintessential man or woman. If anything, the universe of the gymnasium or the stadium often has been deemed as troubling to Jewish religious values and teachings. For sure, beginning with biblical sources and legends, the tradition does identify, and sometimes nods approvingly, at Jewish physical specimens. Throughout the ages, Jews were told that Moses, in his initial appearance as a defender of Jews, "smote," with his hands or with a sword, an Egyptian who "was beating a Hebrew, one of his people." Soon thereafter, during his exile to Midian, he confronted a group of shepherds who were intimidating Jethro's daughters, a physical act that must have impressed his future wife, Zipporah. Samson earned legendary fame when he triumphed, for a while, over thousands of Philistine opponents, with his weapon of choice, a jawbone of an ass. And Saul, the first "captain over his people Israel," was praised not only for his comely appearance, but also because "from his shoulders upward he was taller than any of the people."[1]

As a lifesaving device, the Talmud does require a father to teach his son to swim. And, living as they did in an early agricultural society, Jews of that era (like everyone else) had to have strong muscles to work their fields, if only to survive. Throughout the ages, rabbinical sources encouraged Jews to be physically fit to more properly observe the commandments. Maimonides, the great twelfth- and thirteenth-century philosopher, legalist, and physician, probably made that point best when he asserted that "a man should aim to maintain physical health and vigor in order that his soul may be upright in a condition to know God." Toward that end, he admonished that "if one leads a sedentary life and does not take exercise . . . even if he eats wholesome food and takes care of himself in accordance with medical rules, he will throughout his life be subject to aches and pains and his strength will fail him." But neither swim instructors nor health food enthusiasts were ever enshrined in Judaism's highest pantheon of heroes.[2]

Jacob, the scholarly man of the tents, was always the rabbis' favorite Jew. Now this earliest yeshiva student — rabbinic homiletic memory has it that he learned in the primordial religious school of Shem and Ever — was strong enough to roll off a large stone from Laban's well. His prowess also seems to have impressed the young women of his time. And this peripatetic of Jewish forefathers had his real — or dream-sequence — physical confrontation with an angel. He may have limped away from this bout with the first recorded athletic hamstring injury. Not incidentally, third century C.E. Rabbi Hama bar Haninah would compare this encounter "to an athlete who was wrestling with a royal prince; lifting up his eyes and seeing the king standing near him, he threw himself before him." Still, Jacob was projected within and throughout Jewish tradition as the ideal Jew through his passive mode. Only in the twentieth century would an avant-garde rabbi suggest that Jacob might have been the first Jewish scholar-athlete. Until then, he was always the benign, introspective individual, fundamentally different from his foil, Esau, the man of the field. Figuratively speaking, his brother was the aggressive and often immoral hunter, or maybe we would say today the star outfielder who was in and out of trouble with the law.[3]

More important, so long as formal sports were associated with ancient religious rites and symbols, Jewish athletes were denigrated as deviants who wanted to separate themselves from the Jewish way of life, or at least to play loose and fast with the traditions. Just how profound — and how widespread — was the players' disaffection from their ancestral past is impossible to tell. Accounts differed from place to place and from source to source, depending in part on how angry the scribes were with the sportsmen's behavior both on and off the field. Predictably, the pro-Maccabbean chroniclers of the second century B.C.E. revolt castigated the followers of "that godless Jason — no High Priest he!" as "Israel's lawless men" for abandoning the temple's sanctuary and sacrifices "to take part in the unlawful displays held in the palaestra," the stadium. In so doing, those who "sold themselves to do evil," set "at naught what their fathers honored." As these Hasmonean heralds told it, so "keen" were these apostates "to be joined to the Gentiles in every detail" that those with the greatest passion "for Greek fashions" went so far as to reverse their circumcisions. Mattahias and Judah's publicists and polemicists hammered their Jewish opponents for having brought down God's punishment upon all Judeans. In a word, "sore distress befell them . . . for it is no light matter to act impiously against the laws of God." ("Sore" certainly is an evocative adjective applicable to those who started Jewish troubles when they brazenly attempted to reattach their foreskins.)[4]

However, a closer look at these apocryphal stories — with assistance from modern Jewish scholarship — suggests that these ardent athletic assimilationists were themselves somewhat exceptional figures within their contemporary Jewish societies. Most ancient Jewish sportsmen were deeply conflicted. They were, in fact, the first Jews who attempted the difficult challenge of finding a comfortable place for their faith's ideas and commitments within a sporting world whose practices and values did not comport with Jewish religious teachings. So, for example, 2 Maccabees relates, right after its excoriation of "vile" Jason's dishonoring of Jewish tradition, that the high priest sent a delegation to an athletic competition in Tyre with the specific instruction to participate in a cult closely associated with ancient sports events. They were "to represent Jerusalem with three hundred drachmas of silver for the sacrifice of Heracles." But apparently — if modern research has it right — those sent on the road trip did not share Jason's proclivities and thus dedicated their "entrance" fees "to fit out the triremes" — galleys or warships — and not to honor a Greek god. Today's scholarship also feels that only "in isolated cases" did Jewish athletes attempt to reverse or disguise their circumcisions.[5]

Nonetheless, Judaism's strictures and prohibitions still were a burden for those who sought to prove — through their sports skills — that they were on a par with all other civilized men in the theater of the greater Greco-Roman world. (I said "men" here intentionally because while, as we will see, informal "ball playing" was not unknown to Jewish girls and women of that epoch, since formal contests — Olympics and the like — were for men only, Jewish women and their Gentile counterparts had to have been, at most, spectators.)[6]

The dilemmas of competing commitments were felt most strongly within the Jewish upper classes. Until well into the Common Era, in places like Alexandria, Egypt, a gymnasium education was a prerequisite for the coveted right of citizenship. There, parents, with vaunted ambitions for their sons, sent them to these Greek schools where athletic achievement was valued even beyond career preparation or even knowledge of the classics as they fulfilled their avowed mission of raising up the total Hellenized man. Upon graduation, those who were fully exposed to the Greek way of life often stayed close to their alma maters that were "the equivalent to the modern country club," high membership fees included. And we can also project that, just like today, much social and business intercourse was performed before, during, and after workouts.[7]

But, in seeking advancement within a larger world, religious concerns and conflicts inevitably plagued Jewish ephebes. Everywhere a young student turned in the gymnasium, he could not help but see statues of the patron gods of sports. More than that, Jewish gentlemen-in-training, as team members, marched in Greek religious processions, sang anthems, and otherwise tossed incense at the feet of foreign deities. And what were the best Jewish sports stars to do when they were invited to participate in "the great games of Olympia and Delphi?"[8] In each of the cases, we might reasonably imagine, Jewish athletes who publicly saluted the gods were not necessarily radical religious deviants. They were just trying to fit in comfortably within the culture of the ancient world.[9]

One possible solution to these problems might have been the creation of separate Jewish sports clubs where young men could play like Greeks without praying like their teammates. And, in fact, there is some evidence, from Hypaipa, near Sardis, in what is modern-day Turkey, that an organization of this kind may have existed among the Hellenized Jews of the late second-century–early third-century C.E. period. If so, then these acculturated Jewish citizens of the ancient world would have adumbrated an answer to the challenge of sports that coreligionists would embrace almost two millennia later in another highly assimilated culture. They proved their physical mettle in a Jewish environment, maybe even against Gentile competitors.[10]

Jews of that same early time and region may even have gone one additional step in anticipating how some American Jews would deal with the impact of sports on their own religious faith and community. Archeological excavations of second- and third-century Sardis have revealed the existence of a synagogue in a prime urban location near "the gymnasium complex" and within the main "colonnaded street" of the city. "Dedicatory inscriptions" in Greek honoring "proud, prosperous and highly respected" Jews with names like Polyhippos or Pegasios or Sokrates certainly attest to how Hellenized were these ancient synagogue-goers. Unfortunately, we do not know if those upper-class Jews, who paid for elements of the sanctuary, also used the gymnasium and were able, somehow, to reconcile their competing interests. But the Jewish institution's placement so close to the sports center makes us wonder whether a primitive expression of the "shul with a pool" concept is almost two thousand years old![11]

We do know for sure that the rabbis of the Greco-Roman period were well aware of the pervasiveness and popularity of sports among certain segments of their people. In fact, a renowned sage, Rabbi Shimon son of Laqish (known in the Babylonian Talmud as Reśh Laqish) may have had some experience with gladiators. And, if we can believe another talmudic legend, as a youth he might even have suited up for battle in an arena. Those hours improving his physique, or so the story goes, eventually paid off for the Jewish community. As a rabbi, he was praised for going after kidnappers and robbers in defense of other Jews.[12] In any event, the sages, in moves that adumbrated what some rabbis would do almost two millennia later, made substantial, pragmatic decisions about how much of this foreign culture might be countenanced within the boundaries of Jewish tradition.

Fundamentally, the rabbis condemned the entire scene at ancient sports stadiums. Jews should not be competing and their coreligionists should not be in attendance. The rabbis decreed that even if idolatry were not explicitly practiced at the games, these realms were ruled out of bounds. For there, the sages feared, even the faithful would find themselves among "scoffers" who would lead them away "from the study of the Torah," what the rabbis deemed as the Jews' *raison d'être*. Needless to emphasize, these religious leaders were also less than pleased with the personal relationships that were engendered between Jews and Gentiles on these occasions. But one Mishnaic scholar, Rabbi Nathan, an early third-century Palestinian sage, did approve of two suggestive circumstances where a Jew could attend the games. A believer could be there if he was on a lifesaving mission "to cry out in order to save the loser" in what I would call a "thumbs up-thumbs down" gladiatorial battle. He could also seat himself "in an amphitheater" in order to "to give evidence on behalf of a woman [whose husband came up short in the arena] that she may remarry." Of course, for us, his decision only offers additional evidence of Jewish participation in these high-profile sports events.[13]

Even as the rabbis abhorred Jewish participation in ancient versions of big-time amateur and professional sports, they did not condemn those Jews who took athletics very seriously so long as their pursuit of the perfect body did not undermine their fidelity to the faith. Although Jacob, the yeshiva student, remained the ideal Jew, the rabbis could countenance an "Orthodox" Jacob the wrestler. Indeed, they seemed to make several efforts to set parameters for those athletic aspirants who harbored at least some concern with traditional practices. Thus, for example, a Mishnaic source enumerates the range of exercises a wrestler must perform to keep in shape or to "make a weight" and delineates which might be performed on the Sabbath and which are prohibited. By inference, such regimens like oiling and massaging of the stomach, skin scraping, and the use of "artificial emetics" — probably to induce vomiting before a weigh-in — were ruled permissible for Jews on other days of the week.[14]

The sages even tried to control their people's evident interest in more informal types of ballplaying. Thankfully for the rabbis, these games of catch, kickball, and even primitive forms of bowling and skittles never made it to the ancient Olympics, so they did not fear that idolatry might infect those attracted to these activities. Still, Jewish boys and girls of all classes — not only ambitious ephebes — picked up their interests from their Greek and Roman neighbors. And, with that affinity came potential problems, issues that adumbrated rabbinic concerns of two millennia later. Issues of modesty when girls played ball, especially in coed environments, troubled the rabbis. They also had their eyes on the reality that ballplaying, singing, and dancing often went hand in hand and they feared what might happen after the formal proceedings ended. And, as always, there was the question of determining which, if any, types of informal play might be countenanced on the Sabbath. The decisions made here about Sabbath play, early on in rabbinic tradition, would form the bases for halachic discussions and rulings during later periods of Jewish history.[15]

During the Middle Ages, Judaism's problems with sports took a lengthy time-out. This millennia-long hiatus was a direct result of the Jews' disadvantaged social and political position under unfriendly Christianity and less-than-accepting Islam. In western Europe, the medieval tournament was the foremost place for this epoch's formal athletic activities, and participation in these games was off-limits to Jews. These events, which have been described as a "brutal medieval cross between sport and warfare," were for the "baronial and fighting class" alone. There knights engaged in a "type of mock battle" in front of lords and ladies that only prepared combatants for real-life engagements. In some cases, the contest was a rite of passage for the neophyte warrior, although there were some itinerant professional battlers. As one twelfth-century chronicler put it, only when an upstart knight felt the tournament lance would he "be able to face real war with the hope of victory." Sometimes, particularly in the early centuries of tournament history, the distinctions between sports and warfare were blurred so much that "teams" — actually rival armies of hundreds of knights each from different towns or regions — bloodied each other severely with the winning contingent capturing and retaining its opponents' possessions. In all events, Jews, who almost never served in medieval armies — even if, here or there, they possessed the right to bear arms to defend their community — would never have been invited to duel, arch, or joust competitively.[16]

Over in the Muslim realm, skills in the art of warfare were also perfected through paramilitary sports. Most notably among the Mamluks, a political-warrior elite that rode roughshod over Middle Eastern society from the thirteenth to the sixteenth century, mounted soldiers showed their proficiency with the lance, with a sword, with a crossbow, and in archery in formal competitions. Their "tournaments" were decidedly not open to Jews nor for that matter to anyone else who did not belong to that class of warriors and rulers. Indeed, given their status as *dhimmis* under Islam — a legally protected but subordinate minority — Jews were generally denied the right to bear arms and to ride horses. So while there were exceptions to the rules — the legendary tenth- and eleventh-century Spanish Jewish leader Shmuel ha-Nagid certainly earned his spurs both in the Muslim court and on the battlefield —

the overwhelming majority of Jews who lived under Islam were completely disconnected from the foreign, military world of medieval sports.[17]

So-called "mock tournaments" held in Italy and designed to humiliate the oppressed minority, were the closest medieval Jews actually got to "competing" before non-Jewish audiences. Local populations and soldiers in Rome and possibly in Sicily, used Jews as "mounts" as they simulated jousting meets and "the utmost brutality was practiced . . . in the course of bellicose games before Lent." It was left to the Jewish community "to be relieved of this degradation," to annually buy off papal authorities.[18]

Still, despite their non-participation in real tournament arenas, some Jews clearly knew what was going on in the Gentile sports realm, enough at least to parody what those around them were doing. For example, in thirteenth-century Spain, there was a wedding custom where "young men used to ride out to meet the bridegroom" in mimic combat, as if they were knights. We can imagine "Jewish cavaliers, mounted on richly caparisoned horses and mules, in fine cloaks, cassocks, silk doublets, closed hoods, and with gilt swords" approaching the mock battle "by mounted buglers . . . heralded by a fanfare of trumpets." Occasionally, the high jinks got out of hand like the time in the late twelfth or early thirteenth century in northern France where some revelers ended up damaging their clothes and injuring their horses. When the party-goers demanded compensation for their losses, the wise Rabbi Samson ben Abraham of Sens threw out this tendentious tort case.[19]

A more serious Jewish version of the tournaments Gentile knights played may have been part of community life in fourteenth-century Germany. An obscure reference in a long-forgotten nineteenth-century Jewish journal reports that "for some years" in mid-century, Jews in neighboring towns in the vicinity of Weissenfels, "through an arrangement with the neighboring noblemen who assured them safe conduct," were permitted to congregate to cheer on "Jewish knights" who displayed their athletic ability in a "Jews Tournament." These events, which, it is said, "naturally aroused a great deal of attention and ignorance" in Gentile quarters, continued until 1384 when Jewish competitors, upon their return home from "the great gathering of Jews . . . were attacked by their own noblemen and thoroughly plundered."[20]

However, notwithstanding the existence of these few medieval Jewish sports events, we have to think that interest in tournament play of any sort probably was restricted to the smallest segment of Jews of that era, like those whom old-time historian Israel Abrahams described romantically as having "highly prized the privilege of wearing arms, styling themselves as knights and bearing stately names." For him, this elite class of Castilian Jews carried themselves that way publicly until King Juan II's decree of 1412 forbade Jews from brandishing "swords, daggers, or similar arms in the cities, town and places" of his dominion. After that edict, they may have continued to pack weapons surreptitiously. Often life continued apace, outside legal lines.[21]

Very recently (2002), a German historian uncovered documents that spoke of a small number of cases in twelfth- to fourteenth-century Germany where Jews were accorded "a knightly position and way of life." They might even have shadowboxed with a lance or a pole. But no one has seen any evidence that these privileged Jews ever were invited to an athletic competition.[22]

If formal sports were off-limits to Jews, and only a certain segment even dreamed of admission to the tournament lists, at home within their own Jewish communities, youngsters — and some adults — did what came naturally. They played informal games of ball and otherwise recreated albeit within their own spheres. It is hard to really gauge how deep or widespread was the passion for play within Jewish quarters. There is a reference in rabbinical responsa literature which suggests that Jews tutored each other in the martial art of fencing, although like swimming instruction, knowing how to duel might have been more than just a game. With potential enemies all around them, even if physical attacks against Jews were not a constant occurrence, such self-defense training might have been a serious lifesaving measure.

We know of such schooling from a dispute that the influential thirteenth-century sage Rabbi Meir of Rothenburg adjudicated. Reportedly, a man hired a fellow Jew to coach him in swordsmanship and signed on for a series of lessons. However, after only one class the student apparently lost interest in "the gladiatorial art" and refused to pay his instructor for more than just that day's session. The coach demanded that the dropout fulfill the entire length of the contract. (We can imagine a similar type of dispute taking place at a twenty-first-century health club.) Rabbi Meir sided with the coach, judging the professional swordsman a highly skilled worker whose valuable time was wasted by the less-than-committed student. Significantly, in rendering his decision, Rabbi Meir made clear that what made this particular skill so valuable was that it "may often save a person's life, as in the case robbers attack one."[23]

All told and untold, what actually went on day to day among the athletically inclined on medieval Jewish streets? Unfortunately, contemporaneous sources are of such a texture that they simply do not delve into such common social behavior, unless problems with such activities were brought to the attention of rabbinic respondents.[24] We can only say that evidence does exist that youngsters did at least occasionally engage in footraces and in what we would call today "Blind Man's Bluff." They also swam for fun and health or just to cool off. Meanwhile, we know that adult men and women participated in a primitive form of tennis. And the issue that arose intermittently for the rabbis' attention was the question of the permissibility of play on Sabbath and Jewish holidays.

Generally speaking, the rabbis accommodated youthful impulses to run and jump and to otherwise exercise on Jewish holy days. For example, in the thirteenth century, Rabbi Isaac of Corbeil ruled that despite Sabbath laws that instruct Jews to walk slowly and deliberately in keeping with the quiet-filled spirit of the day, kids could run around if such activities were pleasurable and satisfying. For youngsters who might perambulate in the woods, that was their way of enjoying the Sabbath.[25]

At about the same time, also in the thirteenth century, a disconcerting abridgment of Sabbath strictures took place in Egypt when some youths went swimming in the Nile. And what made the situation worse — and very embarrassing — for Jewish religious leaders in Cairo was that the miscreants included the sons and daughter of the beadle and "a *parnas,* or social service officer, both officials of the synagogue." Evidently, the phenomenon of "slipping away" from religious life — so common in modern times — could also take place in the medieval period.[26]

Somewhat less problematic to communal authorities of that epoch was the apparently not uncommon interest youngsters and adult sportsmen and women had in playing an early incarnation of jai alai on the Sabbath and holidays. Here the rabbis were concerned with two issues. First, there was the question of whether playing with a racquet violated the prohibition of carrying on the Sabbath or unnecessary carrying on the holidays. Second, even if the racquet itself was not *ipso facto* religiously "out of bounds" (*muktsah*), balls in play would become muddied and filthy from use on the court. On these bases, lines were drawn off the court limiting this form of popular sport. Whether the medieval rabbis' decisions were always followed really cannot be determined.[27]

As the Middle Ages gave way to the Renaissance, Rabbi Moses Provençal ruled on just this question of tennis on the Sabbath and holidays from a number of new and different angles. His nuanced decision is of very special moment. For what brought the problem to his attention as well as what he ultimately decided to do anticipated the renaissance of the clashes that would ensue in modernity when Jews once again started to play not only like, but with, their Gentile neighbors. His judgment marks, in that special time and place, the beginning of the end of the long time-out for Judaism's encounter with sports.

Although there was a medieval Jewish presence in that northern Italian city-state from as early as the twelfth century, and Jews of that region had been subjected to the intermittent terrors and ongoing indignities of Christian persecutions, they had by the sixteenth century achieved an impressive status as respected denizens of an expansive, modern-looking urban center. There, in relative freedom, they began to become very much part of the general culture around them. The ruling Gonzaga family recognized the economic possibilities Jewish traders and merchants might bring to their duchy and, by 1545, had decreed that Jews should be as "free and secure in pursuing their business and professions in our City and Duchy as Christians." This welcome was heard and resonated not only throughout Italy but also among Iberian Jewish refugees who resettled in this haven. By 1560, Mantua, "this joyous city," to quote Jewish sources from that time and place, could boast of a Jewish population of some 2,000 souls. Feeling very much at home in Mantua, Jews of that town took part in the culture of the duke's court, were noted as writers, poets, and musicians, and, most importantly for us, they also started to play tennis quite seriously.[28]

As Jewish interest in this game grew, Rabbi Provençal found himself at odds with what this activity was doing both to the moral fiber and religious values of the young people of his community. To begin with, betting on the outcome of matches apparently was very much part of the Mantuan sports scene, and the rabbi, sounding very much like a twenty-first-century critic of sports gambling, protested strongly against its corrosive effects. Lamenting the demise of the days of yore where sports were more "wholesome," the rabbi opined that "the stake motive of the ancients and the moderns is not identical. With the former, winning was a sort of wholesome fun, with no eye to lucre. Nor did those who lost it feel it keenly, for the stakes put up by each player were by no means an excessive amount. The modern ball players however, may win or lose sums that are considerable, and diversion is not the primary object but material gain."

What made the situation even worse was that this perversion of the values of competition often took place on the Sabbath in violation of the letter and spirit of that holy day. The customary efforts some Jews made to avoid this gross Sabbath transgression did not impress the rabbi. Instead of putting up cash, circumventors gave the winners foodstuffs, like we might today give a trophy to a champion, as an "expression of social conviviality." However, the learned and quite aware sage was not taken in. He ruled that ruse imper- missible because he recognized that these awards were quickly "converted into cash."

But betting and gambling on the Sabbath was only the beginning of the rabbi's headaches from sports within a community that was only starting to drift away from traditional Jewish practice. Probably the fact that it was "not uncommon for the game to be conducted while the sermon" — maybe his own sermon — "is being preached in the synagogue" exercised him more as he recognized that the attractiveness of sports for these early "modern" Jews was becoming greater than the call of the synagogue. What could he do? Obviously, an excoriation of this deviance was in order, even if he most likely would be unable to keep Jews from the courts during shul-time.

At the same time, he also ruled permissively that Jews could play ball when ostensibly services were not in session. He divined that the game they were playing was most akin to what we would call today handball. (Actually, others have remarked that we see in this rabbinic responsum the various stages in the evolution of the modern game of tennis out of handball and jai alai.) And since this activity really did not require the use of a full-fledged racquet, players did not have to be "interdicted . . . for fear that the player might attempt to mend" a broken implement. He thus found a way of positioning himself and the law to accord it and himself continued currency "for the benefit of the multitude" who wanted to be Jews, sportsmen and women, and participants in the athletic world. In rendering this decision, Moses Provençal earned for himself the distinction of being the first "modern" rabbi who attempted to deal with the internal religious clashes engendered by the Jews' clamor for sports in our age.[29]

Still, the resumption of Judaism's full-fledged problems with sports remained in the distant future. An enduring leaven for crises of Jewish identification — born of the interest large numbers of Jews would demonstrate in playing like Gentiles and of the possibility that they would be accepted as teammates within more open societies — had not really begun to rise. In most places, even in Italy, the onerous restrictions and daily abuses held over from the Middle Ages were still very much in effect. Even while Mantuan Jewry and its rabbi were dealing with their religious responses to freedom, not too far away, Roman Jews were still experiencing the degradation of the "mock tournaments" and would do so for another century. Moreover, just a generation or so after Moses Provençal, his own community would be ghettoized as part of the Catholic Counter-Reformation, even if there is evidence that primitive tennis facilities persisted in their closed-off quarters.[30]

At almost the same time, Emperor Rudolf II, who ruled the Holy Roman Empire from 1576 to 1612, made clear, through his decrees on Jewish participation in fencing within his domain, how uncertain he was, and how unwilling his still very Catholic society remained, about opening the doors to the Jews' integration within his court and the larger Austro-Hungarian realm. From his perch in Prague in the late sixteenth and early seventeenth centuries, the mercurial, melancholy, and maybe schizophrenic Rudolf granted a variety of rights to individual Jews, designating them *Hofbefreute Juden*, "court-privileged" Jews, prototypes of the more famous modern Court Jews of subsequent centuries. These special-case Jews were allowed to "travel freely, accompany the royal Court on its journeys, and, in return for special taxes, were free from all local imposts and customs duties." Also, as a devoted friend of the arts, Rudolf II patronized and brought into his charmed circles talented Jewish craftsmen. He went so far as to permit these Jews to organize their own artisan guilds, independent of Christian associations. In that seemingly tolerant environment, we can well assume that men like Jewish banker Mordecai Meisel styled themselves as European gentlemen at court in many observable ways in what came to be seen as an early "golden age" for Bohemian Jewry. The ability to fence was part of the social armor of these Jews on the rise. Actually, some years earlier, a number of unusually talented Jews had been involved in the evolution of the sport away from its original mixture of grappling and swashbuckling toward its more genteel incarnation that was regnant in palace circles.[31]

It seems, however, that this present symbolic elevation of the Jew through admission to this world of sports did not sit well with Prague burghers who were then in competition with Jews on a host of fronts. For these conservative Christian elements, the protocol was clear: A gentleman did not do battle against a member of the underclass of Jews. That was their code of honor. And, arguably in response to burgher complaints that "Jews were being taught fencing and indeed were permitted to participate in public contests," Rudolf II conceded and promulgated an "explicit decree" that enjoined fencing instructors from accepting Jewish disciples at the penalty of "loss of teaching permit, closing of their school or monetary fines." Evidently, his society too was not ready to look upon Jews as teammates.[32]

Notwithstanding these exceptional cases that anticipated future developments and relationships, for western and central European Jews the full restart of Judaism's problems with the wide world of sports, as Jews struggled and gained admission to Gentile athletic clubs and society, would not begin for another two centuries. Meanwhile, in eastern Europe in the seventeenth through nineteenth centuries, Jews and Gentiles were moving further and further away from participating as equals in sports or in anything else.

The earliest Jews in Poland had possessed the right, at least in theory, to test their athletic mettle with and against those around them. Not so their seventeenth- through nineteenth-century counterparts. When Jews were invited into the royal realms of east-central Europe, they were welcomed with rights that established them as "freemen" — uncommon medieval privileges — that placed them on par with "knights and the gentry." And it appears from contemporaneous accounts that some Jews were pretty good with swords and daggers. We can well imagine that some brawny Jews, with knight-like pretensions, might have entertained the notion that they could hold their own alongside Polish nobles. We do know that notwithstanding church condemnation and rabbinical apprehensions about intergroup fraternization, some Jews emulated their neighbors in dress, speech, and other customs. So we can well imagine that these same Jews aspired to meet members of the Polish *shlakta*, as equals, on the field of athletic valor and honor, had only such venues existed.

Arguably, it was only the absence of paramilitary tournament games as part of general thirteenth- through sixteenth-century Polish culture that kept some of that country's first Jewish settlers out of participation.[33] Of course, as always, while a minority of Jews might have dreamed of athletic glory, most Jews contented themselves with the type of recreation — from swimming to ice-skating to playing that primitive form of jai alai during the week and sometimes on holy days — that were common fare elsewhere in Europe.[34]

On the other hand, the oppressed, increasingly downtrodden Polish Jews of the Chmielniski era (post-1648), hardly modern in status or behavior though stuck chronologically in the early modern period of Jewish history, had neither the rights nor the disposition to compete against those they feared. Their first real encounters with freedom and, along with it, sports would not begin until the twentieth century. But while their own era of raised expectations was delayed, changes took place in western and central Europe during the nineteenth century. After a hiatus of more than a millennium, Jewish athletes, anxious for social status and acceptance, began once again to compete with and against non-Jewish counterparts. The ancient encounter between Judaism and sports was renewed, and in bolder relief than before. An age-old question would perplex Jewish circles: Was it possible for a dedicated player to maintain strong ties to the faith — or at least to continue to ally himself with his people and its past — as he made every effort to emulate the ways of the Gentiles to succeed in a modern arena?

JUDAISM'S FIRST MODERN SPORTS SKIRMISHES

The players who ended Judaism's long sports time-out had concerns reminiscent of Greco-Roman Jewish athletes. In classical Jewish societies, Jewish ephebes took to the gym to prove they were on a par with all other citizens. They aspired to play themselves into the larger society around them. The same sorts of motivations brought Jewish students to the gymnasium or to the fencing hall in nineteenth-century Germany. In seventeenth- and eighteenth-century England — like in the ancient world — there was an underclass of Jewish gladiators, pugilists, who for a while fought professionally and were the pride of some of their people. Daniel Mendoza was that period's most celebrated Jewish prizefighter even though he and his fellows, including a few women boxers, did not aspire toward higher social station through a sport that was then, as today, rife with gambling, scandal, and corruption.[1] But it was that class of German Jewish students, resident and frustrated at their country's elite universities, who really carried the banner and problems of the encounter of Judaism and sports into modern times.

Amateur sports were a very serious business for these modern-day ephebes. In their spheres, it was not so much whether Jewish duelists or gymnasts won or lost their matches — remember a fencing scar was a sign of honor —

but rather whether they were allowed to play their games. The right to play sports was a community-defining situation and these status-seeking young Jews badly wanted to be included. The quest to compete arm in arm with and against their Christian counterparts stemmed from the students' deep need to be accepted as gentlemen within fraternity rows. They chafed at signs and slights that suggested they were not full-fledged members of university society.

Ideally, when young Jewish *fuchse* [lit. "foxes"], "pledges," were permitted to demonstrate their courage at a *Mensur*—"a competition between members of different student associations . . . [for] young initiates"—they asserted with one fell swoop as swashbucklers that they were "upstanding and honorable individuals" worthy of the respect and friendship of their Gentile fellow students. Once in the fraternity, they might look forward to a fine time, as one uncharitable critic put it, "boozing and more boozing, [with] duels and other affairs that went with the fraternity code of conduct, card playing at the coffeehouse and conversations about their conquests of ever new girls."[2]

Jewish university students also sought to prove their social mettle, showing that they belonged through athletic proficiency, as members of Turner gymnastic societies. These sportsmen, who did their synchronized calisthenics, were very committed sorts. Under the sway of the charismatic Friedrich Ludwig Jahn, the so-called "father of gymnastics," they were taught to "emphasize the cultural uniqueness of their nationalistic physical activities." When allowed to join in, Jewish Turners were more than happy to leave the classroom for the woods, where they would swing with their compatriots on "towers, platforms, ropes and rings." In so doing, they aggressively disproved romantic and racist canards against themselves and their people as physical degenerates incapable of taking their places as soldiers, players, and patriots within an ambivalent host society.[3]

The problem for these athletic aspirants was that Jews were often dismissed as ungentlemanly and were denied admission to the clubs. It was Rudolf II's court prejudices all over again. One memoirist may have said it best when he recalled that "in regard to social anti-Semitism . . . in the student societies, gymnastic associations . . . and color-wearing student fraternities . . . each of the groups, including the smallest, thought it was something 'better' if it was free of Jews." Friedrich Ludwig Jahn was more tolerant than most university types toward letting Jews swing with their comrades. Although this radical romantic was outspoken in his criticism of *"Junker, Juden* and *Pfaffen"* ("gentry, Jews and priests") as detrimental to the German spirit, he "took a more liberal approach towards the admission of Jews to the German student associations."[4]

Of greater importance to us is what happened to those who were accepted, to quote our memoirist, "as a kind of favor on their part and as a kind of privilege for the Jewish student if they made an exception and admitted him."[5] The pressure on the Jewish student-athlete—now a fraternity member—to fit in was enormous. The young man found himself caught up in an environment "that was strictly regulated by the rules, regulations, and symbolism of a corporate society completely removed from Jewish society." For example, at Heidelberg University, historian Keith Pickus tells us, "every waking hour" of a member of the Rhenania Corps, the Allemania Burschenschaften, or the Frankonia Burschenschaften "was devoted to fulfilling the obligations and social expectations of membership." In that new world, "upholding the laws of kashrut, attending prayer services or even socializing with fellow Jews were beyond the realm of possibility. . . . In order for these students to fully participate within a non-Jewish societal structure, they had to distance themselves from traditional Judaism."[6]

Elsewhere, "in the sports clubs" where "a strict exclusion of Jewish fellowstudents" generally prevailed, the exceptional Jew who succeeded "in achieving admission because he fulfills certain requirements or perhaps because he is clever enough to hide his origins" was sure "to restrict as much as possible his intercourse with Jewish fellow-students so as not to endanger his position in the club." And in the worst-case scenario, the Burschenshaft or Turnerian Jew, so distant from past practices and contemporary religious affiliations, signed on with the Christian majority. Conversion became an out for those who entered university life with ambivalence toward their Judaism and who constantly perceived prejudices within the souls of their Gentile compatriots.[7]

The behavior of these Jews who tried to fight their way into elite Gentile society troubled religious and communal leaders. Rabbi Ludwig Philippson, a young moderate Reform preacher, could not countenance the entire fencing scene. In an 1856 editorial entitled "The Duel from the Standpoint of Judaism" published in his *Allgemeine Zeitung des Judenthums,* this spiritual leader of Magdeburg Jewry criticized those who sought to prove their valor by an unconscionable violation of the Sixth Commandment, "Thou Shalt Not Kill!" Jews of his time, he said, had already proved their allegiance and patriotism to the state through their loyal participation in military activities. Defense of the Fatherland was a permissible exception to the biblical injunction against homicide. But a duel was murder. For Philippson, it was tragically ironic that students of his time indulged in such activities to answer annoying forms of Jew hatred while the 20,000 disciples of Rabbi Akiva, who fought real tyranny under the Romans, considered religious and moral study their highest calling.[8]

But, unlike the rabbis of earlier times and places, neither Philippson nor any other religious spokesman within a fragmented Jewish community had the power to call back to the fold those Jews whose quest for social status pulled them away from ancestral values. What these sportsmen were doing was but another good example of the non-observance and dissociation that was endemic to a German Jewish polity that prayed daily for its complete integration.[9] In that environment, the best that anyone could do was to suggest formulas, to those who still might listen, for dealing with their identity clashes.

As it turned out, the most dynamic attempt to influence came not from rabbis, who had only the most minimal connection to these wavering youngsters,[10] but from within Jewish student ranks themselves. Viadrina, a Jewish student dueling society established at the University of Breslau, was the first to assume that role beginning in the 1880s. Its thrust was to appeal to the personal pride and self-respect of fraternity men and gymnasts who tried mightily to "pass" at the expense of their Jewish identity. Viadrina's stalwarts told their conformist counterparts, in no uncertain terms, that their struggles to establish "doubtful friendships" would not earn them their desired elevation into Teutonic society.[11]

Instead, Viadrina offered the chance to join proud fellow Jewish students who could prove on the field of athletic valor that they were as manly as any Gentile. This Jewish fraternity would be "first of all, a place of physical training of every kind: gymnastics, fencing, rowing, swimming." They would "fight with all [their] energy against the odium and cowardice and weakness" which was leveled against them. Their goal: "to show that every member . . . is equal to every Christian fellow student in any physical exercise and chivalry." Toward that end, fencing practice was held daily from 2 to 3 P.M. Gymnastics training took place twice a week. And swimming was scheduled for every Saturday afternoon.[12]

But could this "Association of Jewish Students" force nasty Gentile students to resolve their disputes in a gentlemanly fashion? The unwillingness of those who pilloried Jews to accept their challenge to a duel was one of the prime sources of humiliation for Jewish students, and insults to young manly pride were factors in efforts to hide their Jewishness. To address this dilemma and to gain respect for their program within and without their community, Viadrina adopted a proactive approach. The association's members would publicly offend known defamers of their people, literally punch campus anti-Semites in the nose, and force showdown confrontations.[13]

When Viadrina worthies were not out fighting — contemporary sources are of several minds on how well Jews performed in their bouts — fraternity brothers entertained themselves much the way their Gentile models or opponents did. They wore the black, gold, and red caps and sashes of the Burschenschaften and did more than their share of drinking, singing, and carousing. One early member recalled fraternity high jinks this way: After swimming in the River Oder, Saturday night was set aside for a *Kneipe* (a "formal drinking and singing session"). Sunday mornings saw the brothers showing off their colors in a public street parade where, maybe, they could pick a fight with a Gentile enemy who might happen on the scene. After that "Sunday afternoons were utilized for a small outing to a café or, possibly, a retreat to one's room."[14]

There was supposed to be a more serious side to Viadrina's cultural life. While primarily committed to the doctrine that "physical strength and agility will increase self-confidence and self-respect, and in the future no one will be ashamed of being a Jew," the fraternity also affirmed in its manifestos that their coterie of Jewish "gymnasts, fencers, rowers and swimmers" must "acquire a firm foundation for this self-respect by studying Jewish history." For Viadrina's members, "such serious work will enable us to reach [the] highest objectives" of being more than just comfortable with their lot within German society. Rather, the best of its men would know "the deeds and sufferings of ancestors." However, Viadrina never did quite follow through on that aspect of its mission.[15]

Although one of its charter members, Benno Jacob, went on to become a rabbi and the great historian Heinrich Graetz and Rabbi Immanuel Joel, Graetz's colleague at the Breslau-based Judische Theologisches Seminar, applauded Viadrina's commitment to Jewish pride and self-defense, the group never really provided its members with their promised Jewish education. One critic from within the organization, who personally wanted more Jewish content in fraternity house activities, recalled that while all members were Jews, none [?] was "pious." They did not comprehend Hebrew, despised Yiddish, and never set foot in a synagogue. Even worse, "Viadrina never failed to a have a Christmas tree" at Yuletide and when "foxes" became full-fledged members, they were "christened" at a "Beer-Baptism."[16]

Jewish sports-oriented fraternities at universities in Heidelberg, Berlin, and Munich also failed to demonstrate what we might call today positive Jewish values. When all these groups coalesced in 1896 to form the Kartell Convent (Association of German Students of the Jewish Faith), its rhetoric spoke emphatically of their desire to "educate . . . self-confident Jews." And it prescribed a minimal degree of devotion to Judaism and Jewish affiliation that it wanted from members. Kartell affiliates had to "agree to raise their children as Jews" and former associates who, in fact, apostatized were stripped of their honored alumni status. Still, despite its promise to provide members with regular talks on Jewish history and literature, only one member fraternity actually even began to do so. While "official fencing training took place daily between 7:00 and 8:00 in the evenings," at Kartell venues, no such formal settings were established for lectures on Judaism.[17]

It remained for the late 1890s and the emergence of incipient Zionist-linked student societies and athletic clubs for a substantive effort to be made toward synthesizing German Jewish athleticism and Judaism. Max Nordau's famous call, at the Second Zionist Congress in 1898, for the raising up of a new type of proud, athletic Jew, who would help the Jewish people take a respected place within the modern world, inspired the Vereinigung Jüdischer Studenten (a/k/a the V.J. St.) or the Bar Kochba Berlin or the Juedische Turnerschaft to open their doors to those who might struggle both for Jewish honor and cultural preservation. The V.J. St. called upon its fellows to "fight with us for our Judaism by cultivating [the study of] Jewish history and literature [and] by steeling [our] bodies." The all-Jewish gymnastic societies fostered what Nordau wanted, "physical fitness, combined with education in Jewish heritage and the belief in the Jewish nation."[18]

However, all told, these organizations did not really capture the imagination of those who wished to play or fight themselves into elite German society. Though the Jewish Turner group did pick up some members when local Deutsche Turnerschaften began to bar "non-Aryan elements," many more of those who were cut out dealt with their exclusion in their own ways. Like Zionism itself, which was then massively unpopular among most German Jewish students, the all-Jewish clubs and societies smacked of the very separatism these youngsters were spending their lives, straining themselves, and shedding their blood in duels to overcome. Athletic assimilationists liked neither the Viadrina nor the Kartell for emphasizing the "Jewish Question." And to their way of thinking, Nordau's followers were even worse.[19]

In the end, it was probably the fact that only limited numbers of young Jews actually used athletics to prove themselves in the society around them that really mitigated this early modern skirmish between Judaism and sports. Unlike other commercial, cultural, or social contexts where larger numbers of Jews felt the strain to downplay, or to abandon, their Jewishness, most German Jewish youngsters were not part of the pressure-filled university-fraternity-athletic scene.

Still, Jahnian-style demands that Jews be more like Germans, in the physical training sense of the word, did occasionally impact upon the religious sensibilities of those who were not so driven to compete with, among, and against Gentiles. Striving to look and act like their fellow citizens while remaining true to the faith's basic teachings, most Orthodox Jews in nineteenth-century Germany also countenanced physical training as a part of the education of their well-rounded German youngsters — the "Mensch-Yisroel" — even if the "mensch" was a young woman. Rabbi Samson Raphael Hirsch, the apostle of "Torah with Derekh Eretz," a way of living harmoniously as a German and as an observant Jew, pointed to the cultivation of "physical powers" as among the three key "resources which the child requires for living as an Israelite." For him, it was a parent's obligation to "see that his [youngster's] limbs are firm and supple and exercise them — our Sages, as we know, included swimming among the subjects of education." That position became institutional policy in his Frankfurt school, where physical training was part of the curriculum, but never on Saturday. There, even the committed physical culturalist would have been told to abstain from exercising on Jewish holy days.[20]

Elsewhere, within Orthodox communities that did not establish their own schools, problems did come up when Jewish school kids were pressured to do their calisthenics and the like on the Sabbath. Bowing to the dilemma of families that wanted to conform to the rules, yet concerned with inevitable declines in the next generation's religious values, Berlin's Rabbi Esriel Hildesheimer ruled in 1882 that it was permissible for Jewish children within his community who attended German schools to exercise on the Sabbath to avoid incurring the anger of school "directors." Although the rabbi noted abundant precedents that suggested that "training" on the Sabbath was prohibited, the needs of youngsters, clearly caught between two cultures, militated toward his lenient position.[21]

Judaism fared much better in its inaugural encounter with the mores and code of conduct of mid-nineteenth-century British sports. Putting aside the sagas of Jewish aristocrats—like the English Rothschilds—who as budding British country squires lavished time and effort as equestrian hunters pursuing foxes and deer at a "chase," athletics became an extracurricular option for that country's own select group of Anglicized Jews who, beginning in the late 1850s, started attending England's most prestigious universities.[22]

In any event, once Jews gained the right of admission to Cambridge and Oxford—by an Act of Parliament in 1856—they found there a far more hospitable environment from that which their coreligionists in central Europe confronted. With religious oaths and compulsory chapel attendance no longer around to bother them, Jews found that they could fit in well with their fellow students. Here the locus of intellectual and social activity was the small-size college, an egalitarian setting far different from German fraternity rows. In a place where, according to a sympathetic chronicler of Cambridge life, fellow students were "all at least acquaintances," Jews had much less to prove. Dueling for decency was not dictated nor demanded. In fact, the universities even showed some sensitivity to Jewish students' religious values. By the 1880s, there was a sort of honor system in effect that permitted Jews to take exams on days other than the Sabbath and holidays. And by that time, some kosher food was available in college dining halls for those eating with their Gentile friends. All this evidence seems to suggest that the legendary tale of Harold Abrahams' travails against social anti-Semitism, so poignantly portrayed in the Oscar-winning film *Chariots of Fire,* is more Hollywood than history. In actuality, that famous, if somewhat later, Cambridge Jewish athlete never felt the need to prove himself by sprinting around the school's quadrangle in record time. Nor did his Dons ever critique him for being something less than a gentleman. As one of his own contemporaries has put it, "Abrahams, on his own testimony, would certainly have regarded . . . an anti-Semitic undertone of his time at Cambridge as over-fanciful."[23]

Still, it is reasonable to project that if a Jewish Cambridge or Oxford man did opt to run or play football or become a cricketer as a school's athlete, inevitably he would have to face up to the challenge of Sabbath observance. That is, if Jewish religious values were of any significance to this sportsman. University accommodations went only so far. For a while, and not unlike the nasty German scene, the paucity of Jews who actually involved themselves in "varsity" competition mitigated this problem for Judaism. This early skirmish became a more pervasive dilemma only when an increasing number of Jewish student-athletes, who first learned their sports skills at English public schools and honed their abilities further at Jewish youth clubs or the Zionist Maccabi contingent, overcame a so-called "Jewish tardiness . . . in maturing a capacity for team-effort." But that moment of future Jewish encounter with sports would await the opening of the twentieth century.[24]

Meanwhile, even as Judaism experienced its first modern difficulties with elite student-athletes, both in friendly England and sometimes nasty Germany, sports slowly began to make its initial impact upon the religious values of very different classes of Jews in the nineteenth-century United States. As we finally reach the ultimate destination for our study, we find that immigrant-generation German newcomers were among the first American Jewish athletes. They joined transplanted Turner societies that welcomed their fellow workers or small-time merchants into their athletic midst.

German Jewish newcomers to this land generally saw themselves as part of a larger central European migration, identified still with the culture of the Fatherland, and stayed close to their fellow former burghers in their social organizations. That is, so long as they were accepted. For those with athletic interests, that meant affiliation with the various Turner gymnastic groups that sprung up in cities with significant German and central European Jewish populations. And apparently these Jews were readily admitted since, to quote one Cincinnati club newsletter, "bear in mind that *man* is the main thing, and that Jew, or Mohammedan is a matter of minor importance." Manliness, the improvement of the body, the development of a robust physique, was at the core of the American Turner's creed. It seems that the followers of Friedrich Ludwig Jahn on this side of the Atlantic believed in his cult of physical fitness and devotion to freedom without sharing the guru's ambivalence toward Jews. They did not fret over the fate of the Fatherland they had left behind nor concern themselves with defining who was a true German.[25]

For Jews, that true liberalism meant ready admission into a welcoming community of sportsmen. And, in fact, individual Jews became leaders of these immigrant sports associations. Sigismund Kaufmann served as speaker of the New York Socialistischer Turnverein for more than twenty years. Meanwhile, almost a continent away, in Jewish outposts in San Bernardino, San Francisco, and Los Angeles, Jews were prominent in founding local Turner societies. Gymnastics instructor Emil Harris and champion rifle marksman Isaac Cohen were probably the best Jewish athletes in the Southern California group.[26]

What were the religious values of these noteworthy Jewish Turner members? The meager evidence that exists suggests that in the New York environment, "few of those recognized as leaders of the broader community" — known as *Kleindeutschland*—retained really close ties to the community of religious Jews. However, in California, some important Jewish Turners were also loyal and involved Jews. There is even the case of Siegmund Bergel, who was both a vice president of the San Bernardino Turners and headmaster of a fledgling Hebrew and English academy in his California town.[27]

The problems these first American Jewish athletes might have had in reconciling their Jewish and sports affiliations did not provoke religious communal consideration. For again, much like the German scene and certainly in line with English life, the world of sports captivated few first-generation Jews. Most newcomers, taking their first tentative steps in this country, scarcely had a moment for sports. And even if some Jews had a bit of time on their hands, they were unfamiliar with boxing, running, rowing, or even billiards, a somewhat athletic event that requires eye-hand coordination at least. These pastimes were the provinces of the native-born and of other ethnic groups. The English transplant of cricket and its quasi-derivative, baseball, were also foreign to them. And most German Jewish immigrants did not have the cash and the class to clamor for involvement in turf sports.[28]

I must say here *most* German Jewish immigrants, because there is the case of August Belmont who, not long after his arrival in the United States, became involved in the elite sport of thoroughbred racing. As a member of New York's social winner's circle, he was elected in 1865 as the first president of that city's Jockey Club. But then again, this financier, who came to this country as an agent of the Rothschild bank and who also served as American consul-general to the Austro-Hungarian Empire, was not the average first-generation Jewish immigrant. Additionally, we have to surmise that he had no problems reconciling the calls of his classy sporting life with any remnant of his distant ancestral Jewish past. Belmont, who married Commodore Matthew Perry's daughter in New York's Protestant Episcopal Church of the Ascension and who raised his children in the Episcopal faith — even if he personally never converted — was completely divorced from Judaism.[29]

It was the children of German Jewish immigrants who showed a more recognizable affinity for this country's indigenous sports culture as they assumed a posture as Americans on the rise. And some of the outgrowths of this new interest, which were perceived as part of a general social malaise of Jewish youth of the time, did not sit well with their own communal and religious leaders.

The German Jewish social clubs that were founded beginning in the 1860s were the venues for this troubling encounter. In an era where upscale Gentile-run associations were in most cases off limits to newly affluent Jewish business types — August Belmont was admitted, but he was a rare exception — this Jewish-organized alternative offered a haven where "the Jews could copy Gentile habits more directly and prove their readiness to enter Gentile society." And in fact once within its portals, club members behaved pretty much like their Gentile counterparts did across the street. They ran parties and balls, spent their informal free hours playing cards or discussing the events of the day in their smoking rooms, maybe with a brandy in hand, while the more intellectually inclined repaired to the library. Significantly for us, where the Jewish club differed programmatically from the institutions they emulated was in the absence of a gymnasium in places like New York's Harmonie Club or Cincinnati's Phoenix Club, even if members did find time to shoot pool, go bowling, or maybe take horseback riding lessons, as a group excursion.[30]

At issue for Jewish-minded observers of the club scene was not so much the vision of Jews at play, but rather the morass of moral "abuses that . . . insensibly crept into practice." Young Jews, it was deemed, were spending too much time in the worst aspect of sporting pursuits, participating not as athletes but as spectators at the track, gambling with racing forms in their hands. And when the "card" or "meeting" was over, it was back to the club to toast pari-mutuel victory or to wash down a nag's defeat. Such "young men need[ed] waking up" from their desire to "dabble . . . in silly fashions, drink and gamble, swear and make bets."[31]

The liquor-free and almost smokeless environment of the Young Men's Hebrew Association (YMHA) was just the right place for Jewish youngsters. There, young men, and more often than not young women, could find a myriad of social, cultural, and intellectual activities. They could attend their club-like galas, parties, and dances. Debating groups and literary societies could provide a haze-free forum for discussions of current events. Those who enjoyed reading could find comfortable seats in the library. And maybe, along the way, as members learned to "develop and elevate (their) mental and moral character," they might also commit themselves to "cultivating and fostering a better knowledge . . . of Judaism."[32]

Significantly, early on, physical fitness and athletic participation — those good American sports ideals so absent from the seamier Jewish club scene — were deemed worthy of YMHA programming. By 1875, the New York YMHA had formed its "athletic circle" in addition to its orchestra, glee club, French, German, English, and Hebrew literature classes. The Philadelphia YMHA began similar activities at about the same time. As of 1877, Newark's Y could boast of a gymnasium the size of a present-day basketball court, while that same year the New York Y witnessed the opening of its own "complete gymnasium." Indeed, by 1890, as many as twenty cities had such Jewish-run facilities, complete with "trained instructors who were graduates of the 'Turner' colleges of the period," a final German athletic influence on Jewish life. The first Y swimming pool would open in 1891, and most of these facilities and activities were available both to full members (men) and to "honorary" or "contributing," non-voting women affiliates. For example, in 1880, the "Hebrew Ladies of Harlem donated $300 to equip the gymnasium of the Harlem YMHA, and were given free use of the gymnasium and other facilities." Typically, men and women had their own separate allotted times for sports. Coed activities would be a feature of the twentieth century.[33]

Here, in affirming unadulterated athleticism as an appropriate pursuit for Jewish young people, YMHA programming marked a notable turning point in Judaism's encounter with sports history, even if this concept stemmed from a non-Jewish source. Its neighboring Young Men's Christian Association (YMCA) believed, as a point of faith, that through the right sorts of cultural, educational, and of course recreational activities, it could make better men and better Christians of their charges. Impressed with how "successful [the YMCA was] in its work among young men," Hebrew Y founders, like Oscar Straus, organized their New York branch to do much the same for Jews.[34]

Still, while the Ys were generally applauded for their position as a counterweight against bad behavior among Jewish youngsters, and hopes were always expressed that those attracted to its portals would develop a stronger sense of Jewish identification, concerns were also raised that members' devotion to even the best sorts of sports challenged essential religious values. The "Sabbath question" first arose within the New York Y in 1877, when sportsmen wanted the spanking-new gymnasium available to them on the Jewish day of rest, apparently much to the chagrin of more observantly inclined members. This clash of sensibilities seemingly was resolved with a "compromise . . . whereby the gymnasium was kept open on the Sabbath for 'lighter exercises' only, and members were not allowed to practice on the trapeze and horizontal bars!"[35]

Unfortunately, the sources do not permit us to know precisely what caused those whom we will call here "traditionalists" to make a flexible religious determination reminiscent of Rabbi Moses Provençal's decision in sixteenth-century Mantua. He too dealt with Jews who did not follow Jewish rules. For the record, early Y minutes tell us that a year later, in 1878, the Association decided to close "the Bowling Alley and Gymnasium . . . on the Jewish Sabbath, the day of Atonement, first and seventh days of Passover, and first and eighth days of Tabernacles, and on the first day of Pentecost and the first day New Year" as they seemingly decided to reconcile the institution's calendar with the religious feelings of the Y's predominantly Reform-oriented lay leaders. Still, we might conjecture that Rabbi Provençal's nineteenth-century American counterparts struck their initial compromise of Sabbath values in pursuit of an even loftier religious goal. Maybe they divined that Y membership, and a loose construction of religious obligations, could be a step leading toward synagogue affiliation. Actually, some ten years later, "Jewish ministers" of New York took exactly this stance when they predicated their support for their local Y on the premise that "if the sole means that will commend a young men's organization to our young men be a gymnasium, bowling alleys, athletic grounds, and a collection of fashionable bath-rooms, we suppose that, in the interest of future congregations, such means must be provided." (We will meet up again and again with the Sabbath question at the Ys throughout this book.)[36]

A far more impatient Rabbi Henry Berkowitz of Kansas City, Missouri, was unwilling to wait for the athletically inclined to somehow find their way from Y sports venues to synagogue life. He preferred and strongly advocated that congregations, through "Adult Auxiliary Associations" like the one he planned for his own Temple B'nai Jehudah, actively pursue sports aficionados through the "furnishing (of) a gymnasium and all means of healthy recreation." The aggressive Berkowitz also wanted a designated place or facility in his religious institution for those who were more enamored of art, music, and even "public entertainment" than services and sermons. Implicit in his plan was the strategy that the sports facility — and for that matter the congregational library, music room, and social hall — was but one door away from the sanctuary. The trick would be to lure those who came to play to stay to pray.[37]

The impetus for this novel congregational construction was rooted in the same troubling communal dynamics that elsewhere had called the Ys into existence. Berkowitz reportedly was very upset that "congregations have gradually loosened their hold upon the lives of the people and . . . have surrendered their influence to the social clubs." And he was almost apoplectic about what went on in those smoke-filled rooms, especially the endemic gambling epidemic. He considered it "a national curse" as he railed from his pulpit about the "evil" of card playing, and he depicted its "hold . . . as worse even than the drinking habit and its effect." For Berkowitz, a wide-open temple had the potential — far more than did the Y— to bring Jews with both benign and malignant pastime interests home to religious affiliation and commitment. And it appears that the rabbi had a special part in his heart for the sportsmen's needs and mentality.[38]

Though hardly an athlete himself — as a youth he "was not gifted with a strong, robust physique" — Berkowitz nonetheless understood that people, beginning with children and adolescents, naturally preferred the playground to the synagogue and to the school. As an adult he would recall that as a boy, he "felt much resentment that at four o'clock in the afternoon every day, I was obliged to go to Hebrew school when I should have been out playing ball." The challenge was to create an institution where before, or after, the playground closed, students would naturally find time and an interest in acquiring "the knowledge which we desire them to have and the influence and impressions we desire to bring upon them in their religious life."[39]

Berkowitz's "Adult Auxiliary Association" did not come to full fruition at B'nai Jehudah primarily because three years after his initiative was hatched in 1888, the rabbi departed for a new pulpit in Philadelphia. Still, his ideas were not lost upon Reform and more traditional rabbis nationally, especially those who in the succeeding few years saw gymnasia — and other ancillary improvements — built in their temples in Chicago, New York, Cleveland, Cincinnati, and Detroit. Moses Gries probably was the rabbi most impressed with Berkowitz's ideas. Certainly he promoted the gymnasium-in-the-synagogue idea from his pulpit at Cleveland's Tifereth Israel. Speaking to his Reform colleagues of the Central Conference of American Rabbis in 1901, the year his temple's sports facility opened, Gries asserted that if rabbis taught "children to turn naturally to the temple for the satisfaction of the natural desires" — like sports — and the temple was responsive, "you may be sure boys and girls will be enthusiastically loyal to it." If this could only take place, he prayed, "amusements, now too often an opposing force, interfering with public worship and other congregational work, will be subordinated."[40]

Gries, who personally micro-managed construction of the new synagogue facility, made every effort to integrate athletics into his temple's weekly schedule of activities. Boys were "gathered together for social recreation and pleasures that are pure and uplifting of their nature" on Monday and Thursday afternoons. Girls were provided "healthful physical recreation under influences that lead to moral health" on Tuesday and Friday afternoon. The program also called for a women's "seniors" class early Friday evening and a special "Business Men's" session on Saturday evening. Significantly, the gym was closed to all for the rest of Saturday and the entire day on Sunday in recognition of, albeit in an idiosyncratic way, the demands of Sabbath worship.

As one of the foremost radical Reform rabbis of his time, Gries countenanced both Saturday and Sunday as recognizable Jewish days of rest. Indeed, Tifereth Israel held services on both Saturday and Sunday mornings even if its "Sabbath school" was conducted on Sunday, suggesting a preference for the American civic day of rest within congregational consciousness. (At that point, weekday services were unknown at the Cleveland temple as well as at most American Reform synagogues.) In all events, for Gries, the ideal young Jewish athlete, boy or girl, could do his or her gymnastics up to twice a week on the synagogue's premises, attend Junior Temple Society on Friday night, study in the Sabbath school, take Confirmation classes Friday afternoon, and the family could pray together either Saturday or Sunday morning. It is not known how many young men or women opted for that specific regimen and were "drawn . . . more closely to this Temple."

What is certain is that sports at the synagogue were extremely popular. Wrestling attracted its share of boys. And both sexes liked gymnastics within a facility that was equipped with stationary rings, horizontal and parallel bars, and pommel horses. An impressed gymnasium committee proudly reported in 1901 that "within six months of its opening . . . attendance had outgrown the accommodations, compelling a large increase in space and an addition of sixty-two lockers" as membership numbered some 194 youngsters and young adults.[41]

Although Berkowitz's and Gries's colleagues surely wanted the athletically inclined to find their way to synagogue affiliation, many remained unconvinced that the road to the sanctuary led through the gymnasium. Maybe they too wondered, as we do, what proportion of the 194 sports enthusiasts did anything more than exercise in a Jewish environment. In a sense, this wing of the temple, far more than any library, lecture room, or even social hall, had yet to overcome its "pagan" history or image. Detroit's Rabbi David Franklin reflected some of these reservations when he remarked in 1902 that "it is the curse of our day that the club and not the synagogue has become the centre of our life. There our young men flock for recreation and amusement . . . ," out of "sheer fright at the confusion the word might create. I would rather not have a gymnasium in any part of my temple or Sabbath School building." However, in the end he approved such activities admittedly as a "self defense measure since the gymnasium of the Young Men's Christian Association, the only one available to our boys and young men, has become a menace to our cause . . . taking our children away from us on the Sabbath morning, and inculcating with the gymnastic instruction, also the elements of Christianity." Nonetheless the rabbi certainly remained concerned that the temple's athletic offerings not become too prominent a part of the congregation's profile.[42]

Franklin's tentative solution was to directly link his synagogue sports program to Sabbath school activities. After an inaugural phase, where anyone could use the facility, the rabbi limited gymnasium membership to "the pupils of the Sabbath School." In the words of its congregational chronicler, "the real value of the gymnasium is in holding the interest of the Sabbath School children to their work, membership in the gymnasium being regarded as a privilege by the pupils of the school."[43]

All told, by the end of the nineteenth century, many of the dilemmas sports engendered for the integrity of modern Judaism, and some of the problems communal leaders faced in answering that threat, had begun to be experienced within both European and American Jewish societies. Jewish athletes were sometimes pressured — and other times they simply preferred — to embrace the demands and values of sports at the expense of Jewish allegiances and observances. And while rabbis and their lay helpers, particularly in America, took some fledgling steps to make the disinterested feel at home within remodeled religious settings, there was far from unanimity within concerned Jewish circles that the opening of synagogue portals to the world of fun and games was an effective, or even an appropriate, Jewish response. Still, these early modern encounters between Judaism and sports remained but skirmishes. The relatively small numbers of Jews who identified themselves with the culture of athletics held down the depths of the concerns. But the crucial confrontation was not far off. Particularly in America, the twentieth century would witness an exponential expansion of problems as sports came to pervade so much of the mass culture and consciousness of this country. Now, more than ever before, a significant part of the definition of what it meant to be an American involved knowledge of, affinity for, and participation in the nation's pastimes. And arriving as they did with the goal of becoming like all others, the new Jewish majority, immigrants from eastern Europe and especially their children, quickly discovered and identified with the world of athletics. With this great popularity again came, with even bolder relief, the questions of reconciling religious values and identities with a burgeoning new cultural attraction.

3

THE CHALLENGE AND OPPORTUNITY OF
A NEW WORLD OF AMERICAN SPORTS

The athleticism valued in the world of sports was not honored in the nineteenth-century shtetl. Reverence and concern for the head, for the intellect, far more than the cultivation of the body, was where these Jews' emphasis lay. While few in the community were rich and knowledgeable enough to engage in full-time study, most people looked up to these *Sheyneh Yidn,* these Jewish "beautiful people." With that cultural ideal squarely in mind, parents hoped to raise their sons to be scholars, to work with their minds and not with their muscles. But that rarified status was a reality for only a tiny minority. Most fathers were butchers, bakers, porters, coachmen, etc. On their own, some children played primitive forms of baseball called "Oina" and "Myatch," where balls and sticks were hit for distance, but these youngsters did so without their elders' blessing. Whiling away time as an athlete was no way for a kid to move up in class. Rather, the most renowned youths of the Jewish town were the sedentary types who stuck to their books. Of course, in keeping with Jewish tradition, even the most committed students participated in outdoor games on Lag B'Omer, the Jewish field day. But there was no social sanction for daily and violent pastimes; "fighting [was] 'un-Jewish' in the extreme." There certainly were no organized competitions within the shtetl nor any talk on the Jewish street of producing well-rounded scholar-athletes.[1]

By the late nineteenth century, witnesses of the traditional heder scene, including young men who survived its regimens, were far from sold on how well this educational system did its job as a molder of great Jewish minds. Critics from memoirists to novelists spoke angrily, when they did not write hauntingly, of one-room schoolhouses where unfortunate children were forced to stay in class for up to nine hours a day in stuffy rooms—with no time for recess—under the sway of unskilled, abusive teachers. Those in control, it was said, traumatized their kids. Whatever the truth is here—whether these schools cultivated or stultified the mind and the spirit—for us, the essential point is that they did nothing to develop or improve their disciples' physiques. And that was the way most boys were educated and socialized in eastern European communities.[2]

Girls, for the most part, did not have access to the best and worst of this formal teaching system, but they were not left to run free either. Although elementary schools for girls did exist within the shtetls, their mission was circumscribed to provide its charges with rudimentary Jewish and general language skills and knowledge of basic traditional texts. They did not aspire to raise up female intellectual giants. Immigrant author Mary Antin described this situation well when she remarked that if in the Old World, a girl "could sign her name in Russian, do a little figuring, and write a letter in Yiddish to the parents of her betrothed, she was considered . . . well educated." Within that traditional world, especially among the few Jews who had some money, "extracurricular" time was available to expose daughters to music, art, and other softer subjects. Young women were not stuck in class for eight or nine hours a day. Poor girls did not have time on their hands after school. They went to work. But in the end, whether rich or poor, most girls were trained to assume traditional roles within their families and society. No one spoke to them, or to their parents, about the value of physical training as part of a young woman's life.[3]

There were, of course, real exceptions within and without the world of the Jewish shtetl, those who were handy with swords, brickbats, and maybe even with guns. There might even have been some Jewish sportsmen circling or jumping around the fringes of society. Yiddish literature, for example, is replete toward the late nineteenth century with tales and images of the Jewish "tough guy"—the *ba'al guf*—who lived by his fists and who was there when other Jews were physically endangered. He appeared on the scene, most dramatically, when riots took place to, as writer Sholem Asch once put it, "take matters into [his] own hands . . . into the streets [where he would] give hooligans a lesson." But as much as the Jewish community appreciated his rough and ready efforts, he was not held up as an ideal Jew. He might have been respected but he was never to be emulated, except in a moment of crisis. No one really wanted his kid to be a muscle man, even if some working-class Jews had calluses on their own hands.[4]

Jewish physical specimens might also be found among those who took to the streets in organized fashion when their people were attacked during the infamous pogroms of the early 1880s and their successor atrocities of the early twentieth century. As early as 1881, groups of Jewish youngsters were arrested in Odessa for resisting Gentile enemies. Some were actually exiled for two weeks in boats on the Black Sea as punishment for their efforts. Later on, when even more widespread riots ensued, armed Jewish resisters met the marauders in the streets and back alleys of Homel (1903), Kishineff (1903), Poltava (1904), and Bialystock (1905). And from all accounts, Jewish battlers more than held their own in these confrontations. They would have been even more successful if soldiers and/or the police had not intervened on the side of the rioters. It also did not help that at the end of the day, Jewish activists were dragged into courts and accused of having started the riots by attacking Christians.[5]

But, again, these Jewish men on a mission to defend Jewish lives and pride were exceptional figures. In the 1880s, the Odessa-based crowd was made up mostly of gymnasium, secondary school, and university students, enlightened young men who had broken with the world and values of the shtetl. In the early decades of Czar Alexander II's regime (1855–1881), they and their families had dreamed the dream that there could be room within a secularized Russian society for modernizing Jews like themselves. The pogroms of the early 1880s shook up their lives and their sense of comradeship with the Russian people. To a great extent, it has been said, when they went into the streets, they were both literally and figuratively "returning to their people."[6]

In the early twentieth century, radicals — be they Jewish Socialists (Bundists) or Labor Zionists — intent on changing the whole world, or at least the Jewish condition, led the way into battle. At stake for them, to quote from a Bundist newspaper, "are our lives, and still more our honor and human dignity." Zionists were committed "to defend our national honor to the last drop of blood."[7]

It is not inconceivable that, in calmer times, some of these Jewish student activists might have taken an interest in sports. Modern sports were not totally unknown in eastern European lands of the nineteenth century. The first shards of research in this area indicate that by 1867 there was a gymnastics society in Lvov. Its avowed Jahnian-like goals were the "cultivating [of] national consciousness through cultural activity and — with regard to sports — the biological renaissance of Polish society through physical exercises." Two years later, a skating association was created in Lvov. By the mid-1880s, Warsaw, Cracow, and Lvov also had cyclist, fencing, and skating societies. And "at this [same] time, independent sports activities began within workers' circles such as Silesia, Lodz and in Warsaw." It is not inconceivable that a highly enlightened Jew who lived in one of these major Jewish cities or a Bundist from Lodz or Warsaw might have found his way toward the gyms, tracks, or ponds those local athletes attended.[8]

However, these student and radical defender-athletes did not inspire large numbers of fellow Jews to take up arms against their oppressors. Similarly, in better times, their frequenting of the sports gym did not inspire any sort of cult of physicality to emerge within the larger Jewish population. The lives and many attitudes of the masses of Jews changed dramatically in the nineteenth century. Ten of thousands migrated from shtetls to urban centers as the city increasingly became the locus of Jewish life. There, Jews were pushed through government decrees into productive forms of labor. Though it was surely not the czar's intention, demands that Jews become workers ultimately resulted in that oppressed minority acquiring a range of rudimentary industrial skills that would hold them in good stead someday in America. And as some of them became workers, they began to harbor an incipient class-conscious mentality. But with it all, even as their lives were altered in disparate ways, most Jews did not assume a new posture regarding the value of their own physicality and aggressiveness toward the hostile outside world.[9]

Commenting on how he and his fellow radicals basically stood alone during the Poltava engagements, Ber Borochov, the famous Marxist Zionist leader said sadly, if matter-of-factly, "The other Jews did not join us." He was likewise more than chagrined that his Gentile Marxist "friends" also did not help him. It made more sense to most Jews, an unarmed civilian population, to avoid physical confrontations they could not win. So while Borochov's band of very physical Jews, who were also often estranged culturally from the community, might have been admired at a distance during flash points of crisis, they remained Jews on the margins of society. Meanwhile, most children were still not socialized to became what we might call today "stand-up guys," even if they no longer all lived in shtetls.[10]

What is most important to us is that those who most wanted to change the world and themselves with their ideas — and maybe their fists — were not among the first, nor the most likely, Jews to seek out America. Either they stayed and sought to revolutionize Russia or they took their battles to Zion. Matters changed somewhat after the failed Russian revolution of 1905 that convinced an ever-increasing number of Bundist types to take their lives and messages to the United States. They would prove to be more activist in so many ways within the American ghetto. However, even when they battled in the streets of this country as men and women in search of social justice or economic equality, they did not fight with their fists. In this respect, Jewish radical street protesters were not so different from the majority of those non-activists who came to the United States after avoiding physical encounters during times of turmoil in the Old Country.[11]

Therefore, of all the attitude adjustments immigrant Jews had to make in their encounter with the new American world around them, coming to terms with this country's tight embrace of physicality proved to be among the most difficult. For them to idealize and emulate, for example, a rough-riding chief executive who enjoyed striking pugilistic poses while stripped to the waist to display his fighting trim required a fundamental change in their approach to life. And it appears that even as they came on board with so many other American values and mores, the newcomers neither looked, nor could they act, the part of the robust, athletic American. Theodore Roosevelt's concept that the "brawn," "spirit," "self-confidence," and "quickness of men," acquired in the pursuit of sports victory, was essential to American greatness was foreign to this generation. Nor did these immigrants show any aptitude for change in this arena, even if they loved and respected T.R., a great friend and protector of the Jews.[12]

This lack of athleticism and absence of physicality was not lost on outsiders who constantly inventoried the immigrants' cultural baggage. Both those who generally praised Jewish industriousness or their potential to contribute to America, as well as those who loudly feared that these foreigners were overrunning and undermining America, concurred that Jewish men could use some time in the weight room if they ever hoped to make it as Americans. It was a pervasive point of emphasis that "training in athletics will bring about a coincidental mental development that will stand him in hand in the classroom or study, and in the practical affairs of life." No one said that back in the shtetl! Gymnastic training of a different type — befitting what was deemed appropriate for the "weaker sex" — was prescribed for Jewish women if they were to fit feminine roles. Critics, friendly and otherwise, all spoke of "puny" Jewish men, with "narrow chests" and "dwarf stature" and of immigrant women who were "poor in physical estate and . . . lack the physical well-being of . . . the well-bred American woman." A noted restrictionist, E. A. Ross, characterized Jews as "the popular opposite of our pioneer breed. Not only are they undersized and weak-muscled, but they shun bodily activity and are extremely sensitive to pain." Meanwhile, a supporter of the new Americans, Charles S. Bernheimer, admitted that Jews were "physically . . . inferior to the Anglo-Saxons in the United States" and to other immigrants among whom they lived. His "physical bent marked him," said this German-American Jewish communal worker, "among a crowd of Italians and Slavs."[13]

For friends of immigrants, these characteristics were hardly irreversible, if immigrant Jews would only show an interest in physical fitness and sports. The leaders of the Educational Alliance, that renowned downtown New York settlement house, believed that "physical training" will "effectively remove" the stigma that "our co-religionists . . . lack physical courage." As they saw it, these newcomers "have an idea that physical weakness is a virtue . . . for this reason it becomes essential to encourage athletics among immigrant Jews." Dr. Maurice Fishberg, medical examiner of the United

47

"Athletic Class at the Educational Alliance," circa 1917. *Jewish Communal Register, 1917–1918.*

Hebrew Charities, had a specific plan in mind to bulk up his patients. He preached, with certainty, that "outdoor life and participation in the national sports will help develop the chest, which is decidedly smaller in proportion in height than that of non-Jews." However, he was also dismayed to report "that systematic exercises," including "gymnastics," were "not at all in vogue among immigrants." Fishberg also suggested that Jews take up "billiards, golf, tennis and hunting," which only indicates that he was more than a little out of touch with what might have been reasonably expected of those he sought to influence.[14]

In any event, Fishberg's fellow Jews took in few of his and others' concerns and criticisms. In keeping with their eastern European values, work was deemed essential. And study, now more often than not secular education, to achieve in America was highly valued. On the other hand, sports and recreation, physicality, even at its best and purest, remained a disrespected frivolity, even if it might be good for them. An on-the-scene observer, David Blaustein, said as much when he complained that "the whole concept of play is foreign to immigrant [Jewish] people — a waste of time, frivolity." And the

New York Herald Tribune of his day fully concurred. "The rage [of athletics] is something incomprehensible to him. He has cultivated his mind so long at the expense of his body that the American maxim 'a sound mind in a sound body' is something he cannot understand."[15]

Irving Howe, raconteur of downtown Jewish life, has explained first-generation disinterest with the gym this way. "Suspicion of the physical, fear of hurt, anxiety over the sheer 'pointlessness' of play: all this went deep into the recesses of the Jewish psyche."[16] Let me say it my way: Jews of the older generation were prepared to pay many prices to be deemed good Americans. From the very start, immigrant newcomers worked as their fellow citizens did. In time, they learned the language of their adopted country, became comfortable with new forms of dress, ate the same foods as all others, and when their men were here long enough lined up with the majority political parties. (Women did not have the franchise until 1920.) But even as they acculturated in these and so many other ways, they simply did not understand why and how athleticism contributed to becoming an American.

The immigrants' children, on the other hand, clearly understood that being physical was a fundamental American trait. They were bombarded from all sides about the promise, possibilities, and necessity of sports and athleticism. In the public school, participation in "physical training and athletics" was consistently encouraged to "inculcate the virtues of self-reliance and unselfish cooperation," two good Rooseveltian qualities, in these young people. In New York, for example, "physical training and hygiene" were integral parts of the curriculum from elementary school days on. With similar goals in mind, schools established interscholastic programs — games and meets — to do much more than just develop "the physical efficiency of its boys and girls." Rather, through the sponsorship of sports like baseball, basketball, or track and field under the watchful guidance of a teacher/coach, "ideals of courage, honesty, courtesy and strength" were promoted within young Jews, and all others for that matter. The desired result was the emergence of "able men and women trained in body and soul, for their own happiness and the welfare of the State."[17]

Meanwhile, downtown-based settlement houses in Jewish immigrant quarters proffered their own versions of this transforming and patriotic message. Their creed was to build upon the "public schools in the transformation of the crude immigration material into the real citizens and citizenesses [*sic*]." Toward that end, gymnasium work was deemed "a good example of practical training for democracy." Among its virtues was the inculcation of "respect for success and a willingness to be governed by tried and proved leaders." So said the leaders of the Chicago Hebrew Institute, who bragged that "we train boys and girls to be self-reliant, independent, and on square in everything." And they pledged that out of their own "Health Palace of Chicago" would emerge specimens of "real manhood and real womanhood." For girls, both in Chicago and elsewhere, it was deemed worthy that "every girl be as

slender as the fashion demands" through calisthenics, swimming, and dancing. The Irene Kaufmann Settlement in Pittsburgh told its youthful female
charges to "dig up your bloomers and middies and c'mon!" even if competitive sports generally were not emphasized. Back then it was believed that
"athletics do not test womanliness as they test manliness." Of course, boys
had to "have a gymnasium and drill hall where they can run off their surplus
spirits and be taught physical and moral manhood at the same time." Renowned settlement house worker Jane Addams of Chicago's Hull House
spoke evocatively of young people possessed of "symmetrical muscular development" who were "quick to respond to [athletic] fellowship."[18]

While it is uncertain how loudly and clearly Jewish youngsters heard these
commands, it is undeniable that they really liked these sports programs.
And they quickly made their mark on these leveling playing fields. But it was
not just the natural physical attractiveness of working up a good sweat—a
feeling that was now liberated for Jews in this new country—which brought
these boys and girls to the gym. They also could get their endorphin rush,
without encouragement, diving off East Side docks and other unsupervised
venues. Or they could dance up a storm at a local ragtime hang out. Rather,
the school or settlement team afforded them the chance to be "chosen in"
as American athletes. And when they excelled in competition, it rewarded
them with the triumphal feeling that they truly belonged here.

Such emotions had to have coursed through a young man named Freedman of Public School No. 9 in New York's downtown district when, in the
fall of 1908, he was chosen "to represent his school in relay races" sponsored by the Public School Athletic League. After all, the prowess of this
ninety-pound sprinter who "nevertheless . . . made some of his older and
larger boys acknowledge his superiority" was publicly touted, maybe within
his earshot, as proof "to those of other creeds that [the Jew's] presence is
absolutely essential towards success, when he becomes a real factor in his
everyday activities of his environment, then and then only can a Jew hope to
receive from his Gentile rival the respect and credit due him."[19]

Indeed, by the mid-1910s, Jewish participation and acceptance in New
York's non-Jewish sports clubs was so commonplace that a proud local Jewish journalist paused to note an "exceedingly rare" occurrence. A sprinter
named Shapiro, carrying the banner of a Jewish team, "showed his heels to a
large representative field at a 'monster' benefit athletic carnival at Madison
Square Garden." For that observer, "it is much more common to find the
names of the star Jewish performers on the roster of the Irish–American
Athletic Club." And he wondered whether it brought "joy to thousands of
Irishmen when they [saw] the colors of the I.A.A.C. brought to the fore by
such loyal sons of Erin" with Jewish and other ethnic surnames.[20]

A young Jewish athlete also felt a surge of palpable pride when he took to
the streets and earned a reputation in types of sporting pursuits that school
and settlement house sages disdained. In America, the *ba'al guf* was more

Girls' swimming class, Irene Kaufmann Settlement House,
Summer Play School, August 1927. Courtesy of the Library
and Archives Division, Historical Society of Western
Pennsylvania, Pittsburgh.

than an occasional or imagined figure. The downtown tough guy was a hero
of the ghetto, someone worthy of respect and emulation because he beat
up the kids from other ethnic groups. He also was the person who might
have provided his fellow Jews with safe passage within the no-man's lands
that separated ethnic neighborhoods. And, if this "Pride of the Ghetto"
took his skills to the next level and he became a successful prizefighter, he
often emerged as a larger-than-life figure. As one downtown pundit put it,
"if in your walks along the East Side you come across young men with
flattened noses and cauliflower ears, remember that there is a new hero-
type in Israel — the pugilist. Our race finds grotesque expression in him."[21]

For another East Side writer, a ring combatant, like his fictionalized "Slugger Cohen," embodied a not-so-secret Jewish desire to get even with past
enemies for the persecutions their forebearers had suffered. As this particular ghetto yarn has it, when Cohen entered the ring, he saw "before his
eyes . . . childhood memories of Kiev flamed and . . . boyhood tales of

Kishineff rang in his ears." Inspired by these recollections, he took out his people's anger through "a few sharp jabs, a stiff uppercut or two—then a murderous blow to the top of the head and the young Pole crumpled to the floor." With his opponent prostate before him "the avenger . . . thundered 'Praise God' in purest Hebrew as he flung aloft his mittened hands." The story ends with the vanquished Gentile emitting from the ring floor "the same cry in weaker tones: 'Praise God, oh Israel.' "[22]

Schools and settlements also taught the manly art of self-defense to all immigrant comers, and heated interethnic encounters on the mat or in the ring that stoked group emotions were part of the game. However, these Jewish amateur champions did not carry the same crowns as the ones fitted for a former Jewish street fighter, who was doubly blessed. He not only carried the public banner of his group, but also was now actually making a living through his physical prowess. The ghetto hero–pugilist had a ticket out of downtown misery, a punched ticket that many young people around him wished they had.

None of these athletic pursuits—from the good clean fun of the settlement court or track to the down-and-dirty fight in the prize ring and to the ill-reputed dance hall—sat well with immigrant Jewish parents. The published laments range from the father's complaint in the Yiddish press that baseball is "this crazy game [where] the children can get crippled" to the *New York Tribune's* report that "there is nothing that disturbs the Jew so much as to see his boy, and still more his girl, taking part in the athletics of the schools." And memoir literature has it that Jewish parents of all sorts berated their athletically inclined youngsters—be they baseball or basketball players and especially if they were boxers—as "loafers." That is, of course, when they were not defining the next generation's participation in sports activities, not to mention their frequenting smoke-filled dance floors for a night of ruckus recreation, as a *"charpah"* and a *"shandah"* (a source of disgrace and shame).[23]

Growing up, Abe Gerchik, who in his parents' opinion spent too much time playing ball in the streets of Brooklyn, "thought his first name was 'get a job' and his last name 'bum' because his mother always used to say to this budding athlete 'get a job, bum.'" Not surprisingly, as he and his brothers got bigger and started playing organized ball in settlement gyms, "never once did [his] mother or father ever see [them] play ball." What they were doing was totally foreign to his folks.[24]

His contemporary, my father Jack Gurock, also knew all about this parent-kid problem. My dad's interest in amateur wrestling did not sit well with his immigrant parents, to the extent they were aware of his comings and goings. Afraid of the censure of his short, stocky, and strong-minded mother, Nechama, who would have been horrified if she knew that her son was actually fighting for the 92nd St Y, he adopted the *nom de querre* of Jack Austin. (I am told that today one of the most famous phony professional

Jack Austin, back row far left, and his 92nd Street YMHA
wrestling teammates, circa 1936. Author's photo.

wrestlers is named Stone-Cold Steve Austin. He is not a relative!) How my
father kept another salient fact from his folks, namely, that before cleaning
up his act at the Y, he had run with some other Jewish toughs in the mean
streets of Harlem, is another matter.

For the minority of parents who harbored strong religious values — and
the many others who possessed traditional Orthodox sensitivities — their
straying sturdy sons and less-than-demure daughters were not only becoming bums, but non-observant ones at that. Imagine, for example, the feelings of Sol "Butch" Schwartz's father when his young man, as a teenager,
began slipping away from home to attend basketball practices and games at
Seward Park High School on the Lower East Side. This downtown kosher
butcher — the derivation of his son's moniker — had successfully reined in
his son's interest in sports while the kid was young. No Friday night or

Saturday sports for youthful Sol. On holy days, he had to sit with his father in their storefront shul. Anxious to be elsewhere, Sol constantly nudged his father to let him "go outside during the Torah reading," where he would "play punch ball or stick ball." When he "came back all sweaty, [his] father would holler at him." Still, through his bar mitzvah, Butch toed his family's line. However, when he reached high school and had a chance to play on Seward Park's varsity, Sol Schwartz decided that "basketball was more important than religion." Despite his father pleas to "stay *aheim*, stay home" on the Sabbath, "the lure of competitive sports won out." As Schwartz moved on to stardom as a collegian at Long Island University, his fidelity to observing kosher laws ended. By that time, Butch has recalled, "what could [my parents] say. It was too late in the game."[25]

Some Orthodox families were able to make a partial peace with their children's ambitions and proclivities. As early as the turn of the century, one Yiddish author evoked this accepting mind-set when he wrote of the pride a fictional rabbi, "a rabbinical scholar of the old type," and his wife came to feel toward their son, "the professional pugilist." Initially, they were "shocked . . . who ever heard of decent people fighting like peasants." But eventually they became "reconciled to his vocation" and actually felt a degree of satisfaction when he was victorious against a Gentile fighter.[26] The saga of "Slugger Cohen" seems to have gotten around! Regrettably, our scribe does not tell us how such parents felt toward the non-religious training regimen that must have become central to their young man's life.

Some children of observant parents assuaged their own guilt, or mollified their parents somewhat, through appeals to a similar sense of ethnic pride. Reportedly, in the late 1910s, the Atlas Club of New Haven, Conn., whose "founders included sons of a rabbi, a *shammos* [sexton] and a *shochet* [ritual slaughterer]" pitched themselves "not simply as another team of players but as a group of goodwill representatives of the Jewish community" who garnered "respect for the Jewish people," even if their matches were on Friday night. We do not know whether their elders applauded this secularized sanctification of their Jewishness.[27]

What is sure, however, is that for many families a child's unmitigated interest in the sports world was a troubling source of intergenerational pain and conflict. For unhappy elders, it was just another sad reality in a world wherein "[the] father follows ancient customs; [while] the boy is a breezy young Americanized product, scornful of the elder . . . a drifting particle in the modern world in the great city." Or, as one 1910s Jewish social worker observed, more specifically, immigrant parents for whom "orthodoxy . . . [was] a type of life rather than a creed" took little pride in their "half-baked second generation" youngsters' knowledge "of batting averages to a 'T'" while their "cocksure" and "smart guy" sons were "indifferent to, if not ashamed of, Jewish life." Clearly, as another contemporary commentator put it, "the appeal of the practical life and even of sport combined to make attendance at synagogue . . . very much less frequent than in the preceding generation." As this critic saw it, "earnest, however well-intentioned, however eloquent" rabbis cannot even begin to make an impression upon the growing character of these adolescents, because these "well-known products of the larger American city street corner" do not deign to step a sneakered foot into their sanctuaries. Youngsters came home from school and settlement house, or up from the streets, with new heroes — a coach and not a rabbi — new interests and new aspirations.[28]

These pressing problems were not lost upon outspoken New York Yiddish newspaper editor Gedalia Bublick. Indeed, his criticism was quite explicit in the *Jewish Daily News* when he told his fellow immigrant readers in 1914 that the old-line synagogue had nothing to offer children possessed of "universal training, school education and modern environment." For him, "unintelligible utterances," be they "Talmudic discourses, mediaeval melodies, Aramaic sophistries or Hebrew recitations" led only to "ridiculing and scoffing" among youngsters who undeniably preferred playing in the streets. To "remedy the disease," Bublick opined, the synagogue had "to open its portals," to include, among other features, "gymnasia" to "bring back the straying sheep to the fold." Implicit in his charge was the understanding that the synagogue had to find a place for what the sports enthusiast enjoyed most before they could even begin to develop a sense of Jewish allegiance.[29]

The immigrant advocates and financial supporters of the modern talmud torah movement agreed with Bublick's understanding of the religious communications gap that was alienating the generations. And they understood that for their initiative to succeed, essentially to convince young people to come up from the streets and to attend a Jewish school, that institution had not only to be meaningful, but fun. Jewish education had to change its tendencies because until now children had been "deprived of . . . hours of rest and play in order to attend instruction offered in the Talmud Torah." These unhappy kids arrived for lessons "after . . . public schools hours" and were "fatigued, sulky and intractable." They regarded "attendance . . . as a substitute for the play in which their schoolmates of the other creeds indulge at the same time."[30]

To counter "this pernicious attitude," these new-style Jewish schools had to provide for "the social as well as religious and play instincts of the child." There was even some talk in pedagogic circles, whose visions people like real estate tycoon Harry Fischel and businessman Samuel I. Hyman championed, that these schools had to "develop healthy bodies as well as sound minds." It was good American rhetoric for the new Jewish school. One criterion of excellence was whether a school did "allow for enough 'free' *time* for the child so that the child can properly care for its recreational needs." They adopted as their own the voice, educational style, and methods of the very public schools that had done so much to alienate young people. There was no other way to counter "irreligion" and to instill in young people an affinity for their "ancestral heritage."[31]

When these Jews with new ideas and new money oversaw the construction of modern talmud torah buildings, whether they were in Philadelphia, or Brownsville in Brooklyn, or Yorkville and Harlem in Manhattan, they not only made certain that pupils sat in bright, airy classrooms, they also ensured that the complexes included gymnasiums, roof gardens, shower rooms, and sometimes swimming pools. Such was clearly the story at the Uptown Talmud Torah (UTT) in East Harlem. Although founded as a heder in the early 1890s, it had become, under Harry Fischel's coaxing and coaching, an "up-to-date" school. Indeed, in 1911 he reported how the school board that he commanded authorized "a course in physical training be given to those children who are enrolled as pupils who have attained the age of ten years and over. . . . In this manner, we provide not only for the mental but for the physical development of the pupils." Such a move was in keeping with the school's mission statement of 1909 that called for the "broadening of the mental, moral, physical and religious instruction of our Jewish boys and girls." Four years later, when an annex bearing Fischel's name was built in central Harlem, it was mandated that "pupils of all the classes and all members of the clubs will have access to the gymnasium and shower baths under the direction of trained physical trainers." By 1915, the Lexington Avenue branch could boast that some "forty clubs meet weekly for literary, social and athletic meetings."[32]

However, for all the power and sincerity of their words and deeds, Bublick, Fischel, Hyman, and their teammates were unique communal figures for that time, place, and first generation. If anything, when they recognized that sports were neither foreign to their personal consciousness nor incompatible with religious identification, they demonstrated how far ahead of their fellow immigrants they were. The values and culture of the athletic world had been unknown to them while they lived in eastern Europe and when they first arrived in America. But now they were talking like confirmed physical culturists, even if they personally did not work out in their own funded gyms. Most important, instead of fearing the next generation's interest in sports, they viewed it as a hook that could be used as a first step in creating a walkable bridge between Jewish generations. Most members of their generation did not quite see athletics in that positive light.[33]

It remained for a new generation of Jewish leaders, raised up in this country and personally exposed to the good and the bad of the public schools, settlements, and streets, to broaden these ideas about sports within American Judaism. The training venue and home base for these major players on the communal scene was the Jewish Theological Seminary of America (JTSA). Although physical education was not part of its formal curriculum, a seminarian's cognizance of, and comfort with, what really

"Strike One! A Game of Ball While Waiting for Class to
Start — Uptown Talmud Torah," circa 1917. *Jewish Communal
Register, 1917–1918.*

interested young people was deemed an important point of emphasis. After
all, the avowed mission of the school was to train rabbis and teachers who
could relate to, and then teach Judaism to, their own kind. It was a kind of
received wisdom that without a knowledge of sports, the men and women of
JTSA would never get to first base with the children of eastern European
immigrants. (While only men could be trained as rabbis, the Seminary's
Teacher Institute was coeducational and educated the very instructors who
would man and woman those modern talmud torahs.)[34]

Seminary head Solomon Schechter affirmed this viewpoint in almost legendary fashion in a conversation with a favored rabbinical student, Louis
Finkelstein, sometime in the early 1910s. Reportedly, as the "white-maned"
scholar and his devoted disciple walked down "the street one day, Dr.
Schechter stopped at a newsstand" to check out "the latest World Series
scores." Evidently, by that time, this Romanian-born, German- and British-
trained expert in rabbinics had become Americanized enough that he knew
when the Fall Classic took place and recognized its importance to Jews in

57

this country. "Can you play baseball?" Schechter inquired of his young man. When the callow Finkelstein, who evidently had never spent time playing stickball in the streets, replied, "No," Schechter chided him: "Remember this, unless you can play baseball, you will never get to be a rabbi in America." (Finkelstein family tradition has it that Schechter asked his student whether he "knew" about baseball.) Whatever version is accurate, the import of the question remains the same: Knowing who led the league would help any rabbi initiate dialogue with youthful congregants. And a preacher who could punctuate his sermons with sports metaphors and references would find people in the pews sitting up and taking notice.[35]

Finkelstein did not immediately repair to the YMHA in his home borough of Brooklyn to work on his swing. In fact, he personally never became either an athlete or a sports fan. For that matter, this sideline sitter "never went to a dance or had a date with a girl in his student days." The rabbi's own son has recalled that "despite Schechter's advice my father knew very little about American sports and could never understand my enthusiasm for the right fielder of the New York Giants whom he called 'Odd' [Mel Ott]." And, notwithstanding his teacher's admonition, this weakness in his rabbinical resume did not prevent this future head of "Schechter's Seminary" from having a distinguished career as a religious leader. He would find other ways to engage and interest youthful listeners. Still, if this young scholar-in-training did not care about the national pastime, others within Finkelstein's own cohort of Seminary contemporaries clearly did. And the sentiments that Schechter harbored, and may have expressed publicly to other students, also made abundant sense to subsequent generations of JTSA graduates. They studied major league statistics religiously.[36]

Speaking for the majority, right around the time of the Schechter-Finkelstein chat, Seminary-trained Rabbi Herbert S. Goldstein explained how essential it was for a rabbi to be a sportsman if he hoped to "do missionary work among those who have gone astray." Potential congregants, he declared, were Jews who "desire to break down these Ghetto walls; they desire to live as their neighbors, their fellow citizens — the Americans." As proof of their desire to be teammates with those around them, "they will enter into the sports and games and leave their Bible, their Talmud for the specialist, for the student," maybe for nerdy fellows like Louis Finkelstein![37]

Goldstein wondered out loud: "Who will deal with this type of American youth?" Not the rabbi of the older generation, who "spent all of his life in the schoolroom . . . who has come here and is out of sympathy with athletics, games, sports and all the manifold varieties of social life of today." Given their lack of appropriate training, he continued, these "foreign, uninteresting teachers" had made the child "happy to close his Siddur, [and] glad to free himself from his *Cheder* [*sic*]." As budding adults, they would have little interest in synagogue and religious life. In his view, only the "younger Orthodox rabbis in America . . . who [have] gone through this kind of youth and social life can be in sympathy with this type of young man and young woman, can meet him or her on their own level." They alone "by reason of their training [were] eminently fitted to take part, as educators, to win back the child for the religious school."[38]

Clearly, the self-promoting Goldstein was speaking about himself as a model Jewish missionary. Though personally not an outstanding athlete, while a pupil in Public School 2 on the Lower East Side, he undoubtedly took the required physical training courses. And reportedly as a high school student at the academically prestigious Townsend Harris High School, he "turned out for the football squad," but did not make the team. We will never know what might have become of his religious values and scruples had he made the club. Goldstein also participated while a freshman at Columbia University in "the class tug of war." So the ambitious modern rabbi knew his way around a gym and could talk about sports with potential followers. Moreover, the dilemmas he might have faced as an aspiring football player may have sensitized him to the observance issues that confronted the young people with whom he huddled.[39]

As important, he had a game plan in mind to "make the [Jewish] school-house a centre where the boy will have the opportunity to give vent to his play instinct, thereby being attracted to the school." He reasoned that "if the play instincts . . . of the child are permitted to have free rein in the schoolhouse, the child will have a desire to go there." He understood that otherwise youngsters would be more than happy to spend all of their leisure time playing with their friends of all kinds and dispositions.[40]

In pointing up his alternative, Goldstein had less-than-flattering words for other modern Jewish institutions that were already involved in getting Jewish boys and girls off the streets. From his vantage point at Yorkville's Congregation Kehilath Jeshurun, where he began serving as assistant rabbi in 1913, Goldstein closely observed the honest efforts of his neighboring YMHA. This institution had initially come into existence in the 1870s to provide young German-American Jewish dandies with a liquor-free and al-most smokeless social and athletic environment, to get them away from the unhealthy club scene. By the turn of the twentieth century, the Y had turned its attention to a different group of second-generation Jews. Now the clients were primarily eastern European boys and young men whom the Hebrew Association hoped could be taught to "be strong against temptation . . . to avoid the countless forms of allurement which vice presents." In the Y lead-ers' view, "after a day's work, the tired young man needs recreation," and their gymnasium offers them the most appropriate "opportunity for physi-cal culture." That meant that an aggressive youth would box under the supervision of a trained coach rather than rumble along neighborhood avenues. Or a lithe potential gymnast would be instructed how to properly climb up a rope to the gym's ceiling rather than learn how to shimmy up an exposed tenement pipe to an open and enticing second-floor window.[41]

However, the knock against the Y, at least from Goldstein's perspective, was that it "only takes the boy off the street and does not give him the education of a Jewish religious environment." True, the Y held religious activities and sponsored Jewish educational classes and programs conducted by JTSA students. Indeed, the 92nd Street institution received high marks from local Jewish journalists when in 1900 it inaugurated Friday evening religious services. (It already had a tradition of sponsoring High Holiday gatherings.) Deemed as "a step in the right direction," Sabbath prayers were judged as proof that "the organization is willing and eager to enter the religious field, where it can together with its gymnastic appliances, develop both the spiritual and physical side of the young members."[42]

But sports, dances, even the library and good, new-fashioned Americanization classes like bookkeeping and elocution were the institution's calling card. Goldstein probably did not have access to an internal Y report of some years earlier that noted that "Religious Exercises" ranked fifth in popularity among Y members, far behind gym, library, lectures, and entertainment. And the study showed that when it came to classes, students preferred bookkeeping, arithmetic, and elocution much more than Hebrew and Jewish history. Had he possessed those documents, they would have only added more fuel to his fiery observation that "the educational centers or the Young Men's Hebrew Association, which are illegitimate synagogal offspring," have contributed to "the problem of the religion of our young." For him, an unhappy tradition was continuing where at the Y those who came to play were not aggressively recruited for loftier goals. Y mission statements that spoke mainly of making youngsters "proud of being Jews and to make them feel the obligation to live up to the highest Jewish traditions . . . to bring to the service of their country the same steadfastness to their ideals which their fathers showed," left the rabbi totally unmoved. As Goldstein saw it, instead of "curing the headache" of the decline of the Jewish home and synagogue in youthful minds and hearts, he concluded, "we have substituted a toothache."[43]

Goldstein was far more circumspect in his criticism of the modern talmud torah movement that his future father-in-law was then championing. (In 1913, the young rabbi was seriously dating Rebecca Betty Fischel.) While these schools, as he saw them, were worthy of praise — they surely offered the best of facilities and the most up-to-date Jewish programming — still they had failed, to date, to capture the imagination and interest of so many youngsters. By his estimate, only 15 percent of Jewish children were turning out for these religious schools, most of them drawn from among the poor and unacculturated.[44] So many other "half-baked" young people remained out in the streets, estranged from religious life. Somehow they had to be drawn back to the synagogue.

Goldstein's solution was the creation of a multifaceted, user-friendly, and attractive Americanized synagogue that could boast of a school, shul, club-rooms, and athletic facilities all under one roof and under staunch religious inspiration. He planned for "amalgamating Jewish social, cultural, and recreational programs with religious educational activities under the auspices of an established Orthodox congregation." His working assumption was that a way could be found to interest those who liked mostly to play to stay around to pray, study, and affiliate. Although he did not acknowledge its Reform antecedent, in 1916 he began rolling out in Upper Manhattan what was, in many ways, a prototype of a new, improved model of the nineteenth-century Temple Center. With Samuel I. Hyman's financial assistance, the Central Jewish Institute (CJI) was established as an extension of the modern Yorkville Talmud Torah and as an appendage of Kehilath Jeshurun with all the social and athletic facilities of the neighboring Y. Its self-declared mission was "to promote the welfare — religious, moral, social and physical — of our Jewish young; to maintain a school for the tuition of the Jewish religion in accordance with the tenets of traditional law; to maintain a center for civic and communal activities." From a purely sports perspective that meant offering gymnastics, calisthenics, volleyball, indoor and outdoor handball, and basketball games to students and to the extended congregational family members.[45]

Less than two years later, the ambitious Goldstein, out for even bigger game, took his Judaism, sports, games, dances, and recreation package on the road to neighboring Harlem. At his Institutional Synagogue, founded in 1917 with Harry Fischel's financial help, the target audience was expressly "many of those . . . attracted to . . . its diverse activities [that] would not be apt to go into a synagogue *per se*." The concrete strategy was that those with non-religious endeavors on their minds, be they athletes, dancers, or club aficionados, would naturally "pass the Synagogue hall and cannot help dropping in for services because it does not require an extra effort, as he or she follows the path of least resistance."[46]

And what sort of attractive Jewish message could a charismatic American rabbi offer young Jews who might find their way to the friendly confines of the sanctuary? In January 1915, even as Goldstein was hatching his plans, another outreach-oriented Seminary graduate was offering praise and seeking a place for the "physically efficient" Jew within contemporary religious culture. From his pulpit at Brooklyn's Temple B'nai Shaloum, Rabbi Israel Herbert Levinthal defined the "real Jew" as the fellow who was "perfect physically, perfect morally, and perfect intellectually." For Levinthal, this model of "ideal Jewish manhood" was a modern incarnation of "our patriarch Jacob." Most appropriately for this audience, Levinthal framed the forefather not only as the intellectualized yeshiva student honored in Jewish tradition but also, we might say, as a weight lifter and wrestler. Jacob was projected to a twentieth-century audience as the first Jewish scholar-athlete and surely worthy of emulation. Levinthal's Jacob had a "firm head . . . his chest was broad, his back was straight, his walk was steady, his arms were

Central Jewish Institute, circa 1917. *Jewish Communal Register,*
1917–1918.

strong." And he was equally at home "toil[ing] in vineyards" as he was studying near his tent in that classic sedentary pose. Unfortunately, Levinthal observed, "twenty hundred years of constant persecution" had taken Jews out of touch with their physical past. Sounding very much like both the friends and foes of immigrants of his time, Levinthal allowed that when "we look upon the average Jew today who comes to these shores . . . we notice his bent back, his drooping head, his narrow chest, his heavy walk, his weak and feeble arms." But the good news now was that Jews in America could regain their ancient stature. To his mind, one of the goals of the synagogue — for that matter, all institutions and agencies that dealt with his people — was "to promote the physical efficiency of the Jew." Here the rhetoric of the public school and the settlement house was preached from the religious pulpit. Opening the door this way to the athletically inclined, the Jacobs of the future, the next step for the rabbi was to make them fully at home with their Jewishness.[47]

So disposed, Levinthal kept close tabs on the evolution of all-purpose synagogues in Manhattan and in 1921 witnessed the building of his own Brooklyn Jewish Center on Eastern Parkway. Indeed, in many ways, his approach and operation clearly resembled Goldstein's initiative. Levinthal envisioned his center as a "Seven Day Synagogue" that offered families religious services, modern talmud torah classes and other educational programs, cultural events of all sorts, and, of course, a panorama of athletic activities, all under one roof.[48]

Those young "estranged . . . drifting" second-generation Jews whom the Harlem-based leader had set out to reach also were his prime audience. And his outreach methodology was the same. Make center facilities available, Levinthal argued, for the "many [who] will come for other purposes than to meet God. . . . Let them come; let them assemble at the *door of the Tabernacle* and you will find . . . that a large percentage of these will be won from outside the door into the portals of the Synagogue proper."

The "magic" of the Center would operate in the following way:

> The young man, entering the gymnasium class, would notice the announcement on the bulletin board that on the next evening a meeting would be held in the interest of Jewish refugees or for relief — that this or that man would speak — his interest would be aroused, and his presence thus assured. He would attend the [weekday] Forum lecture. The chairman would announce that on the coming Friday eve, the Rabbi would speak on this or that subject. It so happened that the subject appealed to him. He would come to the services. If the services appealed to him, he would come again. Thus, the Center activities become directly responsible for an increased enthusiasm for an interest in those activities of the Synagogue which should be nearest to the heart of the Jew.[49]

Of course, Levinthal and his followers helped the magic along by advertising and promoting this very Jewish triple-play — from sports to lectures to

A pool in a shul, the Brooklyn Jewish Center, circa 1920s.
Courtesy of the Ratner Center for the Study of Conservative
Judaism, Jewish Theological Seminary of America.

prayers—prominently within the synagogue's bulletin. For example, the
back page of the April 20, 1923, synagogue weekly offered members "six
private golf lessons [for] $10 . . . [contact] Joseph H. Schwartz, Chair, Ath-
letic Committee," highlighted Dr. Raymond Brook's upcoming lecture on
"Outlawing War—Next Step in Civilization," and invited all comers to "our
Saturday morning services for a service of beauty. For a sermon that inspires. Get the habit every Saturday morning."[50]

The only noteworthy difference between the Institutional Synagogue and
the Brooklyn Jewish Center (BJC) was that if and when a member was attracted to the Eastern Parkway synagogue, he or she would take part in an
incipient Conservative service. In the 1920s and 1930s, even as Levinthal
was finding his way in modernizing the ritual at the BJC, the religious calling
card of his institution was his very popular late Friday service with this

renowned preacher as the featured attraction. The Institutional Synagogue was unequivocally Orthodox.

In launching their comparable efforts, both Levinthal and Goldstein would have been totally remiss had they not noted the role Rabbi Mordecai M. Kaplan's teachings and activities played in influencing and even guiding what they set out to do. Actually, the Brooklyn-based Conservative rabbi readily acknowledged what Kaplan meant to him. The Orthodox Goldstein, on the other hand, who had grave difficulties with the Reconstructionist rabbi's radical theological stances, was hard-pressed to speak highly of Kaplan's social vision. By the way, Kaplan personally did not like Goldstein and the feeling seems to have been mutual.[51]

Nonetheless, the fact remains that Kaplan was an influence or an inspiration in both Goldstein's and Levinthal's developments. He had been their professor at the Seminary during the period where he was Goldstein's predecessor as "Minister," and subsequently English-speaking Rabbi at Kehilath Jeshurun. Harry Fischel was then one of Kaplan's congregants. The future Reconstructionist leader was a member of the Uptown Talmud Torah's Board of Education and many of his students — men and women both — taught at the UTT. For a while, the Seminary Teachers' Institute, which Kaplan headed, actually was housed within the Harlem Jewish school building. The peripatetic professor also hovered around the CJI crowd as deliberations ensued that led to Hyman and Goldstein opening their institution.[52]

Thus he knew all about neighborhood problems including an understanding of the dreams and goals of budding Jewish sportsmen. For as a youth he had "desired" to earn an athletic letter as a member of Columbia University's "scrub football team." But in the end he "had too much work to carry out [his] ambition." The busy Kaplan did find some time, as a rabbinical student, to do some boxing, but his competitive athletic career was short-lived. He looked elsewhere for recreation after his sparring partner, classmate Benjamin Aaron Tintner "managed to break the edges of two of [his] front teeth." All told, armed with these broadening experiences within and without talmud torah rooms, board rooms, and gymnasium weight rooms, Kaplan, from the first decade of the past century on, felt comfortable preaching his synagogue-centered programs to second-generation Jews. Ultimately, his ideas would be applied as much to Eastern Parkway as to Yorkville or Harlem.[53]

From his inside-the-loop perspective as chair of the Y's Committee on Religious Work for a number of years beginning in 1913, Kaplan was keenly critical of that institution's Jewish limitations, and he was as outspoken as Goldstein about where the Y had failed. Whether it was in the Jewish newspapers of the time or in personal communications to Y leaders, he made the point that while "entertainments, the pool room, and the gymnasium may serve as a temporary means of keeping young men away from the gambling dens and worse," the Y had to "stimulate in them a positive enthusiasm for

Judaism." The sad fact was that "the young people themselves who came into the clubs and classes were not interested in Jewish matters and did not care to hear of them." In fact, his jaundiced advice was if the Y could not reverse its field of activity, he "would most strongly advocate that the YMHA become a purely secular organization." In due time, Kaplan made clear that the well-integrated synagogue, his Jewish Center project, was the only way of meeting the Jewish needs of young people and their families.[54]

By his own account, his personal, troubling observation of Jewish young adults playing baseball in the streets on a Sabbath afternoon while their still-devout elders listened to a rabbi drone on in a shul about some traditional text — "there were no young men among the listeners" — helped quicken his and his supporters' pace to create a model synagogue. Their home base would be within the new up-and-coming community of the West Side. Some of his old-time backers from his Kehilath Jeshurun days, who had over the years heard his laments and resonated to his draft plans, helped him move forward with his endeavor.[55]

The formula — which Goldstein had already started to implement and which Levinthal and scores of others would follow — called for the "trans-lat[ion]" of the synagogue into "a synagogue center . . . where all the members of the family would feel at home during the seven days of the week. There they could sing and dance and play." The notion of the week-long synagogue, a concept that Levinthal would favor as his own trademark, was now activated. Unquestionably, one of the most closely watched and trumpeted indicators that the Center was fulfilling its mission would be the extent to which the "athletikers," as synagogue bulletin editor Mordecai Kaplan called them, found their way from gym or pool to the sanctuary. For the rabbi, a "happy Center combination" took place when "two youngsters were overheard while walking into the gymnasium, humming to themselves with delightful unselfconsciousness, the 'Meleh Elyon' melody [a prayer from the High Holiday liturgy] sung a few minutes earlier on the floor below." He was also absolutely delighted with "a group of six earnest 'ath-letikers' whose 'regular menu' includes 'the Gymnasium, the Pool, Shahris [Morning Prayers], breakfast and the resultant 'grand and glorious feel-ing.' " Here both Kaplan and the youngsters were experiencing endorphin rushes from that potent combination of religious and sports activities. The many Conservative and some of the Orthodox rabbis who would seek to follow in Kaplan's footsteps would be pleased if and when they could brag like him about similar successes with young people.[56]

Indeed, the 1920s witnessed synagogues and rabbis throughout much of this country working for their own version of the "happy Center combi-nation." In many places, synagogue leaders minced no words when they boasted that "we work on the theory that coming to the Social center regu-larly and often will gradually rekindle the dormant spark of Jewishness in all of us and eventually these thousands" — like the 13,473 males and 7,461 females who worked out at Newark's Temple B'nai Abraham in 1927 — "will make a beaten path to our Temple Service." Borrowing a page from Kaplan's already dog-eared book, the builders of commodious gymnasiums, fully equipped pools, and bowling alleys fervently believed that only "by extending . . . activities to include not only the education and religious training of the young and old, but also to promote their social and physical training," could they "arouse a keener interest in Jewish religion and affairs" among the "great many [who] had become careless in observance . . . or had become indifferent and drifted from the faith of their fathers."[57]

The momentum that the wizard of the West Side generated was felt mainly among the growing Conservative congregations of this land. But the budding Orthodox Young Israel movement also resonated to his plan. In fact, as early as 1916, Harry G. Fromberg, one of its founders, declared that "the real aim" of his organization was the creation of "an institutional synagogue on the east side [of Manhattan], . . . a social center [complete] with a gymnasium." When that movement made its way to Brooklyn in the early 1920s, leaders of the Young Israel of Brooklyn made good on Fromberg's pledge. Its first permanent home in that borough, an altered "club house," had a gymnasium and a dance hall on premises in addition to its auditorium-sanctuary and classrooms. Ballplaying and dancing would remain a fixture of Young Israel activity for several succeeding generations.[58]

How could these congregations on the move know if they were doing a good job? The synagogue that Louise Schneider attended in the southeast Bronx had to have believed that it was getting its message across when in 1922 this eleven-year-old girl won a short story contest sponsored by the *United Synagogue Recorder* with a tale about "The Boy Who Didn't Want to Go to Temple." Her story depicts a kid named David, the best pitcher on his baseball team, probably a sandlot bunch in the decades before Little League, who is cajoled by his mother to attend temple instead of playing a game that morning. His mother induced him to show up — even if he was disappointing his friends — with a promise that "a surprise was coming." The surprise turned out to be impressive "Confirmation exercises" where "five boys in dark suits and the same amount of girls dressed all in white" conducted the service or otherwise spoke to the congregation. On the way home from this "beautiful" service, David, the now inspired and future confirmation student, said to his mother, "It was a surprise and to think I was going to miss it and play baseball on Shevuot [*sic*]." Louise's message is clear. If ways could be found to get those who preferred their games to experience a service where children were made the center of attention, they could be attracted to life in the sanctuary. The right kind of shul could compete with the call of the street. Kaplan — and for that matter Levinthal and Goldstein, all of whom undoubtedly subscribed to the *Recorder* — must have smiled when they read a young girl's innocent promotional piece for their activities.[59]

Not every Americanized congregation had either the resources or the interest in following Kaplan, the leader. For example, in 1924, Rabbi Louis Finkelstein's congregation Kehilath Israel, situated across the street from bucolic Crotona Park, built its own "beautiful community center" complete with a talmud torah wing and social hall. But Finkelstein, decidedly the non-athlete, reportedly was not "inclined to use that vehicle . . . the image of athleticism, to try and attract young people to the house of worship." On the other hand, he did not "condemn those who did." However, other rabbis of Finkelstein's time were not nearly as sportsmanlike toward the athletics-Judaism strategy.[60]

In fact, as early as the mid-1910s, a more heated replay of the debate over the late-nineteenth-century Temple Center was already ongoing, as critics from a variety of venues questioned the appropriateness and efficacy of this loudly touted outreach approach. First, there were those who now argued, even more than opponents had before, that the positioning of the sports facility so close to the sanctuary smacked of "secularization" and engendered disdain and disrespect for the faith and its traditions. From the very start, beginning with the CJI, "older members of the congregation" deemed as "sacrilegious . . . the propinquity of shower baths and religious school." But then again, old-line Orthodox Jews had problems with the whole gamut of new educational plans. Harry Fischel had fought that battle at the UTT.[61]

Meanwhile, from within Conservative circles came some marked ambivalence about this entire scene from none other than Solomon Schechter himself. In one of his last speeches before his death in 1915, Schechter bitingly warned that the "synagogue itself . . . a Sacred Place [not] be largely stripped of its sacred features." While he did not renege here on his advice about baseball and congregants, he did express open apprehension that an unbridled "Institutional Synagogue" — he mentioned Goldstein's projected initiative by name — not let "the worship of God . . . become in the end subordinated to the material service of man and his amusements." For him, a rabbi speaking of sports was acceptable, but the world of such fun and games should not be emphasized too strongly within shul precincts.[62]

That same year, 1915, Reform spokesmen also weighed in with a telling reservation. Editors of the *American Israelite* openly feared "that the social center which is regularly attached to the synagogue will become not an accessory of congregational life but . . . the synagogue with its function of prayer and teaching will merely be tolerated as an adjunct to the social center."[63]

A decade or so after both Schechter and his more liberal Jewish counterparts spoke out, some United Synagogue of America officials sketched out a much-worse-case situation in which "institutionalizing the synagogue" and the "pursuit of recreation and sport" had rendered some congregations little more than Jewish "social and country clubs." For these critics, "swimming pools and Forums however well patronized are as indicative of religious health and well-being, as Jewish pugilists and heroes of the gridiron" who generally were far from the best religious role models.[64]

Then there was Rabbi Israel Goldstein, a self-designated "agnostic" when it came to the 1920s Synagogue Center initiative. Maybe his agnosticism here ultimately meant that he did not really believe in the sports-Judaism scenario even if gymnasium activities existed within the life of his own congregation, New York's B'nai Jeshurun. He once angrily characterized the Synagogue Center idea as "the rabbi's folly and the laymen's Paradise." While this Goldstein, no relation to Herbert, admitted that sports and other social activities created "a certain amount of good-will [among] . . . young people who were formerly afraid of the synagogue and distrusted it," he was unconvinced that "the Synagogue Center has made the Jewish youth more responsive to the full Jewish life." Indeed, he worried out loud that "the same young people who, when they were shy of the synagogue at least had a reverence for it, now, as a result of playing basketball in its very premises, lost their reverence for the synagogue." He openly questioned whether "if the Synagogue Center has had the effect of erasing the distinction between the sacred and the secular, it has been at the expense of the sacred." For him, seeing the rabbi as "a good fellow" — maybe even having the spiritual leader work out with them in the gymnasium — did not make youngsters attuned to the faith messages he ultimately sought to impart. Rather, it rendered synagogue life "banal and even vulgar."[65]

If anything, Rabbi Joel Blau chimed in, when a rabbi peppered his talks to congregants with references to "tango dancing" and "baseball" to keep men and women in the pews from "fidget[ing]" during his sermon, he did major damage to the dignity of the "Jewish pulpit." Writing at just about the same time as his Brooklyn colleague Levinthal was speaking about "ideal Jewish manhood," Blau made clear that "the function of any pulpit is inspirational . . . to keep the God passion burning within human hearts." As he put it, "topics you call life, live only for a day or so." Reportedly, some years later, Blau — no friend of what Herbert S. Goldstein, Kaplan, and Levinthal had wrought — was the first to derisively characterize the Synagogue Center movement as the "shul with a pool" phenomenon.[66]

Indeed, in 1925, Blau again went on the offensive with comparable criticism about what rabbis who supported the sports-Judaism synthesis were doing to their sacred religious space. He mocked the assumption that "since the young . . . want athletics, swimming pools, dances, lectures on not too difficult subjects, we will give it to them, and not incidentally, we will lure them to a little bit of a religious service and with a little bit of a sermon preferably on the topics of the day, so that little by little they might become used to going to the synagogue and imbibing what is called Jewishness." Blau's colleague in the Conservative rabbinate, Rabbi Samuel Freedman, went even further when he lampooned as "prize fight promoters" those who in their "frantic desire to attract the youth of the synagogue . . . have so far catered to their tastes that they no longer look upon it as a religious institu-tion." For him, they were not much different from boxing entrepreneurs who would do anything to get fans into the arena. To these attacks, the tolerant Levinthal—after all, he did let Blau's remarks appear in his own Brooklyn Jewish Center's *Annual*—would only reply, "The fact that the Cen-ter possesses the facilities for all those manifold activities does not mean that we neglect the synagogue or that we have minimized the importance of the Religious School. Nay, the very reverse is the truth."[67]

But beyond the appropriateness of secular activities, sports rhetoric in sermonics, and knocking the shul and the rabbi off their respective pedes-tals, there lay the even more fundamental issue of whether the "magic" that Levinthal bragged about actually worked. Indeed, critics alleged, from the very start of the movement—beginning again with the CJI experiment—that the youth of Jewish America were not really finding their way from the pool to the shul. Even if youngsters never made fun of the rabbi, now reduced to being just a "regular guy," they were not frequenting his part of the complex.

The first attacks—really counterattacks—came from officials of the YMHA who were offended by Herbert S. Goldstein's contention that their organization failed "to impart positive religion in the minds of youth." Their riposte was that Goldstein's decidedly religious institution, which in their view circumscribed its pitch to youngsters who shared "the same be-lief" as the leader, ended up with a tepid type of member who was neither staunchly Orthodox nor particularly committed to Jewish life. Their story line had many CJI sports people "merely attracted to the center because of the comfortable facilities . . . [joining] clubs [that] . . . assumed Jewish names, but that was as far as their Jewish activities extend. These young men don't for the most part attend either the Talmud Torah or the synagogue of the Institute." Preferring their own soft-sell approach, Y officials argued that they were doing a better job of offsetting "the keen competition of the commercialized dance halls and other places of recreation." Their Jewish courses, lectures, and the like have lit "dormant sparks of Judaism in the breasts of a great many of our young men [which] are fanned into consum-ing flames."[68]

Soon thereafter, at the point where in the early 1920s the Jewish Centers of Manhattan and Brooklyn were first making their mark, Bronx rabbi Nor-man Salit reported that "there is a most disheartening and sinister lack of interest on the part of the younger generation connected with the usual synagogue. Services of any description fail absolutely to draw attendance in the part of any proportion of the young people." Even those youngsters who "*do* attend clubs connected with the congregation" that offer "athletic activity . . . along the lines of hikes, athletic teams and athletic meets" and, most importantly, dances, evidenced "a decided lack of serious purpose." The worst news was that many rabbis "regard mere attendance at clubs as highly desirable" which is the "minimum of demands to be made on young people."[69]

Maybe the issue was, suggested Brooklyn rabbi Harry Weiss, that "one has only a certain amount of energy at his command, and when, during the week, one attends a card party" — and I will say "the gym" — "one feels that one's duty towards the Congregation is fully performed and the Friday night and Saturday morning services are of necessity neglected." Even more to the point, Weiss continued, a large part of the problem was that synagogue sports staffs were less than helpful in directing the athlete from play to prayer. "I am yet to hear an athletic director say," he lamented, "we have enjoyed the gymnasium of the Synagogue for long, we have served the cause of play, now come boys, next Friday night let us all turn out and hear something about our ancient Faith and about the ideals of our people."[70]

Indeed, a truly committed sports instructor could be a great advocate for Judaism. He or she could be a teacher of Jewish values within the very confines of their own athletic facilities. Such, at least, was Rabbi Samuel M. Cohen's vision when he wrote in 1927 that "the gymnasium is as important as the elementary [Jewish] school." As he saw it, principles of effective Jewish living "can best be learned through physical exercise and through the athletic game." He said that one of the best ways for a youngster to learn about the cardinal Jewish principle of "adherence to Law" is "through activities in which the gymnasium is used." He asked, "What is sportsmanship, for instance, but the recognition of the authority of the Law?"

But unfortunately, the gym teachers he knew — the peripatetic Cohen traveled the country in the 1920s promoting United Synagogue activities — were usually not trained or prepared when it came to imparting such a sophisticated message. In many communities, he remarked, "the gymnasium [was] in [the] charge of a retired pugilist."[71]

In 1928, Rabbi Alter F. Landesman put up some depressing numbers to support the growing impression that the hoped-for move from gymnasium to sanctuary was not really working. His survey of "Synagogue Attendance" within United Synagogue congregations revealed that "the majority of [reporting] rabbis having experience with synagogue centers indicate that the results thus far have been negative or very slight . . . in augmenting attendance at the religious services." Rabbi Abraham J. Levy undoubtedly spoke for that majority when he said that "historically, worship and study led men to the social activities of the Synagogue and not vice versa." Only 30 percent or so of respondents felt it had "a favorable effect on attendance." Others were "still doubtful as to its effect." In their view, "it is too young an institution to be judged accurately."[72]

By that time, Reform rabbi Philip David Bookstaber was also on the record with comparable figures that questioned his movement's own Temple Center enterprise, now in its third generation. His survey of some thirty-six Temple Centers that had built pools and gyms "to 'feed' the Congregation with members; to 'catch' the young man or woman who is becoming estranged from the Temple," determined that "attendance at our religious services has not been augmented." Moreover, "no appreciable increase of membership on the part of young men and women is manifest [and] the Temple Center has not initiated any religious fervor." Indeed, he reported that, in fact, "the more forceful and energetic rabbis are adopting curative and preventive measures" against the wrong types of incursions and "gradu- ally limiting the expansion of the extra activities." For the truth was, as one of Bookstaber's colleagues saw it, the changing of the "Charleston to the Tel Aviv," giving dances a "Jewish and moral hue," or "calling upon the gymnasium . . . in an attempt to bring them back" was a grave disappoint- ment. The answer for Bookstaber and many others within and without his movement was not costly facilities that failed to point the way to religion. Rather, they put their faith in the establishment of a one-on-one "relation- ship to the adolescent boy or girl who crave for the spiritual comradeship which the rabbi, as spiritual leader and hero can give." For him, a skilled rabbi did not need a gym or pool to connect to young people.[73]

Samuel D. Schwartz, executive director of the Emil G. Hirsch Center of the Chicago Sinai Congregation, did not take well to Bookstaber's gloomy statistics and critical comments. For him, the successful thirty-year history of his institution was evidence enough of the worth of Synagogue/Temple Center efforts. He scoffed at those who spoke derisively of "shuls and pools," pointing out that Rabbi Hirsch himself had been "ridiculed" for "returning to the old Orthodox ritual in installing a swimming pool or 'Mikveh.' " But this visionary, as Schwartz saw him, persevered, oblivious to thoughtless sarcasm, and "through our swimming pool and gymnasium . . . we have succeeded in having people come to us and then gradually learn to come to our Temple." Moreover, he contended that the Center has "developed a community spirit which has made the people in our section of the city feel that to move away from the vicinity of our Temple meant depriving them of some of the most important needs of their lives." Today, "our gymnasium and swimming pool, with unexcelled facilities . . . have proved their merit again and again." For Schwartz, they "compel men to *work out* the best in them" — once again the weight room found a positive place in modern Jewish culture — as they strive toward achieving "all the potentialities of the human heart and soul."[74]

Upon hearing these remarks at a conference of the Central Conference of American Rabbis, a different Rabbi Schwartz sided somewhat with the Hirsch Center director and wondered out loud whether rabbis were too accustomed to judge the value of an initiative on the basis of the number of people who were or were not immediately attracted to services. He believed, rather, that there was no reason to despair if, at present, "there are a great many young men and young women who come to think that all there is to religion is a dance, or a card party, or some other gymnastic performance on the premises of the temple." As he put it — with the help of Scriptures — "it is possible that for the time being the saying of the psalmist is not altogether carried out that for the time being they dance only with their bodies." But he was confident that "after years to come," many of these same people will show up at "services Friday, Shabbo [*sic*] morning or Sunday morning." To this almost prophetic style vision, Rabbi Louis Gross of Brooklyn could only affirm that while "there would seem to be no theological implications in a gymnasium or a social dance, . . . the fact that these things are administered under Jewish religious auspices is the important consideration." For him, the phrase " 'Muscular Judaism' is not necessarily ridiculous, and as for the secularization of the Synagogue the answer is 'Talmud Torah Keneged Kulom" [*sic*] [fig. "finding a means to spread the study of Torah is what it is all about"].[75]

It remained for the rabbi of Cleveland's Congregation Tifereth Israel — it was the first temple to construct its own gymnasium almost thirty years earlier — to bring this 1920s debate over the sports-Judaism synthesis full circle and to have the last word, at least for a while. By the mid-1920s, Rabbi Abba Hillel Silver was already a nationally recognized Jewish religious and political figure. He was certainly as well-known and arguably as influential as Kaplan. So when he lined up against the Synagogue Center movement it was cause for pause in many religious circles.

The planned construction, in 1924, of a new temple site was the immediate impetus for Tifereth Israel officials and their rabbi to reconsider their own Temple Center experience. And the story they told themselves — and eventually related to New York's *American Hebrew* — was not the type of glorious saga that Schwartz trumpeted for Chicago's Sinai Congregation. For Silver, who in 1917 succeeded the sports-supportive Moses Gries, the fact was that "activities of a purely secular and recreational nature aimed at entertaining people . . . contribute little or nothing to spiritual life." Or as Silver's biographer has put it, "there was little evidence that dances, plays, basketball and parties drew young people to worship services." Silver's traditional answer was for the synagogue "to concentrate upon those basic community needs which, from its inception, have been its particular province — religious inspiration and religious education."[76]

For the board members who supported their rabbi's position, one other personal consideration was apparent. The temple's facilities were open to all comers, including what snobbish members might have called riffraff, maybe even riffraff of eastern European extraction. Preferring to associate with their own kind of "homogeneous social groups," those in charge did not champion the idea of further expenditures of "time, money and energy" on a facility they could do without.[77]

In taking that stance, these lay leaders showed how different their perspective was from the unrealized dream one other Reform rabbi had for Synagogue and Temple Centers. In 1914, even as most Synagogue Center plans were still only on temple drawing boards, Horace J. Wolf envisioned a temple "transformed . . . from a Congregational to a neighborhood institution" in service of "the whole house of Israel." There, "on week days and nights, the children and young people look here for recreation and physical culture." Meanwhile, "the annual athletic meet brings together teams from both halves of the community." Ultimately, the institution that "offers young men and women opportunities for clean recreation under proper chaperonage . . . helps to conserve, by means of Jewish lectures and Jewish study circles, the Jewish consciousness that the strange American environment tends to destroy."[78]

Seemingly, that ideal vision did not dawn on Silver. And if it did, he probably would have found no takers within his exclusion-minded board. In any event, while sports facilities were in the building plans of the new temple, by 1929, "the Old Gymnasium had been converted into an Assembly Hall." Eventually, this mostly unused space would be home to the temple's Museum of Judaica and Religious Art.[79]

The 1920s closed with many American Jewish religious leaders uncertain at best that the use of athletics to attract the sports-minded to the sanctuary was appropriate or effective. But even as Kaplan and his followers carried on with their work and continued to deal, in their own special way, with the impact of America's world of fun and games upon second-generation Jewish youngsters, a new foe appeared on the scene that threatened to undermine their initiatives. Beginning in the 1920s, Synagogue Center enthusiasts confronted challenges to religious identity and faith commitments from, seemingly, an unlikely source, the Jewish Community Center movement. These organizations — in the spirit of early Ys and settlements that preceded them — endeavored, as always, to get the Jewish athlete away from the meanness of the streets. But once inside their community houses, they did less than ever to promote what Herbert S. Goldstein might have called "positive Jewish values." And their institutional policies were sometimes at odds with basic Jewish religious tenets, making it difficult for a Jewish athlete to be a religiously observant sports person.

We will get to the chapter on the battle between the Synagogue Center and the Jewish Community Center in due course. But first, we need to look at another sports-Judaism synthesis that was well under way by the 1920s. Within its own religious milieu, the introduction of sports into the training of "all-American" yeshiva students was one of the ways this committed Jewish subgroup projected itself as in touch and comfortable with the modern world around it.

THE TRAINING OF
"ALL-AMERICAN" YESHIVA BOYS

The founders of Etz Chaim had the highest of expectations for their young charges. When they established their yeshiva in 1886, they prayed that their grammar school–aged boys would be the vanguard of a holy effort to recreate on American soil the best of eastern European religious culture. They wanted these talmudic scholars-in-training raised the way the most outstanding heder boys had been educated back in Russia. And they would expend every effort to keep them away from the lures and ills of the American city and society. So they devised a curriculum that focused almost exclusively on instruction in "the Hebrew Language and the Hebrew Law-Talmud, Bible, *Sulchon Aurach* [*sic*], the Code of Jewish Law] during the whole day from nine in the morning until four in the afternoon." The most meager of general education — two hours a day — was offered "from four in the afternoon." In keeping with their Old World values, the concept of an Orthodox scholar-athlete was totally foreign to them. There is no record of Etz Chaim, at its inception, providing any physical training or sports.[1]

Some ten years later, in 1897, the yeshiva's supporters expanded their initiative when they created for high school- and college-aged students a more advanced branch of their still-fledgling institution. Although the Cer-

75

tificate of Incorporation of what became known as the Rabbi Isaac Elchanan Theological Seminary (RIETS), today an affiliate of Yeshiva University, indicated that one of the missions of the school was the training of "students of the Hebrew faith for the Hebrew Orthodox ministry," nothing was done in its classrooms to get these students ready to address, as American rabbis, the problems of assimilation. No ministerial training, no exposure to the practical side of rabbinics, was offered. Even the provision of a "teacher [who] would give instruction in the language of the land" was an afterthought. At this early juncture, the single-minded goal of the yeshiva's founders was the production of rarified scholars — like eastern Europe was still doing — who would garner for America the reputation as a place where the Torah was studied seriously and effectively.[2]

The problem with this plan, for all the sincerity of its proponents, was that it could find but few takers. They could build it, but almost no one came. The fact of the matter was that even the most devout downtowners — like transplanted Russian rabbis and their wives — wanted their sons to compete on a level playing field with all comers in pursuit of economic advancement and social acceptance. For the parents of Mordecai Kaplan, a school that did not prepare their young man for the real American world could not grab nor hold their allegiance. Rabbi Israel and Anna Kaplan's son attended Etz Chaim for at most a few months before moving on to public school. In time, even the few families who stuck with the yeshiva demanded greater systematic secular training for their sons to advance economically in America. But there was no petitioning on the part of the parent body for a physical education department. Like almost all immigrant parents, they also did not deem the acquisition of sports skills as necessary for advancement in America. However, as Etz Chaim fell more in line with New York State Education Department standards during the first decade of the twentieth century, a few moments a day were set aside for "physical training, recess and organized games." But there was no talk yet of producing well-rounded all-American Orthodox youngsters.[3]

RIETS's most pressing problem was that the few students it did attract quickly demonstrated that they wanted more out of their education than just careers in Torah scholarship. Unlike the school's founders, its disciples believed that "being a rabbi in America is not like being a rabbi in the Old World. In America, a rabbi must know the English language to be able to preach to the younger American born and bred generation." That meant acquiring a strong secular education and knowledge of Jewish history, philosophy, and sociology to communicate with, and garner the respect of, their fellow young people. Essentially the students wanted a type of preparation for the twentieth-century American Jewish world that their friends, relatives, and neighbors were acquiring at the Jewish Theological Seminary of America (JTSA). We do not know if anyone ever mentioned then that it also would be nice if RIETS rabbis could talk about who was playing in the

World Series. Still, we can reasonably assume that at least some students felt that a familiarity with sports gave a religious leader an advantage in connecting with potential congregants.[4]

Initially, RIETS's leaders stonewalled their critics. But after two student strikes (1906 and 1908) that decimated their enrollment — many of the disaffected, in fact, went off to the JTSA or left Jewish education completely — the yeshiva's embattled rabbis and lay leaders slowly came to the unavoidable understanding that their school's mission had to change if it hoped to survive. RIETS would continue to try to be a first-class center for Torah scholars, but it would also have a strong interest in the fate of the contemporary Jewish world. Harry Fischel played no small role in moving that process forward. He needed teams of instructors with Americanized outlooks to teach in places like the Uptown Talmud Torah. And until the 1910s, he only had JTSA students and graduates from which to choose. He could be very comfortable with an up-to-date yeshiva.[5]

The long-demanded sea change within the American yeshiva community came to fruition in 1915 with the appointment of Dr. Bernard Revel as president of RIETS. The house of Torah that Revel built had two essential components. His flagship institution was a modern Orthodox yeshiva capable of training Torah-learned and acculturated, English-speaking rabbis to address the social and religious needs of fellow native-born Jews, competitive with JTSA. Almost as important was the creation of a quality preparatory school that would willingly impart secular training to budding rabbis. Toward that end, the Talmudical Academy (TA), a school that proudly conformed to the educational protocols of the state education department, was established a year after Revel's arrival.[6]

But the new yeshiva head was out to bring in more than just the next classes of American Orthodox rabbis. Revel believed that there were many more bright young men in his community who would avail themselves of his school's intensive Torah study program before they pursued secular careers. But they would only enroll if they could be convinced that TA graduates would not be disadvantaged when they competed against public school graduates. To rope in these potential students, Revel's recruitment pitch was that his institution could produce youngsters ready to take their places within the "public life of the community" on an "equal footing" with those schooled within the so-called "Temples of Americanization." As one of Revel's backers boasted, the TA "renders the student as broad-minded and as liberal in his views, though he remains thoroughly observant as a Jew, as the best product of our public school." In the end, these students, it was said, would not only feel comfortable meeting and competing with all others, but they would win in their battles for slots and spots within this country's economy and society. A yeshiva in this country was now in the business of raising up all-American boys, some of whom might become rabbis.[7]

Long-time school principal Dr. Shelley Safir, an American Orthodox layman, enthusiastically implemented that mission. A graduate of New York public schools, City College of New York, and Columbia University, he came over in 1919 from Stuyvesant High School—then already a first-class city public school—with the commitment to produce well-rounded American boys. He and his staff of both Jewish and Gentile teachers encouraged their youngsters to edit school publications and organize clubs, debating societies, student councils, and sanitary and discipline squads. They proudly reported that "aside from their truly remarkable scholastic achievements"— like scoring high on Regents and other standardized tests—"students are also doing their fair share in activities pertaining to their social, civic and physical well-being," including "various types of athletic activities." Fellow CCNY grad Mr. M. Schoenbrun, the school's first staff gym teacher and licensed to teach physical training in New York City schools, may have been the high school boys' earliest faculty athletic role model. But Safir and the other academics did not hide their own interest and prowess in the athletic realm. In fact, they got a chance to strut their stuff in the annual student-faculty baseball game, held appropriately on Lag B'Omer. The principal, himself a tennis buff, played center field in the 1923 tilt. Biology teacher Charles Gramet patrolled right field that day under a "cloudless azure sky," while Reuben Steinbach, from the English department, flanked Safir in left field. The highly regarded English chairman Joseph T. Shipley and Joseph Lookstein, a young rabbinical student, handled the pitching chores. But "good fortune" smiled that day only on the student varsity team as it irreverently "scalped . . . the faculty . . . 13–4 . . . amid enthusiastic cheering and facetious remarks of a large number of spectators."[8]

TA students did not need much encouragement to go out for sports. What other activity proved so decisively that they were just like all other American kids? Annual yearbook reports frequently observed that "although the students of the Yeshivah are deeply in earnest in all their work they do not overlook the need of a sound physique." Settlement house teachings had found acceptance within a house of the Torah. These same organs contained page after page of reports on intramural tilts in baseball, football, basketball, handball, and wrestling as "athletics secured . . . a stronghold in the Yeshiva life." Indeed, in every yearbook's section reserved for graduates' pictures and brief biographies, most students listed among their achievements membership in one or more varsity or intramural teams or leadership in the pupil-run Class Athletic Council. For example, 1923, the year of that memorable Lag B'Omer tussle, of the twenty-five boys who graduated that spring, fifteen engaged in some sort of sports extracurricular activity. The athletes included class president William Berman a/k/a "Kid Geff" about whom a ditty went: "William Berman is our President. A baseball star-oratorically bent." Rhymed kudos were also extended to Morris "Grilly" Grilihas, a star of the faculty game. He went 1 for 3 and scored two runs in

MORRIS GRILIHAS
  "Grilly"

Grilihas appears to be quite dark,
But as an all around athlete, he toes the
                                        mark.
Class Athletic Manager, 8; Class Base-
ball Team 4, 6, 8; Class Basketball
Team, 5, 7; Varsity Team, 8.

Morris "Grilly" Grilihas, star of the 1923 Talmudical Academy
student-faculty baseball game. *The Elchanite,* 1923, p. 17.

the triumph. Of him it was said, "Grilihas appears to be quite dark. But as an all around athlete, he toes the mark."[9]

One of these players was really quite good on the hardwood. In the mid-1920s, TA graduate Louis J. Yager played varsity basketball at the so-called "Main branch" of the CCNY Evening Session. TA students were proud that an alumnus-athlete earned a college letter. They all basked in this additional proof that their academy could produce all-American boys. But what this ballplayer had to do to reach this milestone in any competitor's life could not have sat well with TA school officials nor with the athlete's parents. Faced with a personal conflict between religious observance and athletic participation, Louis Yager had chosen the secular values of sports over ancestral faith commitments.

Yager's dilemma was that in order to be a real teammate, he had to play ball in violation of the Jewish Sabbath. As Hank Greenberg would find out a decade later in his own highly publicized holy day problem, American sports officials of that era were oblivious, if not antagonistic, to Judaism's clock and calendar. In Louis's case, the scheduling issue was that during the 1925–1926 campaign, the CCNY Evening Session team played eight games — they went 4-4 that year. And no fewer than three of the matches were held on the Jewish Sabbath. The two biggest games — the February 12, 1926, game against the Brooklyn Evening School branch, reportedly played before "one of the largest crowds that ever witnessed an Evening Session game," and the March 19, 1926, tilt that pitted the Main Branch against the CCNY School of Commerce — took place on Friday night. The Commerce game, it was said, brought out "the largest crowd that ever witnessed an inter-branch game." After the match, players and fans alike took part in a dance sponsored by a school social club. At these critical moments, Yager decided to secure his membership within an alternative community of athletes.[10]

For young Louis, the decision to play on the Sabbath, and maybe to hang around for the dance afterwards, may well have been his most dramatic statement to that date of how disaffected he had become not only with his father's religious values but also with his elder's lack of economic ambition. This second-generation youngster had a very different vision of what should be important to a Jewish man in America than did his immigrant father. Issues over class or about what constituted success — an intergenerational argument that splintered many Jewish households of that era — was very much alive, if not always explicitly debated, within the Yager home.

Many, many years later, Yager would recall that that he "had many conflicts." Thinking back on his growing up, as a deeply self-reflective elderly gentleman, Louis would "complement . . . both my parents . . . for the attention they paid for [their children's] education." But he remembered that as a kid, he "resented being so different from other kids who did not have the heavy program of study that [he] did." He would have much preferred to spend more of his time playing "stick ball, box ball" and participating in "track . . . hopping from sidewalk to street and between two points on the street." However, he was ticketed for a yeshiva education where "leisure time was quite limited" except for "recess and the summer" or maybe on the Sabbath "when he would sneak out to play baseball when his father would fall asleep."[11]

As a boy and young man, Louis was also unhappy with his family's constant dire economic straits, a condition he attributed to his father's lack of concern with making money. "Father was in the junk business," another son, Ascher Yager recalled. "But he made no money because instead of working he was in the *Beis ha-Medrash* [Torah study hall] studying." Decades later, Ascher would claim with enormous pride that "his father completed the study of the Talmud seven times." For Ascher, who dreamed from age nine of becoming a rabbi and who was in fact ordained at RIETS in 1928, his dad was the consummate role model. Louis did not feel that way about his old man. Evidently, even among siblings, there were differences of opinion over whether — or how deeply — to embrace the American Gospel of Success.

Meanwhile, David Yager, "a very strict father, who valued education over money," was not pleased with Lou's devotion to his extracurricular pursuits. According to Ascher's understatement, "my father was slightly unhappy with Lou." [Lou] "had a superior mind . . . [and] my father was disap-

LOUIS J. YAGER
" El Jay"
Yager is an actor, we must tell,
He mimics historians especially well.
Favorite subject: Mathematics
Hobby: Studying the Talmud
Ambition: Rabbi
Discipline Squad, 6, 7, 8. Bank committee, 6. House of Representatives, 4, 5. Editorial Staff, 8. Assistant athletic manager, 8. Athletic Council, 7. Class athletic manager, 7. Basketball team, 1, 3, 5, 7, 8. Baseball team, 2, 4, 6, 8. Punchball team, 2, 4, 6, 8.

Louis J. Yager, Talmudical Academy student-athlete, 1925. *The Elchanite*, 1925, p. 26.

pointed that he did not use more of his time for study rather than to play basketball in which he excelled."[12]

Seemingly, Louis kept his issues with his family and its traditions pretty much to himself through graduation from the Talmudical Academy. The yearbook biography on "El Jay" — as he was called — noted that his hobby was "Studying the Talmud." He stated that his ambition was "Rabbi," even if he spent most of his spare time at TA playing for the baseball, basketball, and punchball squads and serving as sports correspondent for the yearbook. But when he attended CCNY, he was becoming a different public man. Not only would he play varsity ball during his one semester at the school, but after dropping out in 1927 "due to limited funds," he would leave his family and community behind and travel, off and on, for several years through the Midwest, even ending up one time penniless in Deadwood, South Dakota.[13]

Though Louis was by then no longer Orthodox and would never be that observant again, he did not leave his religious educational background totally behind him. In the early 1930s, to keep body and soul together, Yager gave Hebrew lessons at a Jewish boys' orphanage in Cleveland. And according to his daughter, Mary Yager Jaffe, he never lost his interest in what she called "erudition in Jewish Studies" even if he did not "go to services on Shabbat much," preferring to "go to the University of Nebraska football games" when he worked as a clinical psychologist in Omaha. Evidently, after almost a decade of peregrinations, he had settled down in the late 1930s and earned his degrees from the University of Chicago.[14]

While TA student journalists remained publicly oblivious to the difficulties an alumnus sports hero was having away from home, they did much to immortalize their own in-class rivalries with the prideful assertion that sports in no way detracted from "their achievement in the 'mark book.' " In that regard, they crowed, "there is 'something' different in the Yeshiva student. He knows just where to stop." Their only repeated complaint was that the school did not have adequate sports facilities. Safir admitted as much when he reported to state authorities that, ensconced as they were then in a small building on the Lower East Side, they used "public parks" for outdoor activities and "class rooms for indoor work." Sometimes they would rent out space at the Hamilton Fish Park's gymnasium for intramural battles.[15]

In 1926, student scribes noted a particularly annoying drawback to the sports program of having always to play on the road. There "would have been a punchball tournament," they reported, "if the Hamilton Park policeman had been in good humor. However, the life of a policeman is no 'bed of roses,' and a punchball tournament cannot be held according to the grouchy moods of a policeman."[16]

Bernard Revel, who received his rabbinical training in eastern Europe, had no personal affinity for sports activity. He certainly had no interest in participating in a school sports event. Nor, for that matter, did any of his old-line Orthodox Talmud faculty ever roll up their own gartered sleeves, substitute a ball cap for a fedora, and attempt to get on base. Even the idea of throwing out a ceremonial first pitch was not for Revel or any of his closest colleagues. However, the new yeshiva head did have a sense, in keeping with his reading of Jewish tradition, that the promotion of physical fitness was part of a school's job in molding an integrated American Orthodox personality. So he wrote in 1926 that "the ultimate aim of [Jewish education] is not the mere acquisition of knowledge or skill or the mere preparation of an individual for a particular task in life, but the building of character and the harmonious development of man's physical, mental and spiritual faculties." More than that, Revel, as a realist, understood that American boys, even his disciples whom he called "the few, the saving remnant," loved sports. And to deny them this healthy pleasure would not aid his cause of breaking the public schools' hold on the Jewish community. He thus threw in his lot with Safir and the students and prayed that someday his yeshiva might have an adequate physical education facility. Athletics could be part of the message of "synthesis" that he always preached.[17]

We do not know whether Revel ever had to defend this part of his modern yeshiva program to those within or without his faculty who might castigate athleticism as a waste of time, unfitting for true students of the Torah who should be with the Law day and night. That view, as we have noted, had been the generally held opinion within the religious world from which these teachers of Talmud had come. But, had questions been raised within the ranks, Revel had at least one esteemed colleague on board and one rabbinic exhortation from back in eastern Europe in his corner.

In 1922, Revel scored a coup when he convinced Polish-born rabbi Solomon Polachek, known as the "*Meitsheter Illui*" — the "Genius from Meitshet" — to join his faculty. It was a sage strategic move to bring in a talmudic luminary to shore up the reputation of the school as a Torah center even as the yeshiva was making all these modern moves. As far as we know, during his seven years in New York, Polachek was silent on the importance of gyms and teams within the school. But reportedly he did harbor a positive view of yeshivas encouraging students' physical fitness. It was a Maimonidean-style point of view that Revel could have counted upon if he were ever challenged about what was going on in his Torah school. While still in eastern Europe, or so the story goes, Polachek and his friend Rabbi Meir Berlin once happened upon some youngsters from a gymnasium school in Brisk, Lithuania, and observed them running and jumping around happily in athletic activity. It was then that Polachek apparently remarked "with sorrow, why didn't we have this [activity] when we were youngsters. It would not have hurt our ability to study if we permitted ourselves some time every day to run and jump around."[18]

Polachek's senior and equally esteemed contemporary, the Hafetz Hayim (Rabbi Israel Mayer ha-Cohen Kagan), went even further in expressing sentiments that Revel could have found useful. Using his own life experience as a model, Kagan once publicly regretted that he had not devoted enough time in his youth to physical fitness. A sounder body, in his view, would have helped him become an even greater scholar. Too many hours at his books had weakened his eyesight. As an adult, he was obliged to abstain from reading for two years. Speaking in 1893 to his disciples in the Yeshiva of Radun, Rabbi Kagan had said:

> Do note study overmuch. Man must preserve the body so that it is not weakened, so that it does not fall ill, and for that it is crucial to rest and relax, to breathe fresh air. A walk should be taken toward evening, or sit at home and rest. When possible, a swim in the river is good for strengthening the body. Overindulgence in study is the advice of the evil inclination, which counsels working too hard in order to weaken the body, after which the person will be obliged to refrain entirely from Torah study, so that in the end his reward is his loss.[19]

But maybe Revel never really had to hard-sell this part of RIETS's revised *raison d'être* to those around him. Because for all of their affinity for Old World yeshiva values, he and most of his religious faculty members also were colleagues or disciples of Rabbi Abraham Isaac Kook. And at the very moments when the American yeshiva was changing, the famous Chief Rabbi of Palestine was advocating the value of physical fitness, and even of sports, among Orthodox Jews.

Kook's religious Zionist foursquare stance was basically in response to Max Nordau's hard swipe of some years earlier at the sedentary and decidedly non-competitive lifestyle of religious eastern European Jews. In 1898, Nordau, a secular Zionist, had called upon the Second Zionist Congress to raise up a new, "muscular" Jew and Judaism. He had prayed that his movement would enlist proud, athletic Jews who would help their people fight against all comers and earn for them respected places within the modern world. Those German Jewish students who established V.J. St. or the Bar Kochba Berlin and their counterparts who joined British Zionist athletic clubs had heard this message loud and clear. Nordau's "*ba'al guf,*" in the best sense of the term, was lionized as Judaism's best. Indeed, his very buff appearance was contrasted with "the underdeveloped and frail body of Jewish men . . . produced by the experience of studying in a yeshiva."[20]

For Kook, it was a fundamental article of faith and a lifelong point of emphasis that Orthodox Jews had to take part in the incipient political revival of the Jewish people. As he saw it, to ultimately bring libertine Zionism under the rule of the Torah required that Orthodox Jews — even the most intellectually inclined yeshiva student — had to be a little bit like the "*ba'al guf*" and develop sound bodies to complement their bright minds and holy souls. "Our spiritual emphasis" he wrote,

> ignored the sanctity of the body, physical health and vigor. Let us remember that the Jew possesses a Divine body no less than a Divine spirit. . . . Our regeneration entails a synthesis of the spiritual and physical, vibrant flesh and blood, sturdy organs, and a glowing spirit sustained by firm muscles.

For Kook, the "physical-mental restoration . . . [of] frail Torah scholars . . . represents a cardinal religious obligation."[21]

Rabbi Kook's activist views did not sit well with most of Palestine's old-line Orthodox rabbis. He also had more than his share of outspoken detractors back in eastern Europe and even in America. But his call to athletic arms should have received a respectful hearing in Revel's realm. Precisely at that point, in the early 1920s, the yeshiva's president was linking his school institutionally with the nascent American branch of Mizrachi (Religious Zionists). In fact, for a while in the late 1910s, Rabbi Meir Berlin had been a temporary head of RIETS at a time when Revel was away from the yeshiva tending to pressing family business woes. So Rabbi Polachek's old walking partner, Rabbi Berlin, had a history with Revel's Talmud faculty. Revel never did acknowledge publicly any affinity for this part of Kook's Torah, even if the Palestinian rabbi's works were read with pride, interest, and devotion within his school's circles. But Revel's building activities — as we will immediately see — suggested a kinship with Kook's physical fitness message. Later on in Yeshiva's history, Rabbi Kook's teaching would be explicitly evoked to support the expansion of sports' presence at the New York Torah institution.[22]

The moment the yeshiva's athletics enthusiasts hoped for seemed to have arrived in 1928 when Revel finalized plans not only to append a college to the Talmudical Academy, but to move the entire operation to a commodious campus on Washington Heights in northern Manhattan. With this move, his grand design reached full maturity. Now it would be possible for Orthodox men to stay within their own religious environment through their college years, keep up with their Torah learning, and acquire advanced secular training, just like so many other Jews were obtaining at neighboring CCNY fifty blocks south on St. Nicholas Heights. And they could do it all academically without having to put up with challenges to their faith and practice. As we have already noted, at that point, even a predominantly Jewish school like "City" made no accommodations for those who missed late Friday afternoon classes — or a sports practice or game — to keep their Sabbath. Left unsaid from official Yeshiva sources, but clearly implied to students, was the notion that only at Yeshiva College could they be real college men. There alone could they experience a full extracurricular campus life without all of the dilemmas that Yager had to face.[23]

And speaking of creating a campus life, a "physical culture building" was among the eight structures contemplated for the new uptown venue. Had this vision become a reality, it then would have been possible for these Orthodox undergraduates — both future rabbis and the well-grounded laymen of the future — to while away some time exercising on the parallel bars or still rings or shooting some baskets in the gymnasium.[24]

As fate would have it, Yeshiva College opened its campus's doors uptown in 1929, but without a gym. Seven of the eight buildings for the envisioned complex were not built because when the Great Depression hit America that year, Revel and his followers found that they barely had sufficient funds to complete but one structure. The "temporary gymnasium" situated in the basement of the lone school building, notorious for its low ceiling and poor ventilation, would long be the locus for the courses in physical education required of college freshmen and sophomores. A generation would pass before the financially strapped institution would even begin to think of constructing a first-rate gym.[25]

Still, student interest in sports at the Talmudical Academy and Yeshiva College continued unabated. Indeed, the "program" took a major step forward when the two sister schools began fielding, in the 1930s, interscholastic and intercollegiate teams. Followers of the "Blue and White" basketball squad were enormously proud when their high schoolers defeated clubs like the Tremont Young Israel, or Eastern District Evening High School, or the Pawnees Athletic Club, or the American Zionist Association outfit. In 1937, the baseball varsity "provided one of the greatest

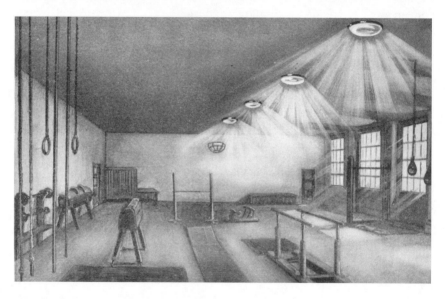

Artist's conception of the Yeshiva College campus and athletic facility, circa 1927. *The Yeshiva College: What it is and What it Stands For* [1927?], pp. 7, 16.

surprises of the year" when the "Mites from the Heights" upended the Townsend Harris High School squad by a 6-1 score behind the "phenomenal hurling of Eli Strum who struck out 16 in 7 innings." He carried a no-hitter into the seventh stanza before the opposition touched him up for their one run.[26]

On the college level, as early as 1931, a group of "students got together and started a movement of forming teams to represent . . . Alma Mater." Basketball was the flagship sport, but varsity tennis also had its devotees, as did baseball. In 1935, Dr. Safir made known his interest in the college promoting that net sport. And, at times, there was talk on campus of establishing a swimming team. But there was no pool facility in the offing.[27] In any event, 1931, the first year of Yeshiva College sports, witnessed the basketballers win over a club team called "The Flashes," a local church group from Saviours Atonement, and the Jewish Theological Seminary of America's squad. Two years later, Yeshiva College put together a five-game winning streak against "clubs, schools and community centers." A year later, the Orthodox club stepped up in class when it took on Louis Yager's old team, the City College Evening Session, adding it to a schedule which now included NYU's School of Commerce and JTSA. In 1935, newspaper scribes got very excited when the "Yeshiva College Cagers Rout[ed] City College Evening Beavers to the Score of 23–14." In that and subsequent years, the Yeshiva College club knocked off the NYU School of Law, Jersey State Teachers College, St. John's School of Pharmacy, and other small-college opponents. By 1936, "the Varsity was taking them on from all sides in a twenty game schedule." The most enjoyable win that year was against the "highly touted Central Jewish Institute courtmen." Moe Krieger's "freak shot in the closing seconds clinch[ed] the game for good Ol' Yeshiva." The presence of his girlfriend in the stands, a school sports reporter suggested, may have inspired Krieger's heroics.[28]

But even when they lost to more quality clubs like the junior varsities of LIU and Manhattan College, Yeshiva students were proud of their team because the very existence of their competitive squads evidenced to the world that they—second-generation American Orthodox students—were regular guys. In 1935, the editors of the student newspaper, *The Commentator,* spoke for so many on their campus when they declared that "more than any other college organization, the Yeshiva College basketball team has been instrumental in uprooting [the] misconception . . . that Yeshiva College . . . is an eastern anachronistic product transplanted artificially to a soil totally inimical to it." They were so proud that "time and again in its intercollegiate encounters, the stands were amazed at the presence of a Yeshiva team." Two years later, student sports columnist Abe Novick chimed in that "the value of an athletic program . . . is the demonstration that there is no inherent quarrel between the cloistered academic life and collegiate sports. The fact that a Yeshiva is not necessarily an old-worldly anachronism withdrawn from reality is what counts." And in 1938, Jacob Goldman, Novick's successor as writer of the "On the Sidelines" column, added similarly that "there can be no doubt that the basketball team has been in a large measure responsible for the attainment of the goal we have been striving for the past ten years. . . . No longer are you met with queer gazes of wonder and ignorance when you explain that you attend Yeshiva College."[29]

Indeed, for a decidedly low-key program, Yeshiva's sports activities received some noteworthy national exposure. At first, Boston's *The Jewish Advocate* was amused by reports that Yeshiva College was fielding sports teams. It predicted that headlines like "Rabbi Cohen intercepted a pass from Ziffkovich . . . may soon be seen on the sporting pages." The *Jewish Advocate* also reacted to the news that "next spring it is planned to have baseball and track teams, and ultimately a football team," with the facetious expectation of "sitting in the rooting section of the Yankee Stadium to cheer the first Yeshiva College football team. Rah, rah, Yeshiva."

However, in December 1935, the *Advocate*'s observations took on a more serious tone when it reported on what appeared in *The Commentator.* Expecting to see "the paper devoted to solemn and somewhat involved treatises on Talmudic law, with occasional admonitions towards adherence to traditional Judaism," it was pleased to leaf through a student organ "full of pep, dash and gossip." The "rabbinical student sports editor" was extolled for "master[ing] sports language" as he "narrat[ed] the exploits of the Yeshiva College basketball team" and reported on intense intramural tussles. For these outsiders, it was "a most revealing paper indeed" for it signified the passing of the "days when the orthodox rabbi was characterized by long beard, 'payeth' [sidelocks], and complete withdrawal from everyday life. Today our young rabbis-in-training attend smokers, play basketball, study embryology, and are just as collegiate as students of engineering, law or business administration." And, from the *Advocate*'s point of view, this change was welcome. "Our rabbis," it continued, "are now in addition to being learned more human and [are] more understanding of human problems. The requirements of their office are such as to demand wide contacts, as well as Talmudic erudition." What Solomon Schechter had implied to Louis Finkelstein was now being said about the all-American type of yeshiva student.[30]

But for Yeshiva youngsters to maintain their glowing reputation, the "Blue and White"'s players and their growing legion of fans had to deport themselves with the manners and perspective befitting men of the Torah when they took on Gentile and other Jewish opponents in Orthodoxy's home. Back in the 1920s, TA student leaders had boasted that they and their classmates "were different." They "know just where to stop." Now, fears were expressed that Yeshiva hoopsters and their supporters did not know their limits and were getting caught up in emulating a dark side of competitive intercollegiate sports. They were adopting a win-at-all-costs attitude that engendered ill will between opponents. Sometimes, the varsity was criticized for subtle social oversights like the time when student editorialists complained that "it's too bad Yeshiva has no officially recognized cheer. The varsity boys were at a loss as to what to use for a cheer after the game." They finally resorted to the old familiar " 'three cheers' for the visitors." But other times, there were real and troubling goings on that were roundly criticized.

For example, in 1939, student journalists were outraged that "visiting teams" were reportedly subjected to "poor refereeing, unsatisfactory timekeeping, excessive roughness and poor sportsmanship on the Yeshiva court." That small, inadequate gym was turning into a snake pit. The word was out to "teams coming to Yeshiva . . . that they would be faced with a set of undesirable conditions that would be a handicap to them." Intense players—and one can imagine fans too—were reminded that "basketball as an extracurricular activity finds its *raison d'être* in the sportsmanship and clean fun exhibited in the keen rivalry of two well-trained and equal teams, rather than in an excessive desire to win games."[31]

What critics were saying now is that if not handled properly, athletics at Yeshiva might cross into the foul territory of constituting a *hilul ha-Shem,* a desecration of God's holy name. Zealousness for sports—this secular creed that placed the highest premium on victory, often at all costs—augured to elevate the world of fitness and fun and games to unconscionable heights, inimical to the teachings of Judaism. Here, as in so many other aspects of modern life, once Orthodox Jews chose to embrace the best of the outside world, they had to develop the right guidelines for their continued participation. Such was the case in the 1930s with the evolution of the all-American yeshiva student.

By the early 1940s, Yeshiva sportsmen had their marching orders. They could have teams like all other colleges and demonstrate to the public that "Yeshiva was not a relic of the middle ages." A cheering squad could even back the ballclubs, outfitted in white cardigan sweaters with a large blue Y on their chests. These boasters, an all-male squad, could "tumble, jump and holler as they presented a pop-eyed view of Yeshiva's spirit in sports." Moreover, if they made all the rights moves, on and off the court, they not only showed the Jewish world and the wider world how Americanized they and their school had become, but those on the team who were rabbis-in-training also developed a social skill that could help them relate to their future youthful congregants, just like the Jewish Theological Seminary fellows whom they regularly were beating on the hardwood. Still, the players and the "program" had to maintain their perspective as Orthodox student-athletes. Another concern—in 1942 it was alleged that on occasion "our basketball team falls so low as to require the assistance of players who are not regularly matriculated." The use of "ringers (nasty word, isn't it)," a *Commentator* columnist said, by those who "place victory above all else . . . manifests a loss of self-respect and that makes the matter a serious one."[32]

In sum, a degree of reverence for the body—an exalted Maimonidean principle—was certainly appropriate for a modern Orthodox student. And a commitment to competitiveness was also understandable. But if Yeshiva's athletes were to be standard-bearers for their faith in America, they had to stay clear of the moral lapses that often came with an uncritical, full-bodied embrace of sports.

5

SHUL VS. POOL: INTERWAR BATTLES AND EARLY POSTWAR ENGAGEMENTS

Advocates of the Synagogue Center concept and supporters of the YMHA never really did get along. As early as the 1880s, Rabbis Henry Berkowitz and Moses Gries were impatient with the Hebrew Associations' slow and unsteady efforts to direct their charges from the gym toward religious affiliation. But Temple Center spokesmen kept their feelings largely to themselves.[1] Not so their 1910s Synagogue Center counterparts, whose visions of what was wrong with the Ys came out of their personal experiences with those whom they would criticize. Herbert S. Goldstein hit hard when, in one of his nastier comments, he called the Ys the "illegitimate . . . offspring of the synagogue." In his view, these institutions did not give their members "the education of a Jewish religious environment." In one of his least charitable moments, Mordecai Kaplan observed comparably that whatever the Ys' social services value to the community, it was failing "to stimulate" in its clients "a positive enthusiasm for Jewishness."[2]

Quick to respond to these canards, Y leaders took public umbrage and launched counterattacks against their critics. The fact of the matter was, they argued, "all too many athletes . . . and many others . . . who were attracted to Synagogue Center games, sports, and social activities were really not interested in religious services." They certainly were not prepared to adhere to the demands a synagogue-based life inevitably placed upon the Jew. The end result was that they played ball and went home untouched or untransformed. "The trouble is," said Samuel A. Goldsmith, secretary of the National Council of YMHAs, "that young men did not often prefer any synagogue," leaving the realistic and pragmatic Associations with the critical task of inculcating a sense of Jewish identification — Goldsmith called it "ethical and ethnical solidarity" — among those who showed up.[3]

Judge Irving Lehman, president of the Jewish Welfare Board, which in 1921 took over control of the Y movement, saw the Associations' mission just about the same way. "The young Jews," he declared, "may refuse to come to the synagogue except on High Holidays. Then it becomes the duty of the community to bring spiritual influences into their lives at some other times and places." To achieve that end — and to ensure, as always, that young Jews not be found "on the street corner" — the Ys, that "great agency for the unification of the Jewish people," made programming available that linked members "to their people."[4]

Indeed, it was a point of faith among those who worked within the Y, or as it was then called the Jewish Community Center (JCC) movement, that "narrowing down" their institution "by making it a recruiting station for the synagogue is wrong." Speaking in 1915 before his colleagues in the National Association of Jewish Social Workers, St. Louis's Oscar Leonard spoke for many in his movement when he said, "The Jews have never coerced anyone into worshipping [and] while institutional religion has its place" within his type of organization, "it should never coerce either young or old to participate in . . . services."[5] However, at no time during this early period of squabbling did any group accuse its counterparts of misrepresentation or, even worse, of constituting a major threat to youngsters building their Jewish identities. That sort of heated rhetoric awaited the interwar period when some Jewish religious leaders — most of them Conservative — went so far as to suggest that the JCC gymnasium was no place for a Jewish athlete, not one, at least, who cared much about his or her religious life.

The busy "medurban" settlements of the 1920s and 1930s, situated somewhere between America's inner cities and the suburban communities of the future, were the locales for these battles. These were the types of neighborhoods to which second-generation Jews flocked in the 1920s and stayed for the next twenty years or so through the Depression and the Second World War. In their new habitats, Jewish youngsters displayed a noticeable disinterest in religious life and observance. Everywhere surveyors looked they found Jewish kids turned off to Judaism. Probes of college students from upstate New York to New England to Chicago to North Dakota revealed that only the smallest proportion felt attending a synagogue was important to their lives or even their identities as Jews. The best they could say about their faith was that they approved of Judaism's "code of ethics." But observance of "our customs" was not for them.[6]

A 1935 study of New York teenagers and young adults reported additional bad news. Attendance at "church social activities" ranked dead last among two score of favorite "free time activities" that Jewish boys and girls preferred. "Listening to the radio, going to the movies, visiting and entertaining friends," participation in athletics and even "walking or hanging around" and, the old stand-by, doing "nothing special," swamped showing up at a synagogue. In the week the survey was conducted only around ten percent of the Jewish men and six percent of the Jewish women interviewed said they had participated in "religious services." The sole good news about the results was that Jewish youth, even if they were not shul-goers, were somewhat less likely than their Christian counterparts to "just hang around" or "do nothing special." That means that Jewish kids could be found "more than other groups" at "public recreation or social centers," and not out looking for trouble on the street corner. In these more controlled environments, Jews would play all sorts of games and sports or seek ways toward "self-improvement." Attending lectures and concerts was also very popular. The more politically minded turned out for rallies in support of their favorite candidates or causes. In each of these venues, Jews would find companionship with their own kind and/or with the opposite sex. But religious activities were not on their minds.[7]

Looking back on those interwar days, it seems as if the weak hold traditional Jewish customs and observances had once held over these youths and their parents while they lived in inner-city hubs was now completely broken, as those born in the U.S.A. continued their quests to advance in American society. If synagogues downtown had been half-filled on the Sabbath morning because Jews were out working — or the lucky ones were sleeping in after a Friday night at a dance hall — houses of worship in the new neighborhoods were almost completely empty on the holy day. The High Holidays were the only time where a combination of nostalgia, maybe a bit of awe over the Days of Judgment, and the desire to see and be seen by their fellow Jews brought families inside the shul.[8]

For Jews with sporting interests, either as players or, now more than ever, as fans, expanding athletic attractions led them even further away from religious values. Now the lures of the formal playing field and the stadium were stronger than ever. In fact, they were inescapable. After the Great War — which witnessed America field quite a few out-of-shape soldiers — school administrators and public officials redoubled their efforts to promote physical fitness programs for all youngsters and to expand competitive sports for the athletically gifted. As part of the "100 percent Americanism" creed of that era, it was deemed essential that this country's future defenders be strong, courageous, and team-oriented to protect all that was held dear against the rising tide of Bolshevism from Russia and radicalism in America. This gospel of athletics was preached in public schools everywhere, certainly within earshot of all Jewish children of immigrants, as the opportunities and demands to play on a team expanded tremendously.[9]

Meanwhile, for those who were becoming fans during the so-called "Golden Age of Sports," it became increasingly simple to follow the exploits of a favorite athlete or team. Back-page sports sections of tabloid newspapers, like the *New York Daily News* or the *Chicago Tribune,* screamed out headlines glorifying the exploits of that period's greatest athletes. And by the 1920s, radio broadcasts began to bring the wide world of sports into a supporter's living room. Commentators of the time spoke of fight fans "listen[ing] in at their own or their friends' radio sets," creating a whole new culture of fandom. One could well imagine a group of Jewish fans crowding into a friend's parlor on a cold winter night or, in warmer weather, standing outside a candy store window listening in for the latest updates on the heroes of the time.[10]

It would not only have been the Ruths, Dempseys, and Granges who would have captured their attention. Jews had their own legion of legendary stars from their own neighborhoods that captured the strongest of loyalties. That interwar Semitic pantheon began with Glickman and Greenberg. In the end, their historical significance would, of course, transcend everything they did on the track or diamond. But Jews also held seventeen boxing championships during the 1920s and 1930s. Benny Leonard dominated the welterweight classification in the early 1920s and Barney Ross was the king of that division a decade later. At the same time, Nat Holman patrolled the backcourt for the original Celtics — a renowned early 1920s barnstorming professional squad — even as he was beginning a decades-long career as the head coach of CCNY basketball. There he produced literally hundreds of outstanding Jewish roundballers and eight All-Americans. By the end of the 1920s, some 500 or more Jews had played major college football. And in the early 1930s, Brooklyn's Sid Luckman would captivate fans first at Columbia University before quarterbacking the Chicago Bears in the National Football League. So, if *Harper's* magazine was right when it suggested in the 1920s that college football was "almost our national religion," Jews were among its most devoted worshippers.[11]

Thus, when rabbis complained — as well they did — that congregants were content to sit at home on a Friday night in front of their radios and were absent from synagogue, is it a reach to say that some were sitting in their apartments, or out on the stoop, tuned in to play-by-plays and re-creations of games and fights? Others might have been otherwise occupied playing for their school, club, or college.[12]

During this trying time for American Judaism, at a moment where rabbis could have used a huge assist from more popular forces within their own community, the last thing they needed was to have the burgeoning Jewish

Community Center movement offer but another venue that was not supportive of religious life. But there they were in so many of the Jewish streets and towns of America with proclivities, policies, and personnel that ignored their youngsters' Jewish identities.

As the Center movement grew beginning in the 1920s, its national leaders usually said all the right words about promoting Judaism. Its longest-time booster and director, Louis Kraft, put it this way: JCCs served as "a reservoir of Jewish life and influence in the community and more particularly to help bring our youth closer to Jewish life in sentiment, thought and action." And serve and grow they did during the 1920s and 1930s throughout the United States. In February 1923, for example, the movement's monthly, *The Jewish Center,* proudly announced that in the previous eighteen months, ten new buildings had been purchased and three more were under construction. At that point, plans were being hatched to "extend the center movement to the point where thousands and thousands might receive the benefits of membership." Two months later, it was reported that these benefits had indeed been extended to communities from Binghamton, New York, to Dallas, Texas, to Philadelphia, Pennsylvania, to Louisville, Kentucky, and eight cities in between. And, in subsequent months, the 1920s building boom movement roared into Kansas City, Missouri, and Nashville, Tennessee, among other locales. The movement lost some momentum during the years of the Depression. Still, existing JCCs expanded their facilities in places like Rochester, New York, and Cincinnati, Ohio. And in 1934, Los Angeles Jewry joyously dedicated its JCC, "a new building and athletic facility" complete "with fifteen meeting rooms, library, kitchen, lounge and playground equipped for gymnastics, volleyball, boxing and wrestling." By 1942, the JCCs could look back on twenty years of progress and count 300 agencies within its purview. These agencies spent five million dollars a year for their estimated 400,000 members who attended well-equipped buildings that cost millions of dollars to build. And, if Kraft's rhetoric rang true, the young men and women who were devoted to the JCCs were not only working up good sweats in their first-class facilities but also were imbibing "the rich cultural heritage of the Jewish group" and "prepar[ing]" themselves for "Jewish living in America."[13]

However, all too often JCCs did not practice what Kraft preached. In fact, as early as 1923, even elements within the movement itself — sometimes program examiners from the national office or local leaders who were proud of what they personally were doing in their towns — were already lamenting that, in many places, positive Jewish messages were often not getting through. For example, Tobias Roth, executive director of the Rochester Y, candidly told his JCC colleagues that "unfortunately, in many associations the Jewish phase of the program is made a side issue, and too little attention is paid to the development of the religious side." For him, tragically, "the term, Hebrew, seems to play a more important part in the name than in the work" of the Ys. Not long thereafter, from Savannah, Georgia, came a disturbing admission and admonition that "athletics must not be allowed to overbalance the program. More than that, they must not be allowed to seem too great a part of the program." In William Pinsker's opinion, "athletic events by their very nature receive undue publicity in proportion to other activities." For the director of that city's Jewish Educational Alliance, there was a "danger that to the community at large the Center may stand for nothing much besides athletics."[14]

Meanwhile, long-time Kaplan disciple Rabbi Jacob S. Golub chastised many Associations for their wrongheaded emphasis on producing great sports teams while Jewish education languished. "Our gymnasium departments," he observed unhappily, "are far more specialized and efficient and call forth more constructive effort than do our schools." How off-center was it, he asked, that "many a YMHA has sent out championship athletic teams" while "their schools are of the type which do not give even a satisfactory preparation for living as a Jew in America?" In 1923, Dr. Mordecai Soltes, director of Jewish Education Extension of the Jewish Welfare Board, sadly reported that "some associations have too long been satisfied with half-hearted, perfunctory attention to the specifically Jewish element in the Jewish Center program." The worst offenders were undoubtedly those Centers that kept their "general offices, gymnasium, pool, lunch-counters, restaurants etc." open on the Sabbath day. What sort of Jewish message was that? Still, Soltes remained convinced that, on the whole, the movement was headed in the right direction, as he reported that "there has been evident a decided change in the proper direction in recent years."[15]

However, Rabbi Alter F. Landesman, who headed up the Hebrew Educational Society of Brooklyn, was not nearly as sanguine both about present and prospective conditions in the field. As he saw things, the tide of disinterest at local Ys had not turned and would not change until Center workers stopped "giving the impression that the Jewish activities of the Center are just one of the departments of the Center, just as the athletic or club departments are." He observed that since the JCCs started out with young members who "neither know much about . . . Judaism . . . nor do they care to know about it," much catch-up work needed to be done. For him, the resident coach or athletic director, the fellow or gal who had the ear or headlock on these youths, was the person who could contribute the most toward Judaizing the Centers. What good did it do, he argued, "to introduce certain Jewish activities in Centers and to put even a rabbi" — like Landesman himself — "at their head, while at the same time we put . . . in charge of the athletic department . . . people who have no understanding of or sympathy for our aims." In the best of all possible situations, Landesman dreamed that the "physical education department" could even "do more than the mere development of muscles." It could actually "ingrain in its members the Jewish conception of holiness." Waxing philosophical, the rabbi continued,

"[T]he body was ever regarded by the Jews as the temple of the soul." Could not the "Jewish laws of purity and personal hygiene supplemented by the best modern scientific thoughts on the subject" be taught more "effectively through the gymnasium classes than through any class in Judaism"? But, awaking from his reveries, Landesman was sure to note that most JCC sports people had neither the training nor the disposition to turn a pool into a shul. Indeed, some did nothing less than "cripple our programs."[16]

Abraham W. Rosenthal of the Bronx Y went even further in questioning whether gym instructors were the right role models for Jewish youngsters. While proud of the goings-on at his home institution, he was quick to wonder out loud if elsewhere — and he surveyed eighty-one centers nationally — "how many of our physical education directors attended club leaders' meetings, the plays, dances [and] debates," many of which had Jewish themes and content, not to mention participating in "services at their Centers." He also "wonder[ed] how many of our directors have made heartfelt five minute appeals to the men on the gymnasium floor for the United Jewish Campaign." And, he continued, "I wonder how many of our directors bring exemplary Jewish lives before our juniors and intermediates, ready to illustrate a good turn, a courageous play, a clean bit of sportsmanship, from the history of our illustrious ancestors and history in the making of our contemporaries."[17]

But how could these gym teachers have such a developed Jewish soul, asked Aaron G. Robison, if, on the national scene, one in five Y sports employees was a Gentile? His most basic criticism of his colleagues, from his vantage point at the Newark Y, was that "many of our executives do not find any reason for taking exception to this situation, their point-of-view being that work on the gymnasium floor can be carried out just as successfully by a non-Jew as by a Jew." Their faulty argument, Robison reasoned, was that the qualities of "sportsmanship, fair play and subordination of self to the group" — all good secular social work values — can be "developed by any good physical education director, as long as he is a real boy's man and knows his business." What they forget, he argued, was that in Jewish Y work "we are attempting to . . . create Jewish consciousness," identification with much more than just the universal truths of Judaism, teachings that a Gentile coach also could personify. Rather, Robison cried, the Center movement needed articulate advocates in the gym, men and women committed to the unique goals, outlook, and observances of the Jewish people.[18]

In 1930, Samuel Leff, field secretary of the Jewish Welfare Board, gave those in the movement who cared about the problem some depressing statistics that showed just how removed from any Jewish mission were so many Y athletics operations. After canvassing some fifty-nine JCCs in the United States and Canada, Leff revealed that the "develop[ment] in Jewish atmosphere" was at the bottom of the list of "aims of physical education departments." Predictably, "physical and health development, recreation, character building etc," all the good "100 percent Americanism" values, received the highest scores. It also seems that even in places where Jewish programming did take place upstairs, the denizens of the downstairs gym or pool were often totally disconnected from other departments.

Leff also uncovered another disturbing fact. While physical education gurus routinely pledged allegiance to the good American and Jewish ethical values of sportsmanship, many coaches abandoned those teachings once they and their charges hit the court. In pursuit of "Ws" in the Ys, sports all too frequently had "been destructively mistaught by some of those so-called physical educators in their intense and often savage fight for athletic victory."[19]

There is also some evidence that coaches and Center officials were not above recruiting the best Jewish ballplayers around town to produce championship teams. It has been alleged that Center leaders sometimes figured that the better the teams, the larger the attendance of Center members at the event and the dance that followed. It might have been both a point of institutional pride and as well as a dollars-and-cents issue. This same canard was also occasionally leveled at some Synagogue Center operations that seemed to get carried away with increasing their own attendance figures and did not forcefully push their avowed religious message. During the 1930s and 1940s, there seems to have been, at least in New York, a subculture of vagabond hoop stars who traveled from the Manhattan Federation to the Harlem Hebrew Institute and from the Williamsburg Y to the Hebrew Education Society of Brownsville, up to the Bronx Y on the Grand Concourse and sometimes to the Union Temple in Brooklyn, always in search of games. To hear some top players of that era tell it, this scene offered this group of "ringers" a chance to "play ball, enjoy ourselves," pick up girls at the post-game dances, and "work out" against the top competition. Sometimes the prime attraction for a high school star was the chance to hone his sports skills against a first-rate college guy.[20]

To many of these concerned on-the-scene observers, a gym in a JCC was one of the last places a Jewish youngster should go to if he or she was interested in Jewish content or even ethical behavior. We can also surmise that the better the athletes, the less likely they would be to gain Jewishly from these encounters. And to make things even worse, there was every indication that there were influential forces within the Center movement that were entirely comfortable with this non-Jewish state of affairs.

Elizabeth, New Jersey, Y executive Harry Lebau, who worked just a few towns over from the outspoken critic Aaron Robison, may have typified the Y man who cared little for Jewish activity within and without the Centers' gyms. For him, "self expression [was] the major function of the Y." Writing in 1929 to his Center colleagues, Lebeau praised the Y as the "institution, par excellence, which offers opportunities to its members for . . . actual exercise of muscles and body and mind." Here was the place where Jews

could express themselves, during their leisure time "actual[ly] and not vi-
cariously . . . in such a way as to increase their own self-respect." How great a
"Jewish home under Jewish auspices" the Y was, he declared, which unites
and "cements our people" by "raising ourselves in our self-esteem and the
regard of others." So he called upon the Y to continue to proffer "as the
main features of its program, athletics, socials, dramatics, choral societies
orchestras, dancing and art classes, etc.," all the "manifold active play forms
which it now features." These activities "alone," he said, "were sufficient to
justify our continued and earnest interest and support of the 'Y' recreational center." Explicitly Jewish educational or religious activities were con-
spicuously missing from his panoply of preferred Y programs.[21]

Frank S. Lloyd strongly seconded Lebau's sentiments when he addressed
the National Association of Jewish Center Workers in 1931. In his speech,
which probably garnered him sustained applause from at least some delegates in the audience, this professor of education from New York University
acknowledged that the goals of the JCCs were "to develop Jewish life on the
highest possible plane." But for him, "citizenship building" was synonymous with teaching members "to conform more nearly to the ideals of the
Jewish faith." And physical education in the Ys was a key component in that
Americanizing agenda. Gym and pool programs served more than just a
"recreational" purpose. They were "a means for the full development and
integration of personalities." Nowhere in his remarks was the promotion of
Jewish identity identified as an objective in producing the well-rounded
Jewish American.[22]

If ideas and attitudes like these saddened rabbis like Alter Landesman,
who spent his days advocating for Judaism within the JCCs, these assimilationist messages only infuriated his fellow Conservative and Reform colleagues who sought to fill their vacant pews with the same unenthusiastic
youth. In 1936, for example, Reform rabbi Louis I. Newman of Manhattan's
Rodeph Sholom characterized "the cultural and educational activities . . . of
the Center" as "in a sense a side show to adorn the circus" of its "central
aim," social and athletic activities. In 1939, Rabbi Simon Greenberg of
Philadelphia upbraided his fellow Conservative rabbis — and his Orthodox
and Reform counterparts too — for their failure to "display some leadership
and get together" to "remove the non-religious Jewish Center . . . this palpable evil from our midst." A year later, Reform rabbi B. Benedict Glazer of
New York warned only a bit more calmly, but in a comparable vein, that
before the Jewish Center movement acts on "its ambition to become the
directing force in Jewish communal life," it had better "first endeavor to increase the Jewish content of its own program." That same year, Conservative
rabbi Nachman Arnoff of Chicago observed, from his own experience, that
"the cultural and religious programming of the average Center is scarcely
visible above ground." And he pointedly warned JCC officials "there can be
no non-sectarianism in Jewish life when we have Jewish survival in mind."[23]

For Cleveland Conservative rabbi Armand E. Cohen, the bottom-line problem was simply that "many Jewish Community Centers in no way understand that they are supposed to preserve Jewish life with its religious interpretation." And that was because, he continued, they are not "guided always by the question, 'How does our work make for the preservation of the Jewish people and does it weave into the religious pattern?' " For Cohen, it was a tragedy that "the un-Jewish Community Center" that had sailed along without critical examination enjoyed "the moral and financial support of the entire Jewish community," including the thoughtless backing of some rabbis.[24]

In passing, Cohen also took dead-eyed aim at the "outspoken assimilationist's" assumption that the "self-expression" style of programming positively "cemented" and unified Jews and "raised the regard" other people had for them. Gentiles, he implied, understood when and why Jews might come together at their own Centers to pray, to study, to imbibe Jewish culture, and, of course, to play. But "merely to segregate Jews in a social settlement that is totally un-Jewish in environment and program is dangerous." It smacked of self-ghettoization. Novelist Ludwig Lewisohn suggested, at just about that same time, that those who frequented a Jewish pool that had no shul gave off the harmful impression that they were sticking to their own kind either because they were "subtly uncomfortable within" or, worse, "shut out from" non-Jewish environments and institutions. Maybe, Cohen suggested, it would better behoove the un-Jewish Centers to come clean, to disavow their nominal Jewish affiliations, forego their substantial communal Stipends, and honestly call themselves "Community Centers" and then open their portals to "all citizens regardless of race, color or creed."[25]

Those under attack—especially the national JCC officials who possessed their own strong Jewish sensitivities—had to have smiled ruefully when their operations were accused of misrepresentation. For they had their own grievances against some Synagogue Center rabbis of their time who allegedly, under the façade of building an all-inclusive religious and social center, utilized communal dollars disingenuously to expand synagogue seating capacities or to construct school annexes. As a result, argued Welfare Board executive Harry L. Glucksman in the early 1930s, "lacking the necessary recreational equipment, these organizations could not successfully function as Centers and were bound to prove disappointing to many, particularly, the youth, who had been led to believe that the organization would be of service in the larger field of Jewish work."[26]

But more frequently, it was rabbinic ingratitude toward religious efforts in the Ys or JCCs that offended people like Kraft, Glucksman, and Philip R. Goldstein—whom we will meet presently. As field secretary of the Welfare Board, Goldstein said as much in 1925 when he debated a local rabbi in Troy, New York, who "opposed the Center movement as an unnecessary menace to the Synagogue." His opponent claimed that "for many people, the Center takes the place of the Synagogue. If Centers did not exist, those people would seek the same social and other satisfactions at the Synagogue." We are assuming here that the Troy temple really had a gym!

Goldstein's answer was that "statistics show[ed] that, once Bar Mitzvah is over or Confirmation, the youth do not respond to the call of the Synagogue." The Y was, thus, compelled and willing to pick up the slack. Goldstein suggested that rather than complain and carp, the rabbi should assist in the Center's work helping "young people come to realize the values of the Jewish religion." Only then would they potentially "return to the Synagogue." Years later, at another heated venue, Louis Kraft would rise at a national gathering of Conservative rabbis and restate the position that "in all candor, I think it is fair to say that the Synagogue has been derelict in its duties, and it ought to be grateful that for a period of twenty-five or thirty years an institution was created to catch up with some of the Jewish youth who otherwise would have come under no Jewish influence.[27]

Still, whatever the origins, truth, and pervasiveness of its Jewishness problem, by the early 1940s, Welfare Board leadership realized that it had a serious image problem. Allegations were constantly coming in from the field. In one telling private communication, a Conservative rabbi in Dayton, Ohio, was moved to write angrily about the local Y's cultural chairman, "who has no Jewish culture whatever and he is married to a non-Jewish woman. Yet, it is men of this type who actually draft the so-called cultural program for the community center." What chance, the religious leader warned, did Judaism have under the watch of this decidedly wrong role model? In the 1940s, relatively few Jews intermarried, but those who did were rarely committed to Jewish observance. Moreover, Rabbi Jacob B. Agus believed that what he chafed about in Dayton was symptomatic of a "national problem . . . that has ominous potentialities for the future of the synagogue." It was time for the JCCs, he argued, to get their houses in order. And Agus suggested as a first step that the Board join with the Jewish interdenominational Synagogue Council of America (SCA) in the creation of a survey committee to ascertain the depths of the dilemma.[28]

Welfare Board president Frank L. Weil seemed to take these criticisms to heart, and in 1944, the first Joint Consultative Committee was set up with six delegates from the national religious group and an equal number of JCC spokesmen impaneled to "study . . . the points of agreement and points of difference between the Center Movement and the Synagogue and to bring remedial recommendations" to Weil's group. Speaking for the Conservative movement at that juncture, Rabbi Robert Gordis, president of its Rabbinical Assembly, was particularly anxious that progress be made immediately "lest the post-war period," that would soon be upon them, "witness a repetition on an enlarged scale of what happened after the First World War, when the synagogue was subjected to a weakening of its influence through an expansion of the secular community center with its generally non-Jewish program." While willing to acknowledge that there were "Jewish Community Centers where there is a very strong Jewish program," for him, the community was on the cusp of a fundamental battle "between the preservationists or survivalists and the assimilationists."[29]

Gordis and many other Conservative colleagues thus quickly grew frustrated when the committee exhibited a lack of initiative. Some of the blame lay with the Synagogue Council itself, which was hamstrung by its own internal problems and wrangling. By rule, every move it made had to meet with a "consensus opinion" among its Conservative, Reform, and Orthodox members, so they could not get an immediate read on "the occasions of irritation within the various communities." But it also seems that even if Weil wanted to move ahead, others within the Welfare Board group remained uninterested in — or were downright opposed to — a re-evaluation of their Jewish policies. In time, charges started to be leveled within Conservative ranks that the Joint Consultative Committee was a sham and that even "our representative on the . . . JWB Council" — that was doing its own, independent, program re-evaluation — "had not been consulted in the deliberations. In other words, our representation was a mere formality." And while so little positive was going on in committee rooms, "plans were being made for drives to build new Centers or enlarge old ones." Indeed, it seemed that the clash between synagogue and Center interests and leadership was constantly increasing.[30]

How bad things were becoming, or continuing, was already clearly evident at the 1946 Rabbinical Assembly meeting when Rabbi Max Artz, who was then traveling the country promoting Conservative Judaism in the emerging suburbs, restated the long-standing problem with unminced words. "We inspire young people in our congregation," he explained. And then, "they go to the Jewish Communal Centers, to the YMHA in the community . . . and, if he meets with people who have a negative attitude to Judaism, who are cynical about it, who have no positive, affirmative convictions about the synagogue, about Jewish life . . . these people chill the ardor of the very young people we try to reach."[31]

And from out in the field came this public lament, in 1947, from a rabbi who was doing his level best to offset the incursion of JCC activities into the lives of his impressionable youths. Rabbi David Shohet of Yonkers, New York, complained that "before the center came into being in our community, my synagogue was practically the center." But now, he continued, "it is struggling for existence. The fact is that the swimming pool has drawn away children from our Talmud Torah." Facing the problem that had perplexed so many modern rabbis before him — kids naturally preferred to learn how to swim instead of how to pray — Shohet lamented, "Between a teacher who teaches Bible and a physical education director who teaches gymnastics, the physical education director will win."[32]

A host of other Conservative rabbis expressed comparable sentiments when their movement polled them about this clash in that same year of 1947. More than half of the 108 members who filled out their written questionnaires asserted that "the Community Center (or YMHA) made only 'some' or no major contribution towards the furtherance of Judaism." As always, the JCCs were criticized for their "emphasis on social contacts," as a "common meeting ground" or as a "landlord for Jewish functions." There were even some offending institutions that conducted events "in direct violation of Jewish tradition and ritual." The problem lay with the " 'Jewish illiteracy' of Center workers and the 'religion-less' program which the Center leaders were holding up as the highest goal of Jewish activity." Altogether, the case was remade that a "state of tension [existed] between Synagogue and Center, their activities, and leadership."[33]

It remained, however, for the appearance of the JCCs' own internal study, the so-called "Janowsky" *JWB Survey*, completed just about the same time as the Conservatives did their review, for the Welfare Board to finally acknowledge the true extent of the problem and to suggest some desire for change. Acting with the blessing and funding of Weil and Kraft, Oscar I. Janowsky, a respected American Jewish historian and sociologist, interviewed some 2,000 JCC workers and Board people from coast to coast and verified that in all too many cases, rabbinic complaints were justified. Janowsky determined that despite Kraft's sincere statements and efforts "to help our youth live affirmatively as Jews," the provision of "recreational facilities for Jews" and not the promotion of "Jewish loyalties and identification" was still the prime objective of most Centers. And in the worst-case situations, about 15 percent of those surveyed "disregarded . . . traditional Jewish useages, especially with respect to the Sabbath and dietary laws." Janowsky found and personally believed that when "health clubs, which are nothing more than steam baths," were "kept open on the Sabbath," they served as an "affront" to rabbis of all movements. The scholar also detected a lack of concern in the land that Center workers—from executives to gym instructors—possess strong backgrounds in Jewish knowledge and education."[34]

For Janowsky, "one conclusion is inescapable and this is the point we desire to underscore. It is not the gymnasium and dance hall that validate the distinctive Jewish Center, but its Jewish purpose. . . . American Jewry is neither an athletic association, nor a health club, nor a dancing society, nor even a recreational fraternity, however, broadly one defines recreation." Moreover, in his view, those who would "insist on maintaining such a Jewish Center" were doing wrong both to Judaism and to the Jews. Writing in the spirit of Armand E. Cohen and Ludwig Lewisohn, Janowsky declared sharply that "it is not Jewish content, but the lack of it which converts the Jewish Center into a 'ghetto.' "[35]

Janowsky and his colleagues strongly advocated that "primary attention" be given to "Jewish content" in the movement. While sure to affirm that "recreation and health education" were important, the "first and greatest emphasis" had to be focused on "spiritual-cultural factors that constitute the Jewish way of life." They called upon all concerned to make every effort to upgrade the Jewish learning of Center workers and members. And on the prickly question of those health clubs that were opened on the Sabbath, the investigative group felt strongly that while Ys could remain open on holy days, "only such activities be permitted which are in consonance with the dignity and tradition of the day."[36]

While these recommendations may have mollified some of the JCCs' critics, other religious observers were unconvinced that meaningful changes were in the offing. For example, at the 1948 and 1949 Rabbinical Assembly convention, colleagues continued to speak out against Center "secularism." Israel M. Goldman of Providence, Rhode Island, still believed that the "rise and spread of the Community Center movement presents a challenge which is most grave in character and menaces the centrality which the Jewish religion and its source, the synagogue, must occupy in the life of American Jewry." Sioux City, Iowa's, Hyman R. Rabinowitz stated unequivocally that "the Jewish Center is, of course, a purely secular institution. Religion surely has no place . . . it's more for play and sociability than for the development of Jewish personalities." To dramatize his point, Rabinowitz offered the following war story from his recent visit to a Center "in a fairly large city in the Middle-west." Invited into the director's private office, he was "amazed to see among the objects which decorated his desk . . . the emblem of a pig in celluloid form." He asked rhetorically: What sort of inspiration ". . . can [he] derive from this emblem to stimulate Jewish children?" And David Aronson of Minneapolis showed that he continued to struggle against sports' challenge to Judaism when he commented that "a community that accepts the philosophy that a gymnasium is as essential to Jewish life as a synagogue and that a Jewish basketball team is as conducive to Jewish survival as a Talmud Torah, is on the way to extinction." Borrowing a page from Hillel's Jewish playbook (a non-Jew once challenged this ancient rabbi to teach him the entire Torah while the "student" stood on one foot), he observed that even "studying Torah while standing on one leg is more than acrobatic Judaism. It cannot be balanced with the high jump."[37]

Meanwhile, a 1947 survey that the Synagogue Council conducted of rabbis of all expressions revealed that in all too many locales, the Center movement either still had a way to go to change, or to live down, its long-standing reputation. Even when we take into account that annoyed respondents answered with more passion than those who were content about the status quo, the level of anger that some men in the field expressed is still striking. One Conservative rabbi in Cincinnati wrote that the Y in his region "is too secular. We cannot survive with gyms and swimming pools and dancing Jews." And as far as the "backgrounds and attitudes of Center workers" were concerned, here he asserted that "they would fit well into a YMCA. One worker did not know who [Theodore] Herzl [the famous Zionist leader] was or what Tisha B'Av [the day of Jewish national mourning] was." An Orthodox colleague in Milwaukee let it be known that where he lived "The Center is Jewish only in name. Its kitchen is absolutely *trefe* [unkosher]. . . . The Sabbath and holidays are flagrantly violated, etc." From Scarsdale, New York, came a rabbi's report that "the Center movement's philosophy is the philosophy of the swimming pool and gym. . . . It is the enemy of the synagogue." Moreover, he asserted that "it is about time that the rabbis wake up to the threat of the Center." And from a Mississippi Reform rabbi came the simple but telling words that the program of his Y was "we should have Jewish basketball."

When these and all other respondents were asked whether they thought the Janowsky report and the promised new sensitivities would change the JCCs' outlook for the better, close to half of the rabbis said that it would. Still, a Tennessee-based Orthodox rabbi, who made it be known that at his JCC "it seems as though knowledge of Judaism is a handicap and the bigger the *goy* [Gentile attitude], the better the director," warned that "like many good thoughts it has not taken hold of general membership or local boards." After all, he observed, "higher echelon seldom gets down to the lower."[38]

Actually, Rabbi Sydney S. Mossman did not know how right he really was. For Janowsky and national spokesmen like Kraft and Weil faced more than just some foot-dragging and apathy among their local affiliates. While the Welfare Board's delegates meeting in Pittsburgh in May 1947 approved the report provisionally, they also decided, given the study's import and in keeping with the board's "democratic" traditions, to "initiate a year's discussion period prior to final decision of the recommendations." And, during that time-out, significant contrarian voices were heard within the movement that openly submitted that the promotion of Judaism was not the JCCs' most important product.[39]

Harkening back to the "self-expressions" viewpoint of the 1930s, the National Association of Jewish Center Workers—representative of those who actually ran the clubs, the gyms, the health facilities, and the like—spoke out against the imposition of a Judaizing agenda upon the local Ys. While agreeing that the movement was supposed to serve "the interests of the Jewish people," in their view, it was up to the membership to decide how Jewish they wanted their institution to be. "Perhaps," they observed, "it is possible to permeate a basketball game or a swimming meet or a dance with Jewishness, but the people who come to these activities come to them as Jews who seek their recreational pursuits in a place where they can share them with other Jews, for a variety of sociological reasons, but who do not seek their activities in order to enhance their Jewishness." For them, just the act of bringing Jews together in their own venue was sufficient to strengthen a feeling of identification with the Jewish group. Essentially, that meant that if a youngster came to a Y just to play ball and showed no interest in anything else, there was no need for the institution to direct him or her out to some Jewish program or activity.[40]

Then there were the unabashedly avowed assimilationists who formed their own Independent Study group that harshly critiqued a perceived attempt to impose Judaism upon reluctant Y members. Sociologist Louis Wirth, along with historian Oscar Handlin and social commentator Elliot Cohen, read Janowsky survey statistics as proof that most Y people — executives, workers, and members alike — cared little for Jewish programming and had no interest in change. They chafed at what they saw as the spread of creeping undemocratic "religious or intolerant fundamentalism" into the JCC world. For them what was most attractive about the Y— at least the way it had always been — was its democracy, unlike the oligarchic world of the synagogue with its posturing rabbis and affluent lay officials in strict control. Theirs was, rather, a model American institution where the members set the agendas. Again it was matter of faith for these advocates that change should not be forced on anyone. Besides which, from their vantage point, the JCCs were already too Jewish: Who needed kosher food or, for that matter, Sabbath observance policies, if the goal of American Jews was to assimilate into the society around them?

These stances infuriated Oscar Janowsky, who publicly scoffed at his opponents' alleged sense of democracy and egalitarianism. He pointedly asserted that when unkosher food was served at a JCC function, it effectively meant that Orthodox Jews — and might we add many Conservative and some Reform Jews as well — were read out of the so-called "entire Jewish community." Janowsky also came close to explicitly characterizing his enemies as self-hating Jews concerned with making Gentiles comfortable in their midst and massively insensitive to their own people. In one of his most resonant statements he charged:

> Suppose an inter-faith group, including Protestants, Catholics and Jews, decided to have a dinner on Friday. Would it not be the proper thing to serve fish rather than meat, so as to enable the Catholic members to participate? Consideration for the Catholic participants would naturally dictate such procedure. All I suggest is that we show the same consideration to our Jewish neighbors which we readily concede to our Christian neighbors.[41]

With this assimilationist attitude still very much alive in the land, Synagogue Council people were, understandably, less than confident that a new era was upon them. While the rabbis and religious lay leaders applauded the Welfare Board's "recognition," through the Janowsky report, that "the growing influence of secularism" in the JCCs was an "aggravated . . . problem," for them the scholar's recommendation did not go far enough in addressing "the lack of proper religious motivation in some of the programs and activities of the Community Centers." Indeed, coming out of their second conference held over two months in the spring of 1948, the Synagogue Council's Executive Committee resolved that, as a start, "Center workers should be required to have Jewish religious education included in their professional training." But beyond that, the organization wanted to empower the not-yet-effective Joint Consultative Committee to control the direction the JCC's postwar growth spurts then well under way. That meant that rabbis — along with the Welfare Board's most committed Jews — would have a large say in determining if a community should have a JCC, and if one existed or should be built, what its religious value system should be. Through its frequent words and resolutions, America's religious community was saying that the JCCs and the Ys still had a long way to go toward consistently providing their young athletes and other members with an environment truly hospitable to the development of their Jewish identities.[42]

Time would tell if the "preservationists" within the JCC movement would not only heed this call, but, as importantly, whether they would gain the upper hand within their own community of social workers and become a potent force for Jewish survival as postwar Jewry confronted the problem of assimilation within an increasingly accepting America, poised on the suburban frontier.

6

THE MISSION OF AMERICAN JEWRY'S TEAM

A vital struggle over Jewish identity broke out in the new suburban communities of early postwar America. The primary face-off pitted the leaders of all modern Jewish religious expressions — from the American Orthodox to the Reform — against the dynamic societal forces that now, more than ever before, threatened to lure Jews away from their traditions. But even as rabbis of all stripes fought with similar weapons against a common foe — the assimilating attractions of an open society — a second battle also ensued. As spokesmen for each movement desperately pursued their wavering flocks, they engaged in what may fairly be described as rabbinic trash talk. Putting their positions front and center, religious competitors made it clear that they alone possessed the right mixture of traditional sensitivities and awareness of the world around them to suit the next generation of American Jews. Their fellow Jewish opponents, they asserted, surely did not. Staking its claims, Yeshiva University offered its sport teams — sometimes mentored by young rabbis with athletic pedigrees of their own — as one visible proof that they were certainly as modern as their liberal Jewish counterparts. By the early 1950s, Yeshiva's team members, particularly its basketball players, be-

came standard-bearers for Orthodoxy, and for Judaism, in venues far removed from their Washington Heights base camp. While these players in
this communal game of one-upmanship did not always carry the day for
Orthodoxy, their prominence created a catalytic dynamic within Yeshiva
itself. It made the school rethink its mission and initiated a debate over what
type of student it truly wanted to attract. Here too, one group of Jews'
affinity for sports, even to promote the ways of traditional Judaism, conflicted with the religious values of compatriots.

The "crabgrass frontier" of the late 1940s and 1950s was the setting for all
this activity and infighting. There, in hospitable suburban locales, Jews
gained a new lease on American life as they were welcomed into improved
residential habitats where cooperation and friendship among groups—
particularly white, middle-class ones—were points of emphasis in their
hometowns. Lines of ethnic demarcation, and long-standing interfaith tensions, started to blur or were increasingly overlooked, as everyone, Jew and
Gentile alike, made an effort to get along in their single-family home developments. The perceptible drop in anti-Semitism in the mellow days of
the early 1950s aided the Jews' fitting in. Overt prejudice of the nastiest
kinds lost much of its steam as it came to be associated, in popular minds,
with an enemy our country had beaten in the Second World War. A more
egalitarian-minded America was no longer pushing the Jews to stay with
their own kind.[1]

The Jews who moved, with their young families in tow, from the inner
cities of their youth to the Levittowns of this nation, loved the fact that
almost no one opposed their making major strides in America. In these
bucolic reaches, as one on-the-scene observer put it, "not only do . . . Jews
live like other[s], they live with them." In the Chicago suburb that our
reporter was talking about, people from all backgrounds almost lived on top
of one another in " 'courts'—*culs de sac,* surrounded in circular fashion by
twenty to forty two-story garden apartments . . . actually a house built together with five or seven others." "Privacy," it was said, was "at a minimum"
as everyone got to know his or her neighbors quite well, and friendly socializing was the thing to do. Still, many of these Jews did not immediately
feel fully comfortable in the Gentile world. They remained, at least for a
while, on "the edge of friendliness" with those around them.[2]

In suburbia Jews were ready joiners. They worked well with others in all
formal points of contact. Build a firehouse, Jews would be there. Need to
energize a school or a library board, Jews were enthusiastic helpers. In one
closely studied community, Jews were lauded for their leadership in the
establishment of a Little League. Not only did "good working relationships"
between Jews and their neighbors evolve out of these efforts, but also some
warm friendships took shape as everyone pitched in. But when the work or
the day was done, this generation of Jews still remained loyal to an intangible

special relationship with other Jews. In their heart of hearts, and in their most informal moments, they preferred the company of those who shared their past.[3]

Here's how that ambivalent Jewish behavior pattern might have looked using sports participation as the vantage point. Out on suburban links, Jews began to show an interest in the game of golf. Their immigrant ancestors had had no contact, connection, or affinity for this formerly WASP preserve situated as it had been, all too often, within restrictive and expensive country clubs. But now, Jews had arrived and were very excited that they were allowed to participate in this prestigious, pastoral pursuit. It was for them another sign of how well they were establishing themselves "within the general mores and values of the community." But when Jewish duffers-in-the-making were asked what sport they truly enjoyed, their most likely response was déclassé "ethnic" games like handball or table tennis. These were either pastimes they had competed in as youths in the Jewish inner city or activities that they liked to play with their closest friends in their own home recreation rooms. For these Jews, playing for status paid significant social dividends. But recreating with one's friends was still priceless.[4]

The problem with this scenario, for those concerned with Judaism's continuity on the suburban frontier, was that religious allegiances bred on hang-ups, marginality, or just plain memories of nasty Gentiles who once troubled them would not long survive the inevitable flattening of differences within the younger generation. The children who would be brought up in the new neighborhoods would come to believe—with many good reasons—that their Gentile neighbors could be among their closest friends. The truth was, reported one suburban-based rabbi in the 1950s, that a portion of his membership "admitted that they wished to move to the suburbs in order to live in a less restricted atmosphere" than in city life. "They wanted their children to meet and socialize with non-Jewish children." For example, they "now played with non-Jewish children on a level of middle-class respectability," on a level social playing field. In the world of suburban Little League, the "name calling and the fist fighting of the slums" and the inner-city neighborhoods was not countenanced. In this more accepting environment, Jewish kids, as never before, would begin to know Christians —real live Protestant Gentiles—not the Catholic ethnics against whom their parents had battled on urban turfs a generation earlier.[5]

Sometimes, getting to be friends with non-Jews paid dividends for the next generation's Jewish identity. That same 1950s suburban rabbi, who noted that his congregants liked mixed communities, also claimed that "in some instances, the unavailability of Christian friends on Sunday morning, when they are attending their churches, has helped to bring Jewish families into the synagogue." But more often than not, when Jews emulated their neighbors, the dilemmas of assimilation intensified. For example, in other locales, on a bright Sunday morning, Jewish children were found dressing up wanting "to go to church too" just like their Gentile friends who then were being packed off to their religious services. Given this dicey state of affairs, families that cared looked, more than ever before, to their synagogues to build within their children a more positive base for remaining Jewish.[6]

Here's how the fear factor operated. Unlike their elders, suburban-born Jews readily called Gentile boys and girls their buddies. The structure of town life brought kids into daily, close contact with each other. Doing what came naturally engendered gender-based relationships. Would these friendships mature into intermarriages, that long-standing fear, which until now had not been largely realized? Somehow, the synagogue had to become the preserver of Judaism. Parents no longer could count on the strongly Jewish neighborhood of the past nor the squads of outside enemies that used to strut down the streets of the city to keep Jewish kids together. They certainly would not tell their kids to stay clear of Gentiles. Such thoughts contributed much to the so-called Jewish religious revival of the early postwar period.[7]

A midwestern suburbanite expressed many of these sentiments when he wrote for a national Jewish periodical in the early 1950s. Thinking of his past and wondering about his kids' future, he recalled that in the urban environment of his youth, Jews knew who and what they were. But now, he was concerned about the "friendships the children make in school," relationships with good, upstanding kids who just happened to be Christian. The Jewish youngsters saw no reason why they should stay away from a dance at someone's "home or in the community social center," events that inevitably strengthened personal associations. And while he acknowledged that "intellectually many [parents] maintain that the religion of the girl" their sons "bring home is of minor importance," this on-the-scene source did admit that his and his friends' feelings about intermarriage is not "an intellectual business." Rather, it is an "inheritance from *Bube* and *Zeide* [which] outweighs liberal logic." In the city, this memoirist mused, "the odds are in your favor. Out here you stack the deck" through linkage to the "social organization of the synagogue."[8]

To lead their hoped-for revival, suburban Jewish families looked to an all-purpose, multitalented rabbi. He would have to represent their community well to the outside world, a relatively simple task in a 1950s America that pledged allegiance as an indivisible nation under God. He also would have to personify commitment to Jewish traditions; he would be observant both for himself and his followers. But that same rabbi should not press members to really be more religious than they wanted to be. Above all, he would have to make kids interested in Jewish life and comfortable in the synagogue's sacred and secular Jewish surroundings.[9]

Conservative rabbis of this time and place certainly were ready to offer themselves as leaders of what came to be trumpeted as a "return to the synagogue movement." As we have seen, they were old hands — or at least their movement was—as heads of seven-day-a-week Synagogue Centers. They were adroit at positioning themselves foursquare for tradition, "leaning toward the Orthodox," even as they were smart enough to contrast who they were and what they were doing against the "store *cheders* of the Bronx and Brooklyn." At the same time, they soft-pedaled the demands of observance. When they did their job well, they knew just what to say when a youngster wanted to bring his or her Gentile friend to a Jewish-sponsored dance or event. And they stayed on message with what was now the long-standing Synagogue Center belief that if athletics could only attract Jews to the religious center, there was a fighting chance that these youngsters might grow in their faith. One Queens colleague offered the all-familiar mantra that "we figure, that if we can get the young people here for one reason, the dances and the sports, they'll start coming for religious reasons as well."[10]

Another United Synagogue member, from Youngstown, Ohio, also reaffirmed Kaplan and Levinthal's article of faith that "every synagogue must consider itself a center for the child's activity—developing a club program of arts and crafts, stamps, music—yes, even athletics." For him, the methodology was clear and effective. "We can introduce Jewish ideas even through the study of stamps, an athletic program for certain holidays and even abstention from such a program on other occasions."[11]

Meanwhile, a rabbi who had served congregations in Pottsville, Pennsylvania, and Columbus, Ohio, told a national Conservative gathering, in the spirit of Solomon Schechter's now-legendary advice, "that the rabbi has to learn the latest baseball scores and the news about football heroes, because these things establish points of contact between the rabbi and the adolescent group." Putting his words into action, he personally escorted his "young people in the Tephilin Club [a post–bar mitzvah boys group] to a professional basketball game." A fishing trip took place when the weather got warmer. But the "the highlight of the Tephilin Club season," he proudly declared, was an overnight trip which he chaperoned. For him, what could be better than leading the kids in morning services, engaging them in a discussion "on the subject of 'What the State of Israel means to me,'" and then observing them take part in two basketball games in a local gymnasium?[12]

Actually, at about that same time, the Conservative movement did come up with a plan that was even better than a weekend with an athletic-minded rabbi for meshing Jewish values and sports activities within impressionable Jewish youths. How about a summer at one of their Ramah camps, where a child would be put "in a total Jewish environment [which] enabled him to live the so-called ideal Jewish life from the time he got up until he went to bed?" Erstwhile Ramah counselor Gerson D. Cohen recalled that one of the points of emphasis "was a concern with teaching [Jewish values] on the ball field. We spoke a great deal about it."[13]

Youngsters were educated, to begin with, that Jewish ethics would not

Basketball game at Camp Ramah, Berkshires, 1964. Courtesy
of the Ratner Center for the Study of Conservative Judaism,
Jewish Theological Seminary of America.

sustain running up a score against an inferior opponent. On a more sophisticated level, when Ramah was at its best, the ball court became a place
where ancient talmudic dicta could come to life for contemporary youngsters. Cohen, who years later succeeded the decidedly unathletic Louis Finkelstein as head of the Jewish Theological Seminary of America, learned
that latter lesson well when he was criticized for refereeing a basketball
game where his wife, Naomi, was a player. As the story goes, during a time-
out, Professor Shalom Spiegel, Ramah of Wisconsin's scholar-in-residence,
upbraided Cohen for being "judge of a game in which someone related to
you is a participant? Any camper who knows halacha," Spiegel said, "will
know you are breaking a religious law." It is really not known how many of
Naomi Cohen's teammates and opponents understood, prior to the game,
the religious roots of her husband's slight indiscretion. But they surely

Swimming class at Camp Ramah, Nyack, 1963. Courtesy of
the Ratner Center for the Study of Conservative Judaism,
Jewish Theological Seminary of America.

knew afterwards. Subsequent to that reprimand, a contrite Cohen gave his
whistle to someone else to finish officiating the contest.[14]

Everyone in the Conservative movement vigorously applauded the good
work that Ramah was doing. It would, in time, produce a new elite of religiously committed youngsters who would constitute an extraordinary cadre
of manpower and womanpower for their movement. The camps would become to Conservative Judaism, to borrow Ramah founder Rabbi Moshe
Davis's sports metaphor, what Little League was to the Big Show. In pitching
the Ramah idea to Louis Finkelstein, Davis once told his boss that "baseball
began to develop its players when they were children. The better, more
committed Little Leaguers went on to the minors and worked their way up
the hierarchical system that required more of them at each stage. The pro-

cess culminated with the draft of the best players into the major leagues." That analogy, Davis claimed, convinced an initially reluctant Finkelstein to support the summer effort. Somewhere Solomon Schechter was smiling! Evidently his disciple had learned enough *about baseball* to appreciate the remark.[15]

No less heartfelt kudos were always extended to the type of rabbi who succeeded in getting his young people away for a weekend of fine Jewish learning and good sports fun. Still, there were many battled-hardened critics within Conservatism who, as always, questioned whether the "stay to pray" approach that was so much a part of their movement's scene truly worked in most cases. For example, the "appearance of athletes" at men's club social events "no matter how well attended" declared one Philadelphia-based rabbi, was "inconsequential" because such activities "lost sight . . . of the values of the synagogue." This rabbi could have derived little comfort from his congregation's participation in a "strictly athletic" intersynagogue men's bowling league even if it gathered together "about 100 men" weekly and reportedly brought "credit and good publicity to Philadelphia Jewry."[16]

And then there was the public speculation that within the many shuls which featured pools, the swimming program lapped the educational center as a congregational priority. Did that mean that the religious Synagogue Center was having the same problems as did the secular JCCs which Conservative rabbis routinely and roundly criticized?

Rochester rabbi Abraham J. Karp seemed to think so when he wondered out loud if "we are also creating the situation where some day a committee will sit and decide whether the life guard and the swimming pool are more important than the guardian of our life who is in the classroom." Certainly neither he nor any other Rabbinical Assembly member could be heartened or gratified by a 1953 survey which suggested that temple members—with lay officials in the lead—were turning out in droves for recreational and social activities but not for services.[17]

There was a harsh reality at the root of this disconnect between the Conservative shul and *its* pool. Suburban Jews were content to merely place their children among their own kind. Rabbis obviously wanted more out of those who entered synagogue portals. Unfortunately for them, it seems that very few members were interested in deep Jewish commitments.

Still, when suburban congregations looked for a religious man to lead them as far as they wanted to go, they usually turned to the young graduates of the Jewish Theological Seminary of America. In some cases, this key personnel decision was made at formal, competitive venues that became known as "Debate Nights." On these occasions, representatives of Orthodoxy, Conservatism, and Reform were invited into a town to pitch their brand of Judaism as the most efficacious in keeping Jews together and for exposing youngsters to "Jewish culture patterns which parents themselves were neither willing nor able to teach them at home." In speaking for

Judaism and against their denominational opponents, Conservative spokes-men could talk of their wealth of youth work experience and their flexibility in balancing the social needs of the time with the demands of Jewish tradi-tion. They could also swipe at their Reform counterparts as out of line with the useable portions of the Jewish past and indict their Orthodox colleagues as out of step with the ways of America. Looking back on those days of battle in suburban rec rooms, one Yeshiva operative has recalled that they had to offset an image of Orthodoxy as reminiscent of "the smell of herring and the sight of spittoons" that reminded all of the "worst" of the old customs.[18]

In their heart of hearts, Orthodox debaters firmly believed they had a compelling theological message that might ultimately carry the day. Their strategy was to avoid criticizing the practices of potential congregants and stick to their message that the modern Orthodox synagogue was God's most appropriate home, even in suburbia. Their standard stump speech would assert that "Jewish tradition does not gain strength from what you do and does not lose its validity from what you do not do. . . . But, the synagogue represents Torah."[19]

However, to even begin to get a fair hearing for their views, they had to get past the first line of strong resistance, the sense within the debate room, or around the suburban town, that Orthodox rabbis could not relate well to Jewish youngsters. One of the ways Yeshiva's strategists sought to offset these impressions was to highlight the athleticism of its young rabbis and the prowess of its college teams.

Actually, there was already talk about this tactic within Yeshiva's student body as early as 1944, when a student journalist asked his readers to look ahead with him to the challenges Orthodoxy and American Judaism would face in the coming years. Yeshiva, said columnist Bernard Weisberg, was now "interested in turning out rabbis who will go out into the spiritual desert that is America today and revive and resuscitate Orthodoxy among the Jews of this land." To be effective out on the hustings required that they "be intimately acquainted with every aspect and every tendency of the Jewish-American youth's daily life." The trick was to take "the activities which are peculiar to American living and channelize them toward a Torah-true Juda-ism." A Yeshiva rabbi had not only to know all about sports but be willing to participate in synagogue-run games and outings. In planning for the battle ahead, a voice at Yeshiva was sounding very much like Solomon Schechter on sports!

Indeed, for Weisberg, the Synagogue Center concept of their man, Ortho-dox rabbi Herbert S. Goldstein, was the proper technique to use in "attract-ing the younger generation to Orthodoxy." His cadre of Yeshiva men had to believe "that once the rabbi can induce the youngsters to come to the center to play . . . he has the material at hand from which to form the future Orthodoxy of America." But to really succeed, the forward-thinking rabbi had to do more than to merely organize activities from afar. "It is necessary to attend them personally and even partake of them when possible." For it was "this type of personal contact with the youth on their own plane, on their own level," that to date was "sadly lacking among our rabbis."[20]

A year or so later, fellow student scribe Myron Fenster framed the challenges that Yeshiva University rabbis faced in a similar way. "The coming generation will be interested not so much in what a rabbi knows, but whether he is a 'regular guy.'" And there was nothing like an athletic background to overcome a congregant's apprehension that the Orthodox rabbi "is a learned fellow and all that, but I don't know, he seems to be living in a world all his own — he does not know what's going on."[21]

Abraham "Doc" Hurwitz, Yeshiva's one-full-time-man physical education department, heartily agreed with all these sentiments. Speaking in 1945 to the "rabbis and hebrew teachers" of the future, he argued that "before a rabbi opens his mouth his physical appearance speaks for him." Indeed, he continued, "many a rabbi maintains his leadership because of the social poise he displays in his contacts with his constituency outside of the pulpit." Thus it was "vital for the aspirant to the rabbinate" to find his way to the weight room.

But more than just displaying — by showing his muscles — that the Orthodox rabbi was one of the guys, Hurwitz believed that the "rabbi or hebrew school teacher trained in physical education and recreational supervision can be a potent force in dealing with our backsliding youth and returning them to the faith of our fathers." He dreamed that Yeshiva would create "a model community Synagogue Center where leaders can be trained to meet these requirements."[22]

However, any plan to institute a more "invigorated, diversified sports program" both for varsity athletes and for all other students, or to create a permanent "Maimonides Health Club," or just to have a decent gym for classes, workouts, and intramurals required a level of institutional commitment that previously had never been available. Until then, Professor Hurwitz, an on-stage magician in his spare time — his daughter Shari Lewis would take some of those skills with her to Broadway and to Hollywood — did whatever he could to prevent the program from disappearing from the Yeshiva scene. The students themselves had run the intramural and intercollegiate sports program. They had raised the monies, really pittances, which were paid to volunteer coaches. Remarkably, they had succeeded in attracting some top-flight men to the challenge of Yeshiva athletics. Their greatest coup was securing Bernard "Red" Sarachek's services as college varsity basketball coach beginning in 1942. Additionally, students and sports-minded alumni sensed that the administration, although certainly not opposed to sports, did not really understand how important athletics were to the undergraduates. *Commentator* scribes frequently made note of the symbolic fact that the college's catalogues occasionally omitted reference to the existence of teams—except maybe the chess or debating squads—in its enumeration of extracurricular activities.[23]

Like his predecessor Bernard Revel, Dr. Samuel Belkin, who was elected Yeshiva University's second president in 1943, a product too of the eastern European yeshiva world before securing a secular education at American Ivy League schools, had no personal affinity for sports. And although he desperately wanted his school and his movement to succeed in suburbia, he had to be sensitized to the idea that sports could help carry the day.[24]

Rabbi Abraham Avrech was anxious to take on the challenge of sports within and without Orthodoxy's Washington Heights home. A 1940 graduate of Yeshiva College, where "Shorty" had played basketball for the "Blue and White," Avrech was called, soon after ordination from Yeshiva's rabbinical school, to serve in the school's newly established Community Service Bureau. That meant that in his day job, he worked with his colleagues to grasp a foothold in out-of-town locales. For example, it was he and his associates who had strategized how to put Orthodoxy's best foot forward at encounters like Debate Night. In his spare time, he collaborated with several like-minded youthful Yeshiva staff members to promote sports on—and beyond—the campus. Here vocation and avocation overlapped as Avrech crusaded, through sports, for the cause of Orthodoxy.[25]

Samuel Hartstein, Belkin's *aide de camp* and the school's public relations director, was of inestimable help to Yeshiva's sports devotees. Himself a former Yeshiva College basketball player, Hartstein was constantly on the scene promoting Yeshiva athletics. More than that, he used his own office to grind out press releases, sports brochures, and the like to the Jewish and general media. Allied with Avrech and others, he was instrumental in 1948 in forming the Yeshiva University Athletic Association (YUAA)—an Orthodox sports booster club—to raise money for coaches and to dream the dream of a first-rate and nationally influential program. Among the YUAA's earliest achievements was its involvement in the long-term engagement of Olympians Henry Wittenberg and Arthur Tauber to coach the fledgling wrestling and fencing teams and the hiring of tennis teaching pro Eli Epstein to lead the netmen. For a while, Edward Lowenstein of the Maccabe Sports Association coached a short-lived soccer team.[26]

If YUAA backers had any doubt that what they were doing was right for Yeshiva and in line with what the faith taught, Rabbi Joseph H. Lookstein's public sentiments had to have encouraged them. That erstwhile 1920s Yeshiva pitcher—he had helped handle the hurling chores in the student-faculty tilt on Lag B'Omer—who was now one of American Orthodoxy's most influential rabbis, explicitly linked what the YUAA was doing to "Rabbi Kook's view that one who is indulged in building up his body, is as much performing the will of God as the pious scholar, thus lending to an athletic program as much significance in an institution of higher learning as a *smicha* [rabbinical ordination] program."[27]

In time, the YUAA put into action its plan to take the battle for Orthodoxy on the road to prove, as Hartstein's media alerts put it, that "they can pray and play . . . that religious observance and sports can go hand-in-hand." Whether it was trips to Hartford, Bridgeport, or New Haven, Connecticut, or to Williamsport or Wilkes-Barre, Pennsylvania, the point was made that "while few individuals think of their spiritual leaders as sports stars, this talent nonetheless, is proving a great boon to many of the six hundred rabbis, graduates of its theological seminary . . . to carry on their programs effectively." Not incidentally, when Yeshiva "invaded" (its term) a local Jewish community, explicit efforts were made to "influence the youth of those towns that show an increased trend towards the Conservative and Reform movements." Indeed, in the opinion of a leader of the Hartford Jewish community, "the visit of the Yeshiva Quintet brought to reality the dream of the late Bernard Revel . . . [who] envisioned in the University graduate a combination of Judaism and the American professional rather than the spiritually deficient Jewish professional who was graduated from another institution of higher learning." [JTSA?][28]

For Orthodox outreach operatives, winning these road games against tough local competition was really secondary to presenting the "team as living proof that Yeshiva University boys walk, talk, and act American and live Torah-true lives." YUAA folks had to have agreed with what a student sportswriter said after their club "got clobbered" by a tough Lycoming College club in Williamsport. "The fact that we lost the game was unimportant and irrelevant as far as the Jewish community was concerned." More important than the won-lost record was the number of communities and synagogues that, in their view, were saved from disaffection from Judaism or affiliation with an opposing religious movement.[29]

However, despite their abundant enthusiasm and obvious energy for battle, Orthodox community service people were only occasionally successful in holding back the tide of Conservatism. The decade after the Second World War really belonged to their opponents, who triumphed at most encounters and generally dominated the religious field. Moreover, even when Orthodoxy won a community in the 1950s, it did not do all that better than its liberal antagonists in intensifying the religious commitments of congregants. A concerned Orthodox observer said as much when he reported in 1961 that "the size of a suburban congregation bears little relation to the number of worshipers actually at services. Membership in a synagogue is not translated into religious observance." Much like those who infrequently attended Conservative and Reform synagogues, those who affiliated with Orthodox shuls "seem to be becoming lax in *kashruth*, Sabbath observance and other cardinals [*sic*] of the Jewish faith." The era of major enclaves of observant Orthodox Jews in suburbia would not begin for another generation. Given this religious tableau, Orthodox outreach's greatest victory in suburbia may simply have been its success—with the help of Yeshiva's athletes—in dispelling negative stereotypes about modern Orthodox rabbis.[30]

Ever the Yeshiva loyalist, Coach Sarachek routinely said all the right things about these moral victories. His recurring tag line was that "we may not win many ball games but if we can turn out leaders we'll be champs in the end." Or he would recite the creed that "not only is the athletic program of immeasurable profit to the student, but the athletic teams are the only ones in the nation fostered by a Jewish college . . . [which] creates intense interest both within the Jewish community and without." But he was also a competitive basketball man with his own impressive athletic pedigree who wanted his club to do more than just show up. As a player, he had been on a Public School Athletic League championship club at Stuyvesant High School. During his early years at Yeshiva, this peripatetic hardwood mentor had taken the Workmen's Circle team and the Grand St. Boys to the Metropolitan Amateur Athletic Union championships and had guided the Scranton Miners to three American Basketball League crowns. Left unsaid was that Yeshiva's record was the only dark spot on his coaching resume.[31]

Sarachek's first real chance to improve both his, and Yeshiva's, basketball record came to hand just in time for the 1949–1950 campaign when, fortuitously, an uncommon young athlete arrived on campus whose background and orientation captured the coach's imagination, not to mention that of Avrech, Hartstein, and other YUAA boosters. Bronx-born Marvin Hershkowitz, an All-City selection from basketball powerhouse DeWitt Clinton High School, hailed from a marginally observant family. By his own estimation, his "family had a tendency towards Orthodoxy and attended an Orthodox synagogue," but his father "worked on Shabbat" to help make ends meet. While at Clinton, Hershkowitz played games on Saturday, but "tried to do as least wrong as possible." For example, he would arrange to bring his "gym stuff" to the game site before the Sabbath to avoid carrying outside in violation of rabbinic precepts. Hershkowitz has recalled that he never did play well in those Saturday games and, as a kid, attributed his failures to some guilt over his Sabbath quasi-violations.

Nonetheless, this highly recruited star went off to the then local big-time basketball school, CCNY, and played quite well on the freshman team. He was part of that great 1948 recruiting class that brought to CCNY Ed Warner, his teammate from Clinton, Taft High School's Ed Roman, and Al Roth from Erasmus Hall. They would lead City to basketball immortality as they formed the nucleus for a team that would in 1950 win the NIT and NCAA "double championship." And then, these same fellows would suffer the ignominy of being key players in the infamous 1951 basketball point-shaving scandal that rocked their college.

However, Hershkowitz would not be among them for either fame or damnation because already as a freshman he was becoming increasingly troubled about upholding his growing traditional religious values. How would he deal with "[unkosher] training tables and Saturday travel dates" that would be part of varsity life? This young man's own personal journey to be both an athlete and an Orthodox Jew led him to Yeshiva University. He felt privileged to play for Sarachek — an outstanding tactician who became his personal friend — even if their club had to travel downtown by subway to practice and play at the Central Needle Trades school on lower Seventh Avenue. As important, Hershkowitz found a number of rabbis and professors who welcomed him, loved his attitude toward Judaism, and were ready to tailor a Jewish studies program to his needs.[32]

Sarachek, the competitor, was excited to acquire a young man of Hershkowitz's caliber who might produce more wins for his team and greater public recognition for the school. The recruiter in Red figured that if Hershkowitz worked out, other public school athletes might follow in his footsteps. Hershkowitz helped out, speaking to potential "Mighty Mites," as the team was now called, about "the coach, the school and that you did not have to be a rabbi" to make it at the school.

As a committed if not particularly observant Jew, Sarachek wanted these fellows to enroll at the school for more than just basketball stardom. He believed, as a matter of faith, that Yeshiva would grant them a quality secular and Jewish education. And he hoped that upon graduation they would contribute to the Jewish community. Indeed, Sarachek was reportedly thrilled when Hershkowitz, upon graduation and after playing in the Maccabiah Games, opted for a career in Jewish social work. He would subsequently return to Yeshiva as Red's assistant and work in the school's fledgling student guidance office before assuming a coaching job at the Ramaz School, a local New York Jewish day school.[33]

Sarachek's visions coincided completely with Hartstein's oft-repeated formula of "Friends, Funds and Freshmen" for the expansion of Yeshiva's purview. By 1956, the highly influential public relations man and his comrades were able to convince their president that this incipient preparatory track — within which Hershkowitz blossomed Jewishly — should be formalized as a new "Jewish Studies Program" (JSP). This division would attract more and more students, not only athletes, with public school backgrounds. Some came with Conservative and Reform backgrounds as Yeshiva University, in its own way, counterattacked against its denominational opponents. The sportsmen would become more than ever American Jewry's team; representing Orthodoxy well beyond Washington Heights would certainly increase the number of friends who felt good about Belkin's institution.[34]

Belkin agreed. In February 1956, he announced that in the coming fall "a limited program in Hebraic studies and the principles of Judaism will be offered to accommodate students who are not prepared to take even a

1949–1950 Yeshiva University men's basketball team. First row from left to right: Marvin Hershkowitz, Howard Danzig, and David Hartman. Second row: Coach Bernard "Red" Sarachek, Ruby Davidman, Artie Stein, Murray Mayer, and Natie Krieger. Courtesy of Yeshiva University Public Affairs Department.

partial program" in Yeshiva's existing religious studies programs, with the proviso that these new students subscribe to the school's Orthodoxy and comport themselves accordingly. This announcement, coming as it did in the midst of the Mighty Mites' greatest basketball season to date, constituted a moment of triumph for Sarachek. This team, led by public school youngsters that Sarachek recruited—with some helpful words from Hershkowitz —would compile a 16-2 record. And now, even more help was on the way. Indeed over the next four years, the team compiled a 46-20 record. Not incidentally, by the 1959–1960 season, eight of the eleven varsity members were public high school kids. Yeshiva basketball seemingly was on the up-swing to stay.[35]

However, this sports heyday did not last long, as Sarachek was unable to sustain the flow of stars into his system. A combination of religious forces within and without the institution and changes in American social circumstances conspired to chill his dreams. While JSP students were heroes to the YUAA crowd, the decision to actively recruit public school graduates never really sat well with others within Yeshiva's community—especially the old-line Talmud faculty—who felt that "the influx of a non-Yeshiva type element into the Yeshiva environment might affect the climate and morale of the Yeshiva itself."[36]

This sports encounter brought to the surface an ongoing tension at the school between those who wanted to extend Yeshiva's purview beyond its campus enclave—with all the attendant risks—and those who wished to preserve at all costs its traditional character and constituency. The inward-facing group exerted pressure to restrict admission to only the most committed. Their carping also played no small role in making the newcomers uncomfortable.

Red's men were the most visible of the school's new recruits. Allegedly, some of the ballplayers—certainly not Hershkowitz—did not always walk the school's straight and narrow. Uncharitable elements on campus derogatorily referred to the JSP students as members of the "Jewish Sports Program" who "came to shoot baskets, take the college courses and go home." Some highly intolerant students even referred to JSP men as *shkotsim* (a very nasty term for Gentiles).[37]

In other quarters, massive ambivalence was expressed about the mission of JSP and the importance sports were playing in Washington Heights. A sports editorial that appeared in *Commentator* in 1958 entitled "What Price Glory?" articulated just this passive-aggressive critique of what Red, Hartstein, and others had wrought. For this scribe, "a small but significant detail, not to be overlooked by the interested observers of the Yeshiva scene is the fact that . . . [next year] there will remain but two members of the varsity basketball team who attend" the more established programs at the college. "The remaining players all graduates of the Public High School System attend the newly formed Jewish Studies Program." He continued, in a critical vein:

> The supporters of the new trend have hoped, at best, to produce a team of glory. But I feel that this past season did not particularly nourish their hopes. What is even worse, in my opinion, is that the basketball team, long a means of propaganda and a matter of public relations to Yeshiva University, has lost its positive value. Can we honestly say to ourselves that the present varsity is, as a whole, representative of Yeshiva University?

However, this columnist's mind was not totally made up as he concluded:

> I hope that the readers of this column do not misunderstand my words. Criticism here is not directed to the Jewish Studies Program as such and surely not to any of the personalities concerned with this program. The final merits of the JSP have yet to be evaluated, but no one will deny its measured value.[38]

A year or so later, this same columnist took pains to praise a JSP ballplayer, "a pioneer in the new . . . program . . . thrust into the Yeshiva spotlight," who had proven himself to the community. Still, the pressure to defend the program, not to mention the need to conform to Yeshiva's lifestyle, combined to make enrollment in the JSP much less attractive than it might have been for subsequent groups of students.[39]

At the same time, a gradual change in Yeshiva's larger student recruitment strategies cut the pool of public school students — sportsmen included — whom the school actively pursued. Here, in a sense, Red's program was a victim of Orthodoxy's success in raising more and more students interested in Yeshiva from within the then-burgeoning nationwide Orthodox day school movement. Increasingly, during the 1960s, "freshmen" would be drawn from that growing group. And while Yeshiva was still committed to outreach, its focus changed. The school's officials quickly began to look at a different type of public school prospect. Now, the typical JSP student might be a graduate of the Bronx High School of Science, who had attended an elementary-level Jewish day school before attending a superior secular high school. He had never really "dropped out" of the Orthodox fold within which he was initially reared, since he often spent his spare time in the ever-expanding network of Orthodox youth groups. The "true freshman" with no real Jewish background but with a strong athletic profile, was no longer appearing at Yeshiva.[40]

To make matters even worse for Red and YUAA sports enthusiasts, as this era unfolded, there was the other, undeniable sociological reality that there were fewer top-notch Jewish ballplayers on urban public high school varsities to pursue. The coach would have to rely on day school products to lead the Mighty Mites. And the 1960s' record reflected the fact that young men who as high schoolers had never played against high-level competition did not adjust well to the pressures of college ball. In a typical year, 1962–1963, with only one good public school player in the starting lineup — two others were role players — the team went 6-14. One veteran of that squad has reported that there was "some tension between the yeshiva and non-yeshiva players." A frustrated Sarachek, his raised expectations shattered, suffered through nine consecutive losing seasons (1960–61 to 1968–1969), winning only 61 of 178 ballgames (.343 winning percentage).[41]

Meanwhile, as if losing on the hardwood was not annoying enough, Red also had to have been troubled in 1964 when questions were raised publicly about whether basketball players—whatever their pedigrees—were worthy institutional standard-bearers at Yeshiva and whether Sarachek was an appropriate role model for this Orthodox institution.

Over the years, a few voices had been heard within the school's more traditional religious circles suggesting that sports and sportsmen detracted from a true "yeshiva environment." In 1946, for example, chemistry major Norman Lamm spoke for that segment of the community when he questioned the importance fellow students were placing upon all extracurricular activities, including sports. This future president of Yeshiva University then staunchly stated that "the leaders of a religion and [Jewish] nation cannot be built by a heterogeneous mixture of Latin, basketball and Varsity shows, with a dash, here and there, of the teachings of the basic doctrines and spirit of that religion." For him, "recreational activities" had their place at Yeshiva; it was not *ipso facto* a waste of valuable time that should be better spent studying the Torah. But the school had to beware lest these activities become too important on campus. For above all, Yeshiva had to be proudly different from all other colleges and universities around it.[42]

The flashpoint in the debate over whether sports and athletes either personified or undermined a true yeshiva environment was a proposal for a "Homecoming Weekend" — including a ballgame and a postgame social — to honor past and present players and "to arouse student and alumni interest in athletics." Its protagonist, *Commentator* sports editor Neil Koslowe, not incidentally the son of an early player-coach of the "Blue and White," held still to the Avrech-Hartstein vision of the late 1940s and 1950s. He argued that a vibrant sports program was essential for Yeshiva's growth, that the recruitment of outstanding athletes from all corners of the Jewish community was a desideratum, and that athletes who "give of themselves so that the Yeshiva name would be respected . . . surely [should] have the respect, praise and appreciation of . . . fellow Yeshiva students."[43]

However, Koslowe was to find that many within his generation of students did not view athletes as among "Yeshiva's best." One such critic, who seemingly spoke for the Student Council majority that rejected Koslowe's proposal, pointedly asserted that "if we wish to do honor; if we wish to create heroes; if we must have idols, let them be those *Roshei Yeshiva* [teachers of Talmud] who wage the war to conquer the contradictions of Torah and *Chochma* [secular learning] and who with G-d's help, will win the battle." As important, he protested that the image of a Yeshiva Homecoming Weekend — with basketball and a postgame social as its centerpiece — smacked of an attempt to secularize his school. Another fellow critic coined the phrase "the collegification" of Yeshiva to underscore his concerns.[44]

As this cultural battle continued, Koslowe was bombarded with canards that his event was a poorly masked effort to bring large numbers of "enticing" Stern College students—Yeshiva's sister school that was founded in 1954—to the weekend's activities. Everyone knew that young Orthodox women had always attended Yeshiva sports events. Saturday night at Central Needle Trades was traditionally "Date Night." But now, it was alleged that this proposed official social event would lead to an unconscionable level of libertine behavior inappropriate for Yeshiva. And even as Koslowe's critics were questioning his intentions, the attacks turned uglier still as students turned on his hero, Coach Sarachek.[45]

Koslowe had said, "Yeshiva College is Bernard Sarachek. He came and he taught and he fought and he yelled" as he preached that "we're Yeshiva [and] we are just as good as anybody else—in fact, we are better in all respects." Red's enemies riposted and blistered the fiery, earthy, old-school coach who punctuated his pep talks with unprintable metaphors as "a vulgar, uncouth person [who] has no place in a university . . . [and] to say that one who has such 'qualities' exemplifies and represents Yeshiva, of all places, is a slander on its good name and reputation."[46]

In response, one of Red's legion of followers tried to put "ribald" Red's rhetoric in its appropriate sports context. In his view, the "spirited coaching of Red Sarachek never seems to have a deleterious effect on the athletes." Besides which, "it is difficult to imagine that the use of phrases like, 'Oh my gracious, fellows, stop, throwing passes away,' would serve a better purpose."[47]

Still, it remained for Victor Geller, Yeshiva's Rabbinic Placement Director —and a YUAA loyalist—to silence angry student opponents by reminding everyone of the services Sarachek had rendered to Orthodoxy in his off-the-court communal activities. In his letter to the editor of *Commentator*, he took readers back to the action of the era of Debate Night, a time in the school's not-so-distant past but a moment that the next generation of Yeshiva students either did not know of or had forgotten.

As the story went, in 1952, a group of some sixty Jewish families, mostly young marrieds and World War II veterans who had grown up in the then-declining East New York, Crown Heights, Williamsburg, and Brownsville sections of Brooklyn, settled into one-family homes in the new Mill Basin section of that borough. Though this community, built on swampland, was legally within the city limits, theirs was a suburban Jewish lifestyle. The lure of "affordable homes, about $10,000 with a 2 percent interest rate" had brought them there. Soon upon arrival, efforts were made to establish a synagogue. But what sort of congregation would they have? Red Sarachek was the one member with connections. He and his wife, Belle, had moved with their two children from Crown Heights just a year earlier. The coach called the placement office at the Community Service Bureau at Yeshiva University and secured the services of a young rabbi, David Halpern. This move seemingly secured the Flatbush Park Jewish Center into the Orthodox column. However, two years later, as the shul prepared to move from its storefront origins on Avenue N to a commodious center on Avenue U, a battle broke out over whether the sanctuary would permanently have a *mechitza* (a partition separating men and women during prayer). The fate of the congregation and its future affiliation was put to a public debate and vote. At that critical moment, Geller reported, "Bernard Sarachek campaigned ceaselessly in his community." Intent in getting out the right kind of supporters, "he organized car pools and a baby sitting service to make sure that every possible vote could be garnered for the forces of Orthodoxy."

At the meeting, Sarachek spoke bluntly — he knew no other way — against those who demanded that men and women had to sit together when they prayed. Leaving theological arguments to Rabbi Halpern, the contrarian coach simply observed that when couples arrived at the gathering, the "women mingled with themselves and 'yenta-ed' and did not stay with their husbands." The men also did what came naturally and hung out with their fellow males. And yet, Red argued, "you are so worried about separation, but look what's happening now. How important is it for you" to be with your husbands during services? It is not known whether Red made or lost any friends with the in-the-face tone of his remarks. But in the end, by a vote of 42-22, the congregation chose Orthodoxy.

For Geller, who had not forgotten that 1954 victory, it was evident that while Sarachek was not "a paragon" nor "an exemplar of Yeshiva . . . let the record be clear that there are large numbers of people within Yeshiva and outside who respect and admire" him. Geller closed by suggesting that critics enroll in a "supplementary course in *derekh eretz*" (proper ethical behavior) before again attacking such a good, if flawed, man.[48]

In 1969, Sarachek left Yeshiva's coaching lines to assist his disciple Lou Carnesecca in the latter's own quixotic pursuit of professional sports glory as coach of the New York Nets. Red had always given valuable advice to some of America's best-known coaches, from Dean Smith to Joe Lapchick to Bob Knight among others. Now he was tapped to officially bring his special expertise to the highest level. Subsequently, he served as a consultant to Carnesecca when Lou returned to St. John's University. And upon retirement to Florida in the 1980s, Red helped out St. John's alumnus Kevin Loughery, an erstwhile "Redman," in schooling the Miami Heat.[49]

Sarachek initially willed the Yeshiva job to Sam Stern, the last of his outstanding public school protégés. But Stern was no more successful than Sarachek in bringing in top-flight talent from a diminishing outside pool of Jewish athletes. After two frustrating seasons, Stern departed and Red turned to Jonathan Halpert to head up and give new direction to the program. Captain of the 1966 Mighty Mites, one of the best Talmudical Academy athletes of his era, and a member of a second-generation Yeshiva family, Halpert, in his early years, tried to use his connections to attract the best players from the ever-growing day school community to his squad. Occasionally, he would reach out — with care and discretion — to a public school youngster who he was certain could toe Yeshiva's now well-defined mark. He also wisely downgraded the team's schedule somewhat to afford his club the possibility of being competitive. In 1978, he turned to me to serve as his assistant coach. It is a job I have relished and have fulfilled with gusto over the past quarter-century except when academic obligations have taken me away from the bench.[50]

In his more than thirty years as Yeshiva's coach, Halpert continued to teach, albeit without the off-color histrionics, Red's style of basketball. Moreover, he preached, as his mentor had, that the club was American Jewry's team and his men were institutional standard-bearers. And he has been proud to take his players on the road to visit outlying Jewish communities. But unlike Sarachek and Hershkowitz, a different type of Orthodox community hosted Yeshiva. Whether the team went to Miami or Brookline or Hartford, it interacted primarily with day school products like themselves. In a sense, the winnowing out of contemporary Orthodoxy of its non-observant segment was reflected by the fact that neither the Floridians, Bostonians, nor Connecticutites who cheered the team on were at all surprised that the players could "play and pray." So did they.

As Sarachek always understood and Hershkowitz exemplified, Halpert knew that to win he had to have a few non-yeshiva trained stars. Day school products would be the complementary role players. Interestingly enough, he found "public school" kids, almost without exception, from within Israeli "public schools." With the help of Hershkowitz — who migrated to Israel in the 1980s — Halpert recruited young men from traditional-leaning "Masorati" families who had expressed enough of a commitment to Orthodox values to pass muster with Yeshiva officials. They tended to be tougher-skinned and tougher-minded and had important experience as former youth players in the very physical international-style game. With these older army veterans as the hub, Yeshiva teams from 1980–2000 amassed a respectable 246-207 (.543) record against decent opposition.

Part of the team's success was attributable to the presence on campus since 1985 of the magnificent Max Stern Athletic Center, complete with a 1,100-seat gym with a pool, next door to a shul. School officials, under President Norman Lamm, realized that to attract late twentieth-century American Orthodox students from day school environments to their university, they would have to provide them with the type of recreational facilities to which they were accustomed at home or at their summer camps. Fortunately, the institution had by then developed enough friends and funds to help them impress potential freshmen. Of course, Yeshiva's sports teams were the immediate beneficiaries of these improvements.

Still, this contemporary era has not constituted a heyday in Yeshiva University sports. Certainly sports are front and center every spring when the Max Stern Athletic Center hosts the Henry Wittenberg Wrestling Tournament and the Red Sarachek Basketball Tournament, major admissions department events, that bring together day school grapplers and hoopsters from around the nation. Nonetheless, with all these available facilities and winning teams to cheer on, there has been a noticeable decline, beginning in the mid-1990s, in student interest in campus sports and even in physical fitness. All too often, the pool and gym are empty or underutilized, frequented by an identifiable minority of students who love to work out, play on varsities, or simply like to cheer in the stands. The others, in keeping with the tenor of these times within the committed Orthodox community, prefer to spend their extracurricular hours in voluntary Torah study. They are, in their own way, of a mind-set far different from their grandfathers, who desperately wanted to be seen as "all-American boys," or even from their fathers, who wanted Yeshiva to be respected through a high sports profile.

This lack of clamor for sports on campus was not lost on a Yeshiva College journalist who, late in the 2001 basketball season, took his fellow students to task for their "apathy" for those who "play out their hearts representing their school." In his op-ed piece, Shai Barnea spoke of athletes whom "no one seems to know . . . [and] no one seems to appreciate what they do." Writing in a tone so much different from *Commentator* sports editor Neil Koslowe of forty years earlier, Barnea did not ask the *beit midrash* crowd to honor Yeshiva athletes. All this contemporary young fan wanted was for the campus to care about and support "what our peers on the basketball team think."

To make his point, Barnea pitched the "dedication" of his Maccabees — the latest name for Yeshiva sports squads — as "only matched by those who learn in the *beit midrash.*" In the same way, he cried, that when "people finish learning *shas* [a tractate of the Talmud], they have a *siyum* [a commemorative celebration] to show their friends what they have accomplished." In the same spirit, he continued, "when the basketball players step out onto the court, they are displaying their accomplishments for us. But . . . very few fans are there to greet them."[51]

It was as if what the young Norman Lamm had hoped for in 1946 had become the prevalent mood on campus. Back then, Lamm had acknowledged that while recreation had its place at his school, "sorely needed 'extra time' put into Talmud studies at night and other free time" in the holy pursuit of *lamdanus*—greater proficiency and versatility as a rabbinical scholar—was what Yeshiva was all about.[52] Close to sixty years ago, this vision was a minority view in Washington Heights. At the beginning of the twenty-first century, it is the majority opinion.

7

AN IRRESISTIBLE FORCE

In 1921, Rabbi Shraga Faivel Mendlowitz assumed control of Mesifta Torah Vodaath (TVD), a still fledgling yeshiva in staunchly Orthodox Williamsburg, Brooklyn. This man on a mission had the vision of picking up where the old Yeshiva Etz Chaim and RIETS leadership had left off before Bernard Revel had guided it down the road toward modernity, or, from where Mendlowitz stood, steered it into religious oblivion. Under his watch, a renewed attempt would be made — with greater vigor and persistence than ever before — to sustain the religious civilization of eastern Europe on foreign American soil. As his followers have told it, "strategic retreats and compromise," what Mendlowitz would have called the sorry bywords of his weak-kneed predecessors, would be unknown in his school. According to his "no compromises" approach, his school would assign little value to raising up generations of well-integrated American Orthodox youngsters. If the state of New York required that his school expose his youngsters to a systematic general education, he would respect its demands. But he would never accord general studies a favored foothold within his institution. For many years, classes on non-religious subjects would be convened "off campus," away from the Bedford Avenue sacred space and locale.[1]

Mendlowitz believed that the whole concept of producing all-American yeshiva boys was a thoroughly unnecessary, if not dangerous, concept. Rather — and again to let those devoted to Mendlowitz have their say — the rabbi "self-consciously set out to create a new type of *bochur* [student] in the melting pot of America . . . who would . . . draw from all that was best from the many strands of European life." The linkage to the Old World past would be clear, consistent, and compelling. If he did his job well, Mendlowitz would "save" a cadre of committed charges from "the pull of the streets" and teach them "to stand alone" and apart from American culture.[2]

Not long thereafter, Yeshiva Rabbi Chaim Berlin (YCB), situated in the neighboring Brownsville section of Brooklyn, deepened the mission of its institution. Until the 1930s, this school resembled the old Etz Chaim: an elementary-level yeshiva that taught the rudiments of a stay-to-yourself Jewish education. Now, under the ever-watchful eye of a transplanted Lithuanian rabbinic luminary, Rabbi Isaac Hutner, YCB expanded the school's reach. Now, like Mesifta Torah Vodaath, it would "aspire to reproduce in this country," as one contemporary observer noted, "the old type of observant God-fearing Jew [who would] exhibit the diligence, sincerity and otherworldliness of the traditional *yeshivah bachur* [along the] model of the *yeshivoth* of Poland, Lithuania and Jerusalem." This school too would be "extreme and uncompromising in [its] Orthodoxy."[3]

In that same interwar period, back over the East River, Rabbi Moses Feinstein established his own European-looking Torah center. Though best known for his more than half a century of leadership as Orthodoxy's most respected decisor of Jewish law in America, Rabbi Feinstein's operational base was his Mesifta Tifereth Jerusalem (MTJ), his East Broadway yeshiva on the outskirts of the old downtown Jewish quarter. Like Mendlowitz and Hutner, Feinstein has been credited with instilling in his students, through his erudition and personal charisma, an elan of excellence that encouraged them to live lives that departed in many ways from the America around them.[4]

Given their stances, with their eyes squarely on the eastern European past, such American signposts as sports, recreation, and even a commitment to organized physical fitness programs — except for the minimum the government required — should have been of little moment within their schools. And yet, this country's athleticism, in its many forms and with all it entailed, proved here too to be an irresistible force. Not only did each of these institutions countenance formal exercise programs and informal games to break up the *yeshiva bochurs'* long day of study, but even more remarkably, none of these schools was immune to pressures that emerged — from within their own student ranks — to establish organized, competitive teams.

Rabbis like Mendlowitz, Hutner, and Feinstein ended up finding themselves dealing, each in his own way, with the same type of basic question that the clamor for athletics engendered within Revel's and Belkin's institution:

How important might sports and sportsmen be within an Orthodox institution in America? The decisions they made reveal just how varied their own communities' approaches were toward meeting up with the challenge of sports, that compelling American force all around them.

Early signs of compromise were already readily visible to a distinguished eastern European rabbinical visitor who visited at Torah Vodaath in the late 1920s. Reportedly, Rabbi Shimon Shkop, rosh yeshiva (dean) of Shaarei Torah Yeshiva in Grodno, Poland, was troubled to see that during "recess time . . . the boys were playing a game of baseball in the yard. And when he saw this, he was astounded and full of wonder and did not want to believe his eyes." He was chagrined that "students of the yeshiva, who study God's Torah could spend their time in such folly."[5]

There is no record of Rabbi Shkop upbraiding Mendlowitz over what would have been counted as, at best, unconventional behavior back in Poland. However, we can reasonably project that had he been confronted, Mendlowitz would have answered, in the spirit of Rabbi Samson Raphael Hirsch, whose thought he had studied while still a yeshiva student in Hungary, that recreational activities — from ballplaying to hiking to swimming, even to acrobatics/gymnastics — helped produce a more physically fit *bochur*, possessed of sufficient stamina to spend the largest part of his long school day in productive Torah study.[6]

Actually, Mendlowitz was far from defensive about his interest in his students' physical prowess. One former student has recalled that in the 1930s, the school organized an acrobatic troupe that performed at fund-raising dinners "in front of hundreds of observers." Maybe here, presumably in reaching out to a group of Jews who were of varying religious stripes, Mendlowitz, for a few moments, drew back slightly from his ultimate mission as he implicitly suggested to the crowd that his boys were not totally un-American. As another former student has conjectured, "If Mr. Mendlowitz [he preferred to be called "Mr."] always was there, there was no [social] dancing so you had to do something, so you either had a choir or you had gymnastics" to make potential benefactors feel good about their involvement with the school. Years later, when two TVD men earned a considerable reputation as *Giborim* (lit. heroes, fig. Orthodox Charles Atlases), school officials turned to them to tell "the kids [young students in the school] that if you learn and you do everything [according to religious precepts] and you exercise, then you can be strong." Roy Chavkin and Arnold Wolf reportedly expressed these sentiments while tearing up phone books with their bare hands in front of crowds of amazed and entranced youngsters.[7]

But beyond the messages Mendlowitz sought to instill within his students, he also was a realist about his charges' own take on the world around them. He recognized that as much as his youngsters were "frum boys," punctiliously observant, they were also "Brooklyn boys" and simply liked the pastimes that were common fare in the city's streets. So the schoolyard was always available for those who wanted to play boxball, or stoopball, or punchball, or association — a rudimentary form of two-hand touch football. Sometimes younger faculty members would join their disciples in handball or baseball games "during recess or on a class outing." These youngsters also liked whiling away their spare time assessing the prospects of their often hapless, if always beloved, Brooklyn Dodgers. A contrarian among them might stick up for the New York Giants or Yankees. For Mendlowitz, the simple reality was that to deny his students this level of relaxation would not advance his ultimate mission. Besides, if pressed, he might have acknowledged that there were far worse types of pursuits that might entice youths with some spare time on their hands.[8]

The trick was to keep a close rein on students even when they were allowed out into the friendly confines of the schoolyard. A biographer of Mendlowitz has it that while the very hands-on administrator permitted stickball games at recess and before school began, he was the timekeeper, with his ever-present pocket watch in hand, determining when to call it quits. This source, which loyally casts the rabbi as always in control, makes no mention of students ever slipping away to play one last inning or down.[9]

Similar patterns of accommodations to the recreationally minded also obtained at Yeshiva Rabbi Chaim Berlin and Mesifta Tifereth Jerusalem, where, likewise, regular school hours were set aside for physical training. And those who were interested in extracurricular fun and games used either a designated classroom or partially renovated former factory or bank buildings as ersatz gymnasiums. And public parks were always around the corner. The lore of MTJ has it that Rabbi Feinstein's son David and another of the yeshiva's prize students were renowned in the neighborhood for their spirited Friday afternoon handball games. Of course, the way a MTJ memoirist tells it, when Rabbi Nison Alpert was not painting the out-of-bounds lines with his killer drop shots, he was able to "carry on an intelligent discussion" presumably on some Torah topic.[10]

What is most important here is that Rabbi Alpert's street games smarts surely were no secret at his institution. To have one of his fans continue his tale: "The nickname by which he was known at MTJ and which he bore without embarrassment was, surprisingly 'Johnny', an allusion, perhaps, to his athletic accomplishments." His ballplaying ability was deemed as having contributed to his "mental agility" in the study hall. A strong body, it was acknowledged, could certainly assist a student to become a superior student. Here, in a subtle way, the yeshiva world community of mid-twentieth-century America broke with its eastern European models. It affirmed as its very own the Hasetz Hayim's once minority views on the value of physical fitness.[11]

But would these schools accede to some students' desire to do more than get into shape or play with their friends? As early as the mid-1940s, the most athletic types sought to formalize their ongoing neighborhood schoolyard rivalries through the creation of varsities that would represent their alma maters. They aspired to find out how good they really were in sports through interscholastic competition. These prime-time initiatives did not sit well with their roshei yeshiva on several critical counts. The time and efforts required to organize teams, schedule games, and prepare properly for these encounters would inevitably limit the number of hours a student-athlete — not to mention the fans of the varsity — could devote to focused, dedicated Torah study. Secondly, while wins and losses in pickup games had no residual impact upon the atmosphere of a yeshiva, triumphs and failures in competition against other schools would have a disquieting ripple effect within the student body. In the schoolyard, the daily "choose up" contests meant constantly shuffled lineups. Yesterday's winners were tomorrow's losers. Game results were of little enduring moment. Not so if two schools would meet in a formal engagement. Here the fear was that star players might be lionized, inferior performances roundly criticized, and outcomes incessantly analyzed. Such excitement would set, in their wake, a wrong tone for institutions where the true heroes were supposed to be the boys who concentrated only on Torah study.[12]

What about Rabbi Nison Alpert, the handball hero? This weekend warrior got a pass because he never participated in any formal tournaments. And what he did on the concrete downtown courts, in the hours before the Sabbath commenced and with the long school week over, was interpreted as but another way in which this committed scholar strengthened himself as a full-time student of the Talmud. The interscholastic sports scene, on the other hand, was a different situation.

But yeshiva officials probably were most against real teams because "road games" would thrust these youngsters into uncontrolled social environments where they would encounter players and ultimately fans who did not share all of their strict Orthodox religious values. If a major thrust of the school was to keep their young men to themselves, sporting events would push them away from their community's goals and mission.

To set the scene for some worst-case scenarios, if in the mid-1940s, a Torah Vodaath squad accepted a challenge from the Talmudical Academy "Talmuds" (then their nickname), they would be matched against another all-boys school, composed of youngsters who like themselves were presumably Sabbath observers and were otherwise religiously devout. However, when the visiting athletes arrived at a Manhattan venue, maybe to play a preliminary to a Yeshiva College game, they would come face to face with a decidedly different Orthodox cultural milieu. Players and fans from Revel's and then Belkin's more Americanized schools might have brought dates to the contests and "gone out" afterwards. Social mixing of the most innocent of kinds was rampant. What could be more kosher than having your girl at a game conducted under Orthodox auspices? If a guy or gal were lucky enough, he or she might end up sitting next to an intended at these coed

"Date Night" at a Yeshiva College basketball game, circa
1950. Courtesy of Yeshiva University Public Affairs
Department.

sports events. The officials of Torah Vodaath, Chaim Berlin, and Mesifta
Tifereth Jerusalem, on the other hand, wanted to have their charges separated socially from women until they were married. For them, real men in
their strictly ordered culture kept their eyes fixed on their studies and did
not get caught up in a modern dating scene. Although formal matchmaking
was then not in vogue, if youngsters had to come together, a more chaperoned setting was much preferred to a wide-open gymnasium[13]

Then there was the problem of "girls' games" that sometimes preceded
boys' varsity matches. Until the twentieth century, Orthodox Judaism had
no explicit code of regulations regarding definitions of female modesty
when it came to young ladies taking part in sports. The rabbis of the Talmud
had looked into this issue some two millennia earlier, but the rules had not
been updated. Though the leaders of Yeshiva University made no formal
pronouncements affirming the appropriateness of girls in shorts playing on
the hardwood in front of men, their hosting of such contests spoke volumes
about their comfort with such modern behavior. Boys and girls watching

each other play was normal, good American fun. Rabbis Mendlowitz, Hutner, and Feinstein differed fundamentally on this issue.[14]

One such type of double-header that these leaders wanted their boys to have no part of had taken place just a few years earlier, in 1937, at Yorkville's Central Jewish Institute, where the girls of the Beth Medrash Lamoros, an Orthodox Hebrew teachers' school, defeated the Herzlia squad, an institution with an even stronger Zionist orientation, before a team from Yeshiva's Teachers Institute — with the help of two Yeshiva College varsity ringers — knocked off a contingent from the Jewish Theological Seminary of America's own Teachers Institute. Reportedly, at this competitive get-together, "there was a large Yeshiva audience watching the proceedings and a cheering squad was formed to urge the Yeshiva team on." To make matters much worse, from a yeshiva world perspective, after the games that were billed as "affair[s] . . . in which the students of the various Hebrew teaching training schools of the city participated," winners and losers alike repaired to the postgame dance sponsored by the Histadruth Hanoar Ha Ivri, another Zionist youth group. TVD, YCB, and MTJ leaders, who incidentally were not supporters of the Zionist cause and looked askance at Conservative Judaism in America, could not countenance their students being part of that scene. To their way of Orthodox thinking, young men and women touching on a dance floor, even if they were not clutching, was patently immodest and impermissible Jewish behavior.[15]

And yet despite all that could be wrong with the messages and the social environment of competitive sports, each of these schools permitted — beginning in the 1940s — some sort of interscholastic experience to exist within their purview. In the case of Mendlowitz's school, tolerance was extended toward those boys who wanted to test their mettle against players from Chaim Berlin and Mesifta Tifereth Jerusalem, schools that championed the same strict religious values. Torah Vodaath lore has it that school leaders were willing to overlook their usual concerns about time lost from all-important Torah study even if the sagas of interscholastic competitions might be discussed too much in the yeshivas' hallways. The rabbis let it be because of their bigger concerns about the lifestyles of "dormitory students with time on their hands."[16]

By reputation, most of the players, while pious, were not "learning boys," the most dedicated Talmud students who were the institution's pride. Some were "out of towners" who had been sent by their parents, for any numbers of reasons, to Orthodoxy's hub and who were new to the intensity of traditional life in the metropolis. Sports had always been part of their lives and "these students would have been culturally shocked without the sports environment." So again here, as with their encouragement of informal recreation, TVD leaders acknowledged that there were far more troubling pastimes that might interest these somewhat marginal youngsters — maybe like dating young women — than semi-formal matches in the streets of Brooklyn or Lower Manhattan.[17]

There was one basketball game, held in the early 1940s, which must have garnered the approval — for obvious reasons — of Rabbi Mendlowitz. During the terrible years of World War II, student-athletes from Torah Vodaath and Chaim Berlin rented a gym in a Brooklyn public school, charged admission to the game, and donated the proceeds to the Vaad Hatzala Rescue Committee, which was then struggling to garner community funds to support their campaign to save the doomed Jews of eastern Europe.[18]

However, Rabbi Mendlowitz and his successors absolutely forbade students from crossing over to Manhattan to the decidedly coeducational environs and other extracurricular activities that attended Talmudical Academy games. Nonetheless, the 1940s witnessed a subterranean sports culture emerging within their school, which only suggests that some students did not share the full range of their rabbis' strict religious values. Athletes from the Brooklyn and Manhattan schools squared off in 1944 and 1948, most likely before coed audiences. Moreover, the early 1950s also saw squads of ballplayers from Torah Vodaath join the fledgling Metropolitan Jewish High School League (MJHSL), an association that was fostered and closely tied to Sarachek, Avrech, and their confreres at Yeshiva University.[19]

The league was an integral part of the Yeshiva University Athletic Association's (YUAA) grand plan to expand its school's sports program through the creation of a high school "farm system" from within the local Orthodox community. Through the loop, it was hoped, schools that were part of the university's widest core constituency would produce ballplayers — maybe mentored by Sarachek's own former athletes — who would end up contributing to the great college coach's program. In an ideal situation, role players from yeshiva high schools would complement a Hershkowitz, from the public schools. The YUAA, reflecting its school's expansive posture, defined its target group quite broadly and sought to include not only its own Talmudical Academy and its new Brooklyn branch, the Brooklyn Talmudical Academy (BTA), established September 1945, and the aforementioned yeshiva world schools. But the MJHSL also reached out to the far more modern Orthodox day schools like the Flatbush Yeshivah, the Ramaz School, and the Hebrew Institute of Long Island (HILI).[20]

Each of these latter schools was fully coeducational. Boys and girls then took all their general and religious studies classes together, separating only at gym time or when boys were taught to lead religious services. Back then, even the most progressive Orthodox educators believed that such training was useless for girls. In keeping with the spirit of those times, 1950s young women were given Betty Crocker cooking classes instead. In addition, at least in the case of Ramaz, these day schools included within their student bodies a significant number — if a not a majority — of youngsters who were far from scrupulously observant of such Orthodox basics as the Sabbath and kashruth laws. Both boys and girls from these schools would attend the games. Some of the spectators and all the ballplayers would not be wearing yarmulkes. Maybe some coeds would serve as cheerleaders. That was another skill 1950s American Jewish girls often wanted to have. And possibly, a girls' preliminary would precede the boys' varsity game. In fact, as early as the 1951–52 season, female competitors from Ramaz and Brooklyn Central, BTA's own sister school — a branch also of Yeshiva University founded in September 1948 — were squaring off against each other under the watchful eyes of both boys and girls.[21] It was also widely understood that after Ramaz home games, single matches, or double-headers, the school would sponsor social dances open both to its students and visitors alike. From the perspective of Ramaz's principal Joseph Lookstein, that erstwhile Yeshiva faculty pitcher and YUAA supporter, it made abundant sense to encourage such a social scene. For unless his "academy," as he initially called his school, strongly embraced American mores — with sports and dancing constituting essential cultural symbols — he would have no chance of attracting to Ramaz those "discriminating," marginally Orthodox students who would never opt for a "ghetto school" that smacked, in any way of a "European . . . atmosphere, culturally isolate[d] and tempted[d] by religious sectarianism."[22]

Torah Vodaath officials could not conceive of their charges participating in the MJHSL. Everything the league stood for, and almost everyone it invited in, offended the Brooklyn yeshiva's religious sensibilities. But evidently, girls in the stands or playing in preliminary games, and female boosters on the sidelines and on the court during time-outs, did not exercise those boys in the school who surreptitiously accepted the loop's invitation. What was essentially a rogue operation lasted two years — 1951 to 1953 — until word got back to school officials about these transgressions. The coach of this rump squad — then a recent graduate of the school — has recalled that when Rabbi Gedalia Schorr, who headed up the yeshiva after Mendlowitz's death in 1948, "found out that they were playing" and that a coed school "came down with cheerleaders, he became very angry and stopped it immediately." Actually, the short-skirted sirens only added insult to the injury of coed activities everywhere one of their students might turn. "Even without cheerleaders, they probably would have opposed" league participation. This student subterranean sports initiative was quickly over.[23]

Rabbi Isaac Hutner of YCB was also less than sanguine about the social scene that accompanied MJHSL games. Still, when the league was established, he permitted his players to participate so long as they adhered to a strict code of conduct after the athletic encounters. Maybe Hutner's confidence in his young men stemmed from the general perception within his school that athletes could be good performers in the classroom. The arrangement was that roundballers could officially wear the colors of the

The Brooklyn Central girls' basketball team, 1953. *The
Elchanette*, 1953, n.p.

"Mesifta High School" against all comers so long as they would discipline
themselves and not hang around for postgame dances and parties.

When that tacit agreement was first reached, there were some elements
within the school who would have liked the administration to take a harder
line on this issue. As one player from that era has recalled, "as a matter of
fact, there was a point where some of the older *bochrim* in the *beis medrash*
wanted to stop it because we played Saturday night and would come into
contact [with girls] whether there were dances or not." It seems that within
this religious culture there always are some senior students ensconced within
the traditional house of study who regularly oppose all pragmatic social
accommodations. But let the former YCB athlete continue: "A couple of us
went to the Rosh Yeshiva and he permitted it so long as the restriction on
dances at Ramaz held and that was it. At Chaim Berlin, nothing happened
unless the Rosh Yeshiva allowed it . . . and we had his approbation."[24]

However, Chaim Berlin's leaders did not go all out in support of their

ABRAHAM SODDEN

Yeshiva University
Basketball Team '51, '52
Student Court '52

Abraham Sodden, Yeshiva Rabbi Chaim Berlin basketball
team, 1951–1952. *The Shofar,* 1952, n.p.

squad. They did not have a regulation-size court and thus were required to
play all their games on the road. Inadvertently, that away-court disadvantage
increased their exposure to socially problematic heterogeneous crowds.
Their practice facility was a barely renovated former bank building with
poor lighting, pillars in the way, and a large steel vault door underneath the
nine-foot basket. (Regulation height for a basket is ten feet.) Hoopsters had
to perfect line-drive shots if they wanted to score from the outside. And
when they drove to the basket, they had to be sure to stay clear of the steel
door. Nonetheless, Mesifta High School players more than held their own in
the MJHSL's early years. In fact, during the 1951–1952 season, their center
Abraham Sodden led the league with a 24-point-per-game average. A year
later, he would move on comfortably to Yeshiva University, without a word of
school disapproval. It was another indication, in its own right, of Rabbi
Hutner's tolerant "wait and see attitude" toward students who were not fully
in line with his school's mission. At Yeshiva University, Sodden would play,
with two other high school classmates, on the "Blue and White"'s outstanding 1955–1956 squad. Back in Brooklyn, their success on the hardwood was
of little moment for Rabbi Hutner, but we can logically surmise that he had
to have been more than satisfied with Sodden and his friends' continued fidelity to Orthodox practice.[25]

Had Rabbi Hutner been aware of former Chaim Berlin star David (Duvvy)

Abraham Sodden, standing third from the right, member of
the Pioneer Country Club team in the "Borscht Belt League,"
circa 1955. Courtesy of Abraham Sodden.

Hartman's move away from sports participation after he enrolled at Yeshiva
University, the Brooklyn rosh yeshiva would have rested further assured that
his long-leash approach toward dealing with teenage boys with basketball on
their minds made abundant sense. As it was, Hartman arrived in Washington Heights with quite a street reputation as a ballplayer. While still a
youth, he had squared off in the backcourt against the young Bob Cousy in a
Catskill Mountains summer basketball game. Hartman played for the strictly
kosher Pioneer Hotel, and the future Boston Celtic suited up for the Tam-
arack Lodge in the famous Borscht Belt League. As a Yeshiva freshman
during the 1949–1950 season, Hartman teamed up with Hershkowitz and
reportedly "thrilled everyone with remarkably accurate passing and 'set
shots.' " But Hartman would play only one year for Sarachek. By the time
the next college campaign rolled around, the thrill of sports was gone for

JANUARY, 1953

HONEY SEELENFREUND — Honey was the organizer of of Central's first cheering squad. (She stole all the "trade secrets" from Ramaz.) She proved her skill and initiative in all athletic activities. Honey will be a Physical Education major in Brooklyn College.

. . . הוה עז כנמר, רץ כצבי

Honey Seelenfreund, organizer of the first Brooklyn Central cheering squad. *The Elchanette,* 1953, n.p.

Hartman. Having outgrown his youthful obsession, this budding scholar now preferred to spend every available moment in Talmud study. He would soon transfer, for a year, to the Lakewood Yeshiva. There, under the influence of Rabbi Aharon Kutler, he would hone his talmudic skills further before returning to Yeshiva University, where he was ordained in 1954. Though by then Hartman was no longer his disciple, Rabbi Hutner had to have been pleased with how this former athlete had turned out. Clearly sports had not ruined the young rabbi.[26]

But Rabbi Hutner could not have been as content with what went on in the midst of Chaim Berlin's own varsity games, especially during the time-outs. Left unresolved — and maybe unspoken of — when his boys were permitted to play in the MJHSL was the perceived immodesty of female cheerleaders who performed on the court during stoppages in play. Ramaz inaugurated this ancillary activity in 1951 with girls in longish skirts. Short skirts appeared in 1954 and remained the style for a generation or more. As important, what Ramaz did became a model for other schools, both coed institutions and the single-gender schools associated with Yeshiva University. The organizer of Brooklyn Central's "first cheering squad" said as much in her 1953 high school yearbook when she noted that "she stole all the 'trade secrets' from Ramaz."[27]

To be more precise, Honey Seelenfreund learned the tricks of that trade — cartwheeling included — from her older sister, who did similar histrionics as a student at Ramaz. Once she learned all the right moves, the younger Seelenfreund, who became a physical education major at Brooklyn College

The Brooklyn Central cheering squad, 1953. *The Elchanette,* 1953, n.p.

and went on to teach gym both in New York public schools and in several local day schools, proceeded to recruit four of her classmates "and many boosters" for their routines. Baton twirling was also part of an act that "put much spirit into many of the BTA games." The girls also performed on the sidelines of Yeshiva University games. As the 1950s progressed, the Brooklyn Central cheerleaders' skirts also got shorter and shorter. By 1955, cheerleaders were "costumed" in "short black corduroy skirts, white tops, red knee socks, red chenille letter C's and red gloves."[28]

Honey's parents saw absolutely nothing immodest with their daughters' extracurricular activities — including their attendance at Ramaz postgame dances, presumably with dates. For this very different type of American-born, Brooklyn-based Orthodox family, sports, with all it entailed, had been a constant in their daily life, except on the Sabbath and holidays. Honey's dad had played handball in his youth on the East Side. And as adults, both of her parents took up skiing — an unusual recreational activity for Jews at that time. During the summers of Honey's youth, she and her five siblings went to coed summer camps under modern Orthodox auspices, where the girls learned to swim and played tennis and basketball. Their brothers did likewise. And back home in Brooklyn during "the year," the boys were aficionados of punchball, stoopball, and stickball, three of that borough's most honored local activities. So while the elder Seelenfreunds never personally attended any of Honey's gymnastic-laden performances, they approved of the adolescent lifestyle that she was playing out within the secure lines of modern Orthodox boundaries.[29]

Rabbi Hutner may have respected the Seelenfreund family's core religious values. After all, back in the 1950s, Americanized, Sabbath-observant families were still a minority even within the Brooklyn Orthodox community. Still, for the head of Chaim Berlin, the extrareligious way of life that the Seelenfreunds had carved out for themselves and their children was simply not right for the yeshiva community that he championed. So when here two Orthodox worlds clashed culturally, the YCB contingent decided to retreat to a more clearly marked sideline. Rabbi Hutner eventually came to the conclusion that notwithstanding his youngsters' apparent adherence to his rules, the social scene all around them, particularly those "jumping and prancing" cheerleaders — the most offensive foul of immodesty — was inappropriate for his disciples. At the close of the 1956–1957 campaign, after six years of participation, Yeshiva Chaim Berlin resigned from the MJHSL.[30]

Although Yeshiva University Athletic Association officials regretted losing a charter member of the league — the move ran counter to its mission of being an all-inclusive Orthodox sports association — Chaim Berlin's exit had no substantive impact on the league. The late 1950s and early 1960s were a heyday for its member schools. The league embarked on a new era of expansion when in 1962 it admitted the Jewish Educational Center (JEC) of Elizabeth, New Jersey, to competition. That team quickly became an athletic powerhouse and, in time, its school officials became highly influential in setting MJHSL policies. Fans could follow league activities not only in the Brooklyn-based *The Jewish Press*, but also in the sports section of the *New York Times*, which occasionally ran its standings. Natural rivalries between the Manhattan and Brooklyn Talmudical Academies and among Ramaz, Flatbush, and HILI were the talk of the modern Orthodox community. I can recall, for example, that on every Washington's Birthday, Ramaz played a triple-header against Flatbush. The boys' junior varsities, urged on by their female boosters, opened the proceedings. They were followed by girls' and boys' varsities that were inspired by their cheerleaders, under the watchful eyes of appreciative coed crowds. And postgame dances remained part of the Ramaz home game scene. The championship game held annually in Madison Square Garden was the highlight of any player's athletic career.

I also can testify that the annual all-star game, held either at New York University's Alumni Hall or at Brooklyn's Westinghouse High School, always drew in excess of a thousand rabid fans. I played a few minutes in one of those tilts. Some of the best league players, the luminaries of those all-star games — moved on as collegiates to Sarachek's program. Red would have preferred public school athletes, but he worked with whoever showed up. And some of these Jewish High School League players, like Sodden before them, had a modicum of talent. The best among them made the *New York Post*'s all-scholastic private school team, a point of great pride for players and the league alike.

But even as Yeshiva University's high schools teams, the Jewish Educational Center of Elizabeth, which had its separate boys and girls divisions, and the fully coed schools were quite content with their approach to sports and to American-style fraternization, one of the league's charter members was slowly beginning to feel uncomfortable with this very modern Orthodox scene. Beginning in the 1960s, voices were heard within the study halls of the Rabbi Jacob Joseph School (RJJ) calling upon their yeshiva to emulate the strict social-religious culture of Torah Vodaath and now of Chaim Berlin. The sports program became a major point of entry for an attempt to interject a new spirit of yeshiva world separatism within the Henry Street school.

For much of its early history, RJJ's mission and constituency had been very much akin to that of the Talmudical Academy or of Yeshiva College. Until it established its own high school program in 1940, the Rabbi Jacob Joseph School was a prime feeder to Revel's high school. And in the 1940s and 1950s, even as it competed with the two TAs (Manhattan and Brooklyn) for secondary school students, the downtown institution was still sending many of its youngsters to Belkin's college. Given its orientation as a single-gender school but with a religious outlook not so different from Yeshiva University's high schools, it was no surprise that it would join the MJHSL. And everyone liked playing against the competitive and combative Rabbi Jacob Joseph School Raiders.[31]

To a large extent, the rough-and-tumble style of their streetwise players was reminiscent of the Oakland Raiders football team of the same era. They loved beating the fancy kids who attended Ramaz and they enjoyed their battles royale with MTA, the league's early perennial champs. They were supported by bands of rabid fans, which were not above all sorts of high jinks in the stands. One of their favorite stunts was to heap verbal abuse upon Ramaz fans when these silk-stocking sports supporters stood reverently, in prep-school style, to sing their alma mater before home games.[32]

For all their social problems with, or resentment of, the Yorkville day school crowd, Rabbi Jacob Joseph students, when they were not misbehaving, may have harbored many of the same hopes and dreams for fame and fortune as the most academically dedicated or snootiest of Ramazites. Many RJJ fellows were not exactly possessed of the "other-worldliness of the traditional [European] yeshiva *bochur.*" The expressed career goals of its 1962 junior high school graduating class may have said it all. Of the sixty-seven young men who planned to continue in its high school, almost a score wanted to be doctors, dentists, or lawyers. Only nine saw themselves as future rabbis. One fellow wanted to be both an "engineer and a rabbi," while another sought to be a "rocket engineer."[33]

For the most part, until the 1960s, the school's rabbinical faculty and administrators were blithely unaware or unconcerned about their sports program. Unlike Torah Vodaath, Chaim Berlin — or for that matter, Ramaz, which had its own strict, if different, disciplinary codes — RJJ students were not closely monitored. Besides which, some of the ballplayers were also excellent Talmud students who had proven that "learning and ball playing could go hand in hand." As one Raider veteran of the late 1950s and 1960s has recalled, "we were 'normal students' . . . playing ball was part of being at RJJ. The *rebbeim* [rabbinical faculty] never came out against it . . . as long as you were learning, you could play ball."[34]

This *laissez-faire* attitude toward the sports scene at RJJ ended in 1963. Students of that era have recalled that the school's Hebrew principal, Rabbi Hersh Ginsberg, was especially militant in trying to position the school within the rising yeshiva world whose religious values were beginning to permeate the modern Orthodox community. In many religious circles, these yeshivas' stand-apart postures and norms of behavior were becoming policies deemed worthy of emulation. Ginsberg's specific goals for his school were not only to align the institution with Torah Vodaath, Chaim Berlin, and Mesifta Tifereth Jerusalem, but he ultimately wanted to have his best students attend advanced Torah institutions like the Beth Medrash Govoha of Lakewood, where they might sit at the feet of that "transcendent Torah scholar," Rabbi Aharon Kotler. For RJJ's man on his own mission, one step in the direction of the yeshiva world was to separate his youngsters from "association with 'Hebrew culture schools' " [viz. Ramaz, Flatbush, et al.] — a derisive and dismissive characterization — that were deemed "derogatory influences on the Yeshiva's reputation." Accordingly, in the fall of 1963, school officials informed Raider players and their coach that the team "had been withdrawn from the League and suspended for a one year period."[35]

This unilateral decision outraged RJJ's ballplayers, and their pain was felt throughout a student body that clearly did not share its rabbis' religious fervor. The aggrieved youngsters quickly formed protest committees and deputations were made, first to school administrator Rabbi Herschel Kurzrock and then to RJJ's board of directors, to find a way "to salvage the team." A suggestive cartoon that appeared in the student newspaper dramatically depicted rank-and-file sentiment. In this caricature, a faceless, fedora-wearing administrator is shown attempting to close a coffin containing the "RJJ Varsity." But two youthful, muscular hands, rising up from within the coffin, bearing the name "school spirit," stymie his efforts to shut the lid. The cartoon was provocatively labeled "We Shall Overcome," as protesters analogized their parochial concerns with the most critical American social crisis of their times. The cultural differences between students and their rabbis were evident. If Rabbi Ginsberg was focused on the world inside of Lakewood, New Jersey, many of his students had their eyes attuned to an outside universe of activities, to places like Selma, Alabama.[36]

Eventually, the students got their chance to plead for the team at a special board meeting. At this crucial sit-down, advocates for the athletes readily agreed that the religious tenor of the school should be upgraded. So they promised to "ensure" that all Raider players would wear "yarmulkes during games" — which only suggests that those who were enamored with yeshiva world models really had a long way to go in transforming their school's student culture. The religious values of some RJJ guys, like their secular ambitions, were not all that different from those of their Ramaz contemporaries.[37] Students also went along with the "exclusion of girls from home games" even as they made their elders understand that it would impossible to demand that the more liberal schools ban their coeds from their home games.[38]

This compromise lasted but one day because the MJHSL categorically refused to countenance " 'segregation' at any of its games." Again, provocative American rhetoric, borrowed from the civil rights movement all around it, found its way into an internal Orthodox debate. Fearing their season was about to be lost, students "marched on the office and pleaded with Rabbi Kurzrock to save the team." Kurzrock, who had been a Raider himself in the early 1950s and who, from most accounts, was a sort of student-sensitive– rosh yeshiva ombudsman, drew up a list of stipulations under which RJJ could remain in the league. Foremost among them was the concept that "a representative of the administration would be present at all games" to ensure proper behavior. Kurzrock attended the opening game of the 1963– 1964 season where he was apparently "impressed by the lack of objectionables" in the Rabbi Jacob Joseph section. And, true to their previous form, not all Raider rooters stayed away from girls. Reportedly, "a minority literally interpret[ed] the time-honored Saturday night activity, the *melave malkah*" [lit. escorting the Sabbath Queen, fig. hanging out with coeds]. Still, Kurzrock "seemed pleased with the bi-lingual encouragement offered by the unofficial cheering squad and proud of his *beis medrash* boys." And the students were thrilled with Kurzrock's presence and attitude. After the Raider win, "the Reb was carried off the court by his elated *hassidim* [*sic*]."[39]

Unfortunately for RJJ sportsmen, their victory off the court was short-lived. The next year, 1964–1965, brought renewed pressure from the school's most religious elements to end Raider association with the MJHSL. The now familiar canards were repeated — "the mixing of sexes at games," or they said "coed Yeshivas who were members of the league presented a downgrading influence on RJJ students." And now, student activists were not persuasive enough and/or Rabbi Kurzrock did not now take their part to prevent a ban on participation. Ballplayers were told that if they still wished to represent their alma mater on the hardwood, their only option was to join the Mesifta High School Athletic Association, a callow, strictly Orthodox version of the MJHSL.[40]

The latter loop, founded for the 1962–1963 season, was the brainchild of Moshe Snow, a graduate of RJJ's high school who was then a rabbinical student at Mesifta Tifereth Jerusalem. Back in the 1950s, MTJ had been a member of the MJHSL for two years and had competed without controversy against the coed schools. The school's "enthusiastic volunteer coach" led a team that played all its games "on the road." The school had no court of its own. State-mandated physical education classes were held in the nearby Educational Alliance. And sometimes the team borrowed RJJ's less-than-adequate gym for practices. Its greatest athletic moment occurred in 1954 when it sent two star players, the Berezon brothers, Gershon and Robert, to the league's inaugural all-star game. However, MTJ left the league soon thereafter primarily because this very small, if elite, school could not field a representative squad. Gershon Berezon has recalled that "our high school was very small and had as little as 20 or 30 students. The team represented a large percentage of the student body. [We were] last in the league, but we were excited about it and played as well as we could."[41]

The Berezons' competitive sports spirit was revived at the East Broadway institution a decade later when Snow found a contingent of "boys interested in organized sports." But, given the changed tenor of the times, neither they nor Snow and certainly not the administration, headed still by the eminent Rabbi Feinstein, would countenance rejoining the MJHSL. This renowned decisor of Jewish law had not spoken out against the coed league in the 1950s, but now—for almost a decade—yeshiva world policies explicitly dictated that its youngsters could not be part of what it unequivocally saw as a libertine, irreligious social setting. In any event, Snow's solution was to reach out to YCB and five other similarly minded schools to form a league of their own. This athletic association would play, like all other leagues did, with uniforms, scoreboards, playoffs, and certified officials. They even rented the same public school gyms that the coed league frequented. However, the competing schools explicitly and consistently barred females from watching their yeshiva boys at play. In their community, a gym would not be a social gathering place for young men and women. Even mothers and sisters of varsity members were barred from games as the evolving rules of modesty were broadened and intensified.[42]

Back at RJJ, Rabbi Ginsberg probably would have been happiest if his students had no sports program. Some of the more remote and rarified roshei yeshiva were unaware that there even was student interest in basketball. For example, one Raider rooter has recalled that once, late at night and after a RJJ ballgame, he happened upon his rebbe on East Broadway, who inquired as to what his student was doing out so late. When the young man responded that he had "attended a game," his teacher asked, "Chess?" But if his boys had to play, if they still felt the urge to compete, Ginsberg could not question the company these athletes were keeping. If anything, when the Raiders lined up against *bochrim* from Chaim Berlin, the Yeshiva of Eastern Parkway, the Chofetz Chaim Yeshiva, the Kamenetz Yeshiva, or the Yeshiva Samson Raphael Hirsch, they were making a statement, albeit in a highly unorthodox way, that the Rabbi Jacob Joseph School was part of the expanding yeshiva world.[43]

Raider players and fans showed little real enthusiasm for the Mesifta Association. Although they joined that league, since any type of competition was better than none, and routed the opposition in both the 1964–1965 and 1965–1966 campaigns, winning the championship both years, these were joyless victories. Their "untarnished record," said the 1965 student yearbook, during "this spurious and abortive season . . . was achieved at the expense of a somewhat inferior competition." What they did want was to return to the long-standing loop. For unlike their teachers, most RJJ guys still saw nothing wrong with fraternization. They had little of Ginsberg's and the roshei yeshivas' religious disposition. I recall one Raider ballplayer of that time saying to me that the "school's leaders do not understand us. Don't they realize that if we aren't at games Saturday nights, we would be at parties with girls." Moreover, they saw themselves as serious athletes who desperately wanted to prove themselves in an established league.[44]

The battle to "crack the adamant refusal of the school's administration" to accede to student wishes was rejoined during the 1965–1966 season. A "Bring Back Basketball" campaign was organized, and once again students were at Rabbi Kurzrock's doorstep petitioning for assistance. To their satisfaction, they found the rabbi-ombudsman willing to take another look at the situation. Reportedly — and in a repeat of the 1963–64 scenario — the assistant high school principal sought means of addressing "one of the chief problems . . . the mixing of the sexes at the games." (Of somewhat lesser moment, but also at issue, was Rabbi Jacob Joseph officials' unhappiness that Manhattan Talmudical Academy, still awaiting the building of a real home gym on Washington Heights, sometimes used Catholic school facilities where crucifixes adorned their walls. Coach Sarachek had disciples within Catholic coaching ranks and they readily accommodated Yeshiva's needs. Jack Donohue, who was then coaching a rather large high schooler named Lew Alcindor at Power Memorial High School, was a particularly good friend of the Jewish coach and his school. From RJJ's stricter religious point of view, Jews should not be present in such Christian religious venues. MJHSL officials did not agree.[45])

In all events, Kurzrock told *The Jewish Press* that "the Administration is trying to work out something . . . some sort of system so that they may possibly rejoin the League." Probably sensing that Rabbi Ginsberg's hardline approach simply was not acceptable to his restive, religiously heterogeneous student body, Kurzrock adroitly readopted his popular 1963 stance.

As one student activist of the time has recalled, Kurzrock, in all of his efforts, cagily "tap-danced" as he "walked a thin line." He "recognized the needs of the student body and tried to find a way of making it work while protecting the values of the school."[46]

The crucial question once again was whether RJJ boys would stay away from girls in a monitored coeducational environment. To test whether "students [could] behave in an orderly manner," Kurzrock permitted the booking of an exhibition game against the Brooklyn Talmudical Academy. In addition, Kurzrock permitted the Raiders to scrimmage other league clubs "to keep the team in shape, and to give the students something to cheer about and to keep up their spirits."[47]

There is no record of Rabbi Kurzrock having attended the December 1965 tilt. He certainly was not carried off the court as he had been two years earlier after his Raiders lost 69-48 in front of some 700 fans at Westinghouse High School in Brooklyn. But Kurzrock had to have liked the subsequent newspaper report from *The Jewish Press*'s on-the-scene columnist, who suggested that the "Administration of RJJ can be only VERY PROUD [*sic*] of the way the game was run and of student decorum."[48]And we know that Kurzrock was pleased that student leaders used this sporting event to raise money to support publication of *The Tablet*, the student yearbook.[49] Here too, subtly, the still very traditional Kurzrock showed a modern, student-sensitive side. "Preppy" yearbooks were the provinces of the Talmudical Academies, of the Centrals and, of course, schools like Ramaz, and not of yeshivas like Torah Vodaath.[50] Evidently, at this juncture, despite Rabbi Ginsberg's staunch advocacy, RJJ's leadership was not of one mind on his quest for unqualified admission into the yeshiva world.

In the fall of 1966, the Rabbi Jacob Joseph School re-entered the coed league. With the help of social studies teacher Bernard Cohen, who bolstered the "de-facto support of Rabbi Kurzrock," an "element of trust was built between the administration and student leaders" that suggested that the young men "understood the values of the school and would protect those values." A deal was struck that the Raiders could play in the MJHSL, but they would stay away from the feared fraternization. In many ways, it was a protocol that was reminiscent of the arrangement that had existed at Chaim Berlin a decade or so earlier. However, not all aspects of this student-administration social contract that also called for good, gentlemanly behavior in the stands were always enforced. Certainly, from the point of view of how outsiders like Ramazites defined appropriate deportment, Raider rowdies often were seen as up to their old tricks. For example, during their first year back, they would chant "*sonei yisroel, sonei yisroel*" (lit. anti-Semites, fig. "you are less religious than we are") whenever the Ramaz team had the ball in its possession. But these catcalls were sounded as most RJJ guys sat in their own section of the bleachers in keeping with the letter of the unwritten law. The downtown school remained in that loop for another decade until "the decline of the lower East Side affected RJJ" causing "a painful reversal in [its] fortunes" and leading the then seventy-five-year-old institution to close its high school.[51]

The 1960s ended with the teams and schools that remained in the league comfortable with the religious values of all athletic competitors. It helped that by that time, Ramaz's "Fall Frolic" and other such dances were socially passé. It wasn't that we were more religious than our predecessors. We just saw ourselves as having concerns more pressing than tuxedoes, corsages, and how to cut in properly on a lacquered floor. By the time I graduated in that very special month of June 1967, the idea of a senior prom was considered a frivolous indulgence.

But over the long haul, it was the gradual conformity of schools like Ramaz and Flatbush to stricter league definitions of proper female "on court" dress and demeanor that maintained unity for the next generation among rival institutions. In the late 1970s, the MJHSL began moving against the long-standing tradition of cheerleading performances on the floor during stoppages in play. JEC's Rabbi Elazar Teitz, who led the charge against those who wore their short skirts in front of men and boys, has recalled that initially his forces pushed for the right of a school that was offended by the "gyrations" to prohibit such routines in their building. Flatbush and Ramaz girls could cavort all they wanted when their schools played each other, but never at JEC. Rabbi Teitz did allow his girls to cheer on their male friends in street clothes from the sidelines, a concession of sorts that did not sit well with even more traditional elements within his own community. Over time, league officials extended their ban to games where visiting teams might be offended. Ultimately, gymnastic-style cheerleading was prohibited entirely from all yeshiva league contests.

The 1980s also witnessed the promulgation of a dress code for female athletes. No longer would girls be permitted to run down court in short gym shorts and short-sleeved shirts in front of grown men and pubescent boys. Sweat pants and long-sleeved uniforms would be the required way to go. Once again, the ban was implemented in stages with Ramaz and Flatbush, for example, initially retaining the right to dress as they chose when they met each other. Actually, here too, for Rabbi Teitz, this policy constituted a middle ground between those within the Orthodox community who would have banned men totally — fathers and brothers included — from observing girls in action and those for whom watching what unfolded on the court was still just good, clean American sports fun. However, the sweats-and-sleeves rule constituted a dramatic departure from past custom or practice. I have to think that those who had run RJJ must have smiled ruefully once they learned of the direction the league had taken. Too bad for them, their school had not survived for its leaders to vote now with the majority in support of increased social separatism.[52]

Clearly, Rabbi Teitz's personal determination to change long-held standards was a major factor here. The young rabbi spoke effectively for his father, the eminent Rabbi Mordecai Pinchas Teitz, who, from his perch as unofficial — if highly influential — Chief Rabbi of Elizabeth, made the decision that modern Orthodoxy, even when played out here on the hardwood, had to position itself somewhere between the strict separatism of the yeshiva world and the more *laissez-faire* attitudes at Ramaz and even Yeshiva University's high schools. In keeping with this creed, the senior Teitz encouraged school administrators "to attend basketball games and other athletic events." For him, reports his family biographer, "sports and a spacious gymnasium were necessities, not extras." Rabbi Mordecai Pinchas Teitz was also not above making the following Solomon Schechter–like statement: "if you let the boys know the results [of the World Series], you'll have a good relationship with them." Rabbi Hutner over at Chaim Berlin never thought in those terms. But Rivkah Teitz Blau also asserts on behalf of her father that "the exciting sports program served Torah," at least her father's and brother's definition of the Torah's views on proper dress and deportment at games. What is most significant for us is that the other schools' principals — most of whom were also Orthodox rabbis — the men and some women who now ran the league, acceded to the Teitzes' calls. It was their acquiescence that made these decisions stick.[53]

Before the start of the 1978–1979 basketball campaign, Flatbush abruptly pushed its cheerleaders to the sidelines, ending a generations-old tradition at that school. Risa Levine, captain of that last pep squad, has recalled that "the administration decided that it was not *z'niut* [modest] and ended it. There were verbal protests, but we accepted the decision." It was a tough call for Levine and her friends because from where they stood, "cheerleading was toned down . . . it was not like in public school. . . . We were not allowed to do splits." Anxious still to publicly express their "school spirit," the sidelined pep squad members channeled their abundant enthusiasm for Falcon athletics — and their dissent from the school's decision — into a coed group of "Rabble-Rousers." From then on, a vocal group of Flatbush's boys and girls stood in the bleachers and "faithfully cheered on the Falcons at every game." Mixing of the sexes at big ballgames would continue to be part of the Flatbush social scene for years to come.[54]

At Ramaz, full compliance with league rules moved much slower. Through the mid-1980s, cheerleaders — "their marching army" as its yearbook put it — continued to dissent, and they performed on the court at home games. However, they now wore sweat pants and long-sleeved shirts. And as of 1991, cheerleading was a thing of the past even at that Yorkville school. But no school rabbi forced these girls out of their outfits and away from their routines. Rather, to hear one member of Ramaz's last cheering squad tell it, by the late 1980s, "it was not as exciting an activity. . . . It was cooler to be on an actual athletic team." And if there were any budding American feminists among this final group of Ramaz cheerleaders, their growing consciousness about being objectified, rather than any overriding concern about religious definitions of modesty, may have also militated against this activity.[55]

On the girls' basketball front, in 1986 Ramaz students, with the support of their general studies administrator Ruth Ritterband, made some noise about "preserv[ing] the Renegades right to wear shorts" in defiance of the "demand" of the "league's teams who refuse to wear shorts that all other squads wear sweatpants." The students' own characterization of themselves as "renegades" bespoke their recognition that, at least on this issue, they were now marginal within the community of league schools. Two years later, in 1988, girl athletes reportedly "did defy the Yeshiva League dress code" somewhat more subtly "wearing cut off sweats above the knee." League officials took notice of Ramaz's deviance, but adopted for a while a passive approach toward punishing violations — unless, of course, an offended team complained. However, by the early 1990s, Ramaz too fell, or was pushed, totally into line. Howard Stahl, the girls' varsity coach at that time, has recalled that league referees were instructed not to permit an improperly dressed female competitor to take the floor.[56]

But that era of common religious values among competitive schools would come to an end during the 1990s. The palpable irresistible force of gender separatism intensified further as some league schools now formally objected to men and boys watching girls at play, no matter how modestly they were dressed. Meanwhile, on a second, very different front, local Solomon Schechter schools, the day school movement of the Conservative movement, publicly appealed for membership in what was now known as the Metropolitan Yeshiva High School League. Their petition set off a public battle between the movements as well as a heated debate within New York Orthodoxy's modern ranks as to the degree to which non-Orthodox institutions and their youngsters might be included within a religious sports league. It was decision-making time once again and a movement for redefinition, all part of an era where even newer trends within Orthodoxy and of internal Jewish religious clashes would become part of the order of the day.

SAFE AT HOME:
TENSION IN JUDAISM'S CLUBHOUSE

The concluding decades of the twentieth century were heady times for this country's Jews. More than ever before, they rested assured that they had achieved the respect, friendship, and even the admiration of most Americans among whom they lived so comfortably. Jews were truly members of America's team. Signs of enduring social acceptance and integration could be seen almost everywhere. Even the longest-standing bastions of social anti-Semitism were finally and effectively breached. The inner offices of executive suites of America's major corporations, law firms, and banks had more than their share of Jewish names on the doors. By the 1980s, Jewish students not only inundated Ivy League schools, but each of these elite institutions could boast of a Jew as its president, law school dean, or other major academic official. Hotels, resorts, and home rental and sales agents rarely, if ever, turned away a Jewish customer or consumer. By then, for more than a generation, less than one in ten Gentiles had any problems with a Jews as neighbors. The days of discriminatory, humiliating prejudice were over.[1]

Those Jews who preferred to obsess about the future fragility of Jewish life in this country, and in the world, could note enough anti-Semitic incidents and statements around to keep them alert and active. A Louis Farrakhan and his troops, or some skinheads in Wyoming, or Yasir Arafat's overseas friends were certainly on the scene to keep some Jews concerned and vigilant. But only the most uptight American Jew could not help not admit that, for the moment, times were good in this prosperous country. And, making the story even better, it seemed evident that in a contemporary environment which hallowed diversity, it was indeed possible for Jews to have it all, as Americans, without abandoning their religious identity.[2]

As the new millennium opened, the Jews' sense that they could be all that they aspired to be in America was given real-life personification when an Orthodox Jew, Joseph Lieberman, was nominated for this country's second highest office. While a few anti-Jewish backbiters raised their eyebrows about a Jew in this rarified position, most Americans were comfortable with his nomination and many were impressed, if not pleased, with his strong commitment to his own Jewish religious values.

Maybe as significant was the hard evidence that despite a worldwide resurgence of anti-Semitic rhetoric and some violence in the aftermath of September 11, 2001, in America, the image of Jews in the popular mind and body politic was neither sullied nor clouded. For example, when polled just six weeks after the attack, the overwhelming majority of Christian and Muslim fellow citizens (84 percent vs. 11 percent) interviewed drew no connection between Jewish "influence in America" and the World Trade Center atrocity. Few Americans believed that "Jews had too much power in America" (71 percent vs. 21 percent). This is the very good news about contemporary American Jewish life.[3]

Still, many of those concerned with Jewish communal survival felt they had much to worry about precisely because of this unparalleled acceptance. Today, as one perceptive observer has put it, "American decency rather than American bias challenges America's Jews." In an American world where Jews increasingly saw Gentiles more than just as neighbors, but as true friends and, in so many instances, as lovers, the possibilities for assimilation increased exponentially. The edge of unfriendliness — that mainstay that helped preserve Jewish allegiances even in hospitable early postwar suburbia — had melted away substantially. The present-day American Jew, said one sociologist, had become fully "unself-conscious in taking part in . . . the surrounding society." Such a mind-set led "to education with non-Jews, work with non-Jews and political participation and social life with non-Jews." Maybe, after a day's work, most Jews still ended up with their own kind. But the new Jewish friendship circle very often included the non-Jewish spouse of one or more of its members.[4]

For those who would maximize the threat full integration posed for Jewish survival, 1990s figures on Jewish mixed marriage were hard news. In some places in America, more than six out of ten married Jews under thirty were wed to a Gentile. As troubling to the Jewish community was the evidence that "negative attitudes towards intermarriage had dropped substantially" since the 1960s.[5] In the early postwar period, suburban parents of baby boomers were very worried about their children's future marriage partners. Their now grown children did not have those concerns.

Turn-of-the-millennium American Jewry possessed a myriad of institutions designed to influence the contemporary generation back toward more robust group identification. More optimistic observers of communal goings-on emphasized how synagogues and schools and Israel-looking organizations and even Ys and JCCs were all out there to capture the allegiance of all Jews, even those who intermarried. However, their more pessimistic counterparts reminded all that notwithstanding innovative efforts at outreach and renewal, there was an unmistakable "drift toward religious minimalism" within the present-day Jewish community. While there were pockets — sometimes deep pockets — of faith commitment and observance within each of American Judaism's four streams, its wavering rank and file were habitually "absenting themselves from religious services" and "abandoning religious rituals," even when they were not intermarrying. In this regard, noted one communal critic, Jews were acting somewhat differently than the Gentiles with whom they have found so many common causes. Upon entering the twenty-first century, "the American population [was] overwhelmingly religious." The Jewish community was not.[6]

To make things even worse, those Jews who were still deeply religious were often at loggerheads with each other, threatening the unity of the Jewish people in this country. Interdenominational trash talk had long been part of the American Jewish scene. But what was said now was far more hurtful than the heated rhetoric of those 1950s and 1960s "Debate Nights." Presently, the movements were described as "contending camps that do not recognize each other's legitimacy as Jews." A bestselling book called *Jew vs. Jew* put the conflicts front and center on the public marquee. When most mean-spirited, some Reform spokespeople characterized Lubavitcher Hasidic outreach work as cult-like maneuvers. When on their worst behavior, many Orthodox rabbis would not join their Conservative or Reform counterparts in community-wide efforts so as not to lend credence to those "clergy" — they would never deign to call them "rabbis" — with whom they differed theologically. Not to be outdone, members of the liberal denominations, annoyed with perceived or real slights about their Jewish lifestyles and characters, sometimes expended time and effort to keep down the numbers of Orthodox Jews and their institutions in their towns. Some of these battles royale ended up with Jews politicking against one another in local elections or dragging other Jews into secular courts, proof that they could not live well together within an open society.[7]

A large part of the problem, but surely not the whole story, was the aggressiveness of a forceful form of Orthodoxy which suffered no rivals and triumphantly asserted the superiority of its own way of life. We first noted this group's momentum as it came out of Brooklyn a generation or so ago. But even as these dynamic defenders of their faith openly castigated all enemies outside of Orthodoxy, it also let the more modern Orthodox around them know, in no uncertain terms, that the latter's accommodations to America's way of life had rendered them less than sterling bearers of the Jewish past. Moreover, that committed community preached to its own army of followers that they must redouble their efforts to lead a strictly observant life in keeping with the mores and traditions that were remembered from their eastern European past.[8]

Each of these trends in contemporary American Jewish life was reflected in the latest turns in the ongoing saga of Judaism's encounter with American sports. There is no better place to observe how well Jews are today integrated within American society then the grandstands and box seats of any stadium in this country. In these venues, no one cares what your faith is so long as you "gotta believe" in the virtue of the home team and are prepared to heap calumnies, and maybe beer, upon misplaced backers of the opposing club. In the stands, sports become a "civic" religion. Fellow congregants—fans—unite in their devotions and even prayers for a glorious "end of days," a world championship. And some of the most committed will not countenance those who dare to tread upon hallowed ballpark grounds to support unwelcome visitors intent on denying their hoped-for destiny. American Jews can belong to this faith community of fandom, that is, if they root for the right team.

Abraham Genauer, a self-described "expatriate Seattleite living in New York City," found all this out when in May 2002, he attended a Yankee-Mariner game at the big ballpark in the Bronx. As an "Orthodox male" with an ongoing allegiance to a Higher Authority, he was certain to keep his head covered at the game, like he did at all other times. But he had a problem. Should he wear a yarmulke at the stadium—"an outward recognition of my faith, heritage and history"—or a Seattle ball cap—to "take pride in the fact that I was a Mariner fan before they were any good"? Which form of identification, he wondered, would bring out the intolerance of what he called "those beer-swilling, battery-throwing, fussing, cussing Yankee fans." His compromised decision was to sit among the "bleacher creatures" with his yarmulke on, but in close proximity "to some Mariner fans to get an appreciation for what I was missing."

To his delight as a Jew, he sat through the athletic encounter "in blissful anonymity." No one bugged him about "that thing on your head." No one referred to his yarmulke "as a Yamaha." Meanwhile a youngster garbed in a Mariners jersey was "heckled." Genauer would later report that "as a Jew I belonged, and even as a WASP," the afflicted Seattle fan, "didn't." That experience in the House that Ruth Built caused Genauer to say quite emotionally that while anti-Semitism in America is by no means dead, but seen through the eyes of Jewish history and the current events in Israel and Europe, it was just an amazing pleasure to watch a baseball game, Jewishness flaunted for all to see, without being accused of dominating, oppressing, crucifying or drinking the blood of anyone.[9]

Not incidentally, if at any point in the game, had Genauer felt the desire for a ballpark hot dog — typical fan that he was — he could have gone over to the kosher concession stand along the right field line and purchased his red-hot frank, knish, and beer. In acknowledgment of kosher eaters as consumers, many American stadiums currently make sure to have such rabbinically supervised culinary delights on hand and on tap. And if Genauer ever chose to follow his club to Baltimore's Camden Yards for a night game and wanted to *daven Maariv* [recite the evening prayers], the Oriole management had a spot reserved for him and others who wanted a minyan.

"How comfortable Jews have become in the American diaspora" is also on display every August at New York's Shea Stadium, when the Mets hold their "Jewish Heritage Day," an unabashed effort to grab the Jewish fan's allegiance away from the clutches of the Bronx Bombers. (Comparable events are staged for this city's other ethnic groups as well.) One of the highlights of the Sunday afternoon's proceedings takes place "between innings [when] the team mascot Mr. Met, together with an Israeli dance troupe, dances on the top of the third base dugout to the tune of 'Hava Negila.' "

For a former Israeli government official who reported on this occurrence, "the 30,000-odd Jews and non-Jews who came out to see the game [who] applauded enthusiastically to the beat of the music" was "a classic example of what makes America great." In Michael Freund's view—just like Genauer's — "only in a country as free and tolerant as the United States can Jews so boldly and publicly assert their identity without fear or recrimination."[10]

Just a week later, the coaches and manager of the Jesse Burkett All Stars, representing Worcester, Mass., showed how accommodating they were of Jewish religious practices when they readily went along with twelve-year-old Micah Golshirazian's decision not to play in a crucial Little League World Series game until the Sabbath was over late Saturday night. Coaches had certainly come a long way from the time, generations earlier, when they told a young Butch Schwartz and maybe a Louis Yager that if they came late for a game, they would be benched permanently for their malfeasances. For Golshirazian to be part of an aspiring national championship team without violating traditional strictures, Micah and his family stayed at a hotel close to the field. He walked to the game and hung out in the dugout until the time was right. ESPN got in on the action, counting down the time until 8:43 P.M. with a clock in the corner of the screen. Then Golshirazian entered the game as a pinch runner and was quickly erased at second base. Still, he remained a hero to his friends back in Boston—and maybe to an international TV audience — even if his club, the next day, lost in the Series finals.[11]

A few months later, up and coming welterweight Dimitriy Salita made his own public statement about how important his Jewish observances were to him. More remarkably, the boxing world demonstrated how willing it was to work with him as he moved up in the pugilistic ranks. As a teenager, this Ukrainian Jewish immigrant came under the influence of the Lubavitch Hasidic movement, those renowned outreach emissaries to non-observant Jews. While still an amateur, he determined that he would never fight on Saturday. Lubavitch rabbi Zalman Liberow told him, "Don't fight on the Sabbath and everything will be all right," and the budding 140-pound fighter has attributed much of his success to his following of that religious teaching. Already during his amateur career, he found some fight officials ready to accommodate his needs. For example, in 2000, after a reporter interceded on his behalf, his fight in the under-nineteen U.S. Amateur Boxing Championships was rescheduled. As a pro, he has made sure to have his camp provide him with a kosher training table. That particular regimen reportedly has on occasion driven one of his trainers "to distraction." Old-timer Jimmy O'Pharrow of the Starett City Boxing Club has complained:

> Why you got to eat food off a certain kind of plate? Why? Meat don't go along with cream? Everybody eats it. What the hell's the difference? It's going to the same place when it's coming out, and in New York, it's going into the Hudson River. It is as simple as that.

Salita's promoter, on the other hand, saw enormous possibilities in his fighter's principled stance. Though Salita's public refusal, for example, to enter the ring for a November 2002 battle in Las Vegas before the Sabbath ended caused Bob Arum some logistical difficulties, the sly fight business-man, himself also a Jew, went along with his fighter's wishes. Arum intuited, as one headline writer put it, that this "Stellar Young Boxer- and an Ortho-dox Jew . . . [is] a Fighter Ripe for Hype." Here, trumpeted Arum, we have "a unique type of product. . . . The fact that he's Jewish is secondary to the fact that he's the kind of Jewish kid that he is . . . this kid Dimitriy, you don't hit lightning again, but if he becomes a boxing star, given his background, he will be huge."

So disposed, Arum had to have been pleased with a February 2003 *Los Angeles Times* piece that spoke of "one of the most incongruous scenes ever witnessed in a sports venue, men prepared to engage in a brutal box-ing match pausing to watch Judaism's *havdalah* [Sabbath concluding cere-mony] service." Rabbi Israel Liberow, Zalman's brother, who conducted the ceremony at the Mandalay Bay Events Center in "Sin City" Nevada, was also duly satisfied with that news feature report. For this Lubavitch leader, it was another way of highly publicizing his efforts to promote Judaism among the unaffiliated, here using a boxer to show the way.[12]

Micah Golshirazian's Sabbath of celebrity was but a one-shot deal. Dimitriy Salita may or may not reach the stature as an icon and as a boxer that Bob Arum and the rabbis Liberow—each for their own reasons—hope their welterweight will achieve. The story of Tamir Goodman, on the other hand, which unfolded over four years (1999–2003) was evidence for many, and as a test case for some others, of how tolerant America might be of the religious values of twenty-first-century Jews.

For the uninitiated, beginning with those who have not logged on to one or more of the some 1,500 web sites that relate part, or a version, of Goodman's tale, the saga began in 1999, when the then seventeen-year-old was tendered a verbal commitment for a grant-in-aid to play big-time college basketball at the University of Maryland with the unprecedented understanding that he would not have to play for this nationally ranked varsity on the Sabbath. In keeping with NCAA rules, he could not officially sign on the bottom line until his senior year. It was "widely assumed that Maryland [would] petition the NCAA for as few Saturday games as possible." That national sports organization, one scribe pointed out, "has in the past been accommodating to Brigham Young, a Mormon school which . . . will not play on Sunday." Why not help out a religious Jew? There was also much talk that Maryland would lobby its fellow Atlantic Coast Conference teams to change the dates or times of its multimillion-dollar weekend postseason tournament to make way for this Orthodox star.[13]

School officials reportedly also promised that they would provide Goodman with a kosher training table at home and on the road. Goodman's longtime coach and full-time publicist Chaim Katz saw no real roadblocks ahead. In his view, "If it's not a problem for Gary [Williams, Maryland head coach], it is not a problem for Tamir. [Williams] gets paid to win. He's not going to play a PR game with Tamir. He wants a player and Tamir's a player." On another occasion Katz waxed even more effusively about his protégé: "This kid is the *emes* [the truth]. He is the best player in the Baltimore area, bar none. There is not a single 17 year old in the United States of America that can guard him."[14]

Meanwhile, to help Goodman walk the straight and narrow, Lubavitch religious emissaries quickly tendered their services as religious mentors and tutors as Goodman planned his trips down the "Tobacco Road" of the ACC. But not to worry. Very early on, the athlete promised his rabbis and his growing public that he would not abandon his religious studies as he made it in sports. "I don't think I necessarily have to sacrifice my [Torah] learning by going to Maryland," he opined. "College kids find a lot of time to do other things. I will make it a point to continue serious *havruta* [one-on-one religious] studies."[15]

For ESPN, Fox News, and *Sports Illustrated,* among other outlets, Goodman made great copy as a truly Jewish "Chariots of Fire"–type hero. (In that Academy Award-winning film, it is Eric Liddle, the Christian son of mission-

aries, who is concerned with Sabbath observance. The Jew, Harold Abrahams, could have cared less about Saturday strictures.) *Sports Illustrated,* that
most esteemed commentator on the American sports scene, went on and on
with a 2,700-word piece that took its millions of readers into the young
man's Orthodox home and described how he peacefully waited out the end
of the Sabbath before playing an "enthralling" game of basketball in front
of hundreds of worshipping fans.[16]

For Jews, and especially for many Orthodox Jews, as the Goodman saga
unfolded, the point guard from the Baltimore Talmudical Academy became
larger than life. He was a dream come true. How many observant youngsters
over the past century had fantasized that they might become so proficient in
sports that this secular world would change its rules to accommodate them?
And now, what they prayed for was being realized through Tamir Goodman.
The ballplayer's own statements did little to dampen communal enthusiasm
for his faithful stance. "In a sense," the youngster once declared, "I feel like
God's messenger." Another time, he proudly observed that because of him,
"when Jewish kids walk into gyms or parks, they don't get dissed as bad.
They'll actually be invited into the games. You have to be proud of your
religion and the way you were brought up." In a more reflective moment,
Goodman added, "I know kids look up to me because I am an Orthodox Jew
and a good basketball player."[17]

As this living legend continued to unfold, Goodman, who one scribe
anointed as "the lone savior of the Orthodox sports world," even became the
subject of a Jewish rap song. Orthodox lyricist Lenny Solomon and singer
Etan G offered the following tribute to "The Kid with the Lid." He was

> the brother that grew up as part of the tribe Who plays a little hoop with a
> little bit of pride. . . . Phylacteries in the morn, strings all day, dig (You're)
> never gonna get rid of the kid with the lid. Kid with the lid is a basketball
> sensation. Kid with the lid is a light unto the nations. Kid with the lid is the
> real thing, baby. He's gonna take you to the "Promised Land."

There was even talk around about a documentary film about the ballplayer's
life and times. And everywhere Goodman went, he was called the "Jewish
Jordan" when he was not being dubbed the "Chassidic Celtic" or the "Lubavitch Laker."[18]

I personally witnessed how big this phenomenon had become when in
March 1999 Goodman brought his team and his entourage to Yeshiva University's annual Sarachek national Jewish high school basketball tournament. Fans, from silk-suited university trustees to gabardine-garbed Talmud
teachers, clamored for reserved seats as the 1,100-seat gymnasium filled up
for a 10:00 A.M. preliminary game. (The "Thunders" from Baltimore won
their opening encounter against a club from L.A. but were destined, later
on in the weekend, to lose two other games to more talented Orthodox
clubs.) During that first early-morning game, a newspaper reporter asked a

Tamir Goodman playing before a packed house at the Red
Sarachek Jewish high school basketball tournament, March
1999. Courtesy of Yeshiva University Public Affairs
Department.

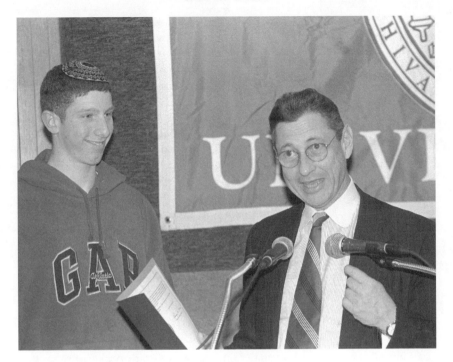

Tamir Goodman receives a "certificate of merit" from
Sheldon Silver, Speaker of the New York State Assembly,
March 1999. Courtesy of Yeshiva University Public Affairs
Department.

Manhattan lawyer why he skipped work to check out Goodman. The AWOL
attorney replied, "I don't expect to see this again in my lifetime." Reports on
the contest and the press conference that followed were carried in Jewish
newspapers all over the country. Sheldon Silver, the Speaker of the New
York State Assembly, showed up with "a certificate of merit" in hand.[19]

Two days later, fellow competitor and Orthodox student Hillie Goldman
sounded a more serious note when he publicly characterized the Balti-
morean's principled stance as a *kiddush ha-Shem,* a sanctification of the Almighty's name, a religiously heroic act which historically was usually reserved
for martyrs for the faith. By then, the elevation of Goodman's exploits had
already transcended the Orthodox community. For example, from his pulpit
in Houston, Texas, Conservative rabbi David Rosen gushed with pride over

Tamir "for remaining true to himself and his beliefs and proud of the University of Maryland for recruiting him." Goodman proved, said the rabbi, "that being Jewish and living a Jewish life does not have to get in the way of your dreams." He told youngsters in his congregation to be like Tamir, "to feel quite prepared and happy to give up . . . after-school sports or activities" and to come "to services on Friday night or Saturday" [instead of] "being with their friends at the mall or going to a movie." For Rosen, the young yeshiva student also had much to say to his community's adults. He hoped that they too would feel comfortable in "asking for time off for Jewish holidays." In so many ways, "Tamir and his coaches have given new worth and new meaning to the pluralistic possibilities in modern America." In Rosen's estimation, Goodman personified the full reconciliation of the clashes so long inherent in Judaism's encounter with American sports and larger society.[20]

But, while this crescendo of kudos continued nationwide, back home in Baltimore, some of his home rabbis began to worry out loud that the hoopla which was enveloping Goodman and his every move was in fact endangering their school's image. For them, the youth's prominence was, at best, a mixed blessing. The school's principal, Rabbi Zvi Teichman, recognized that "Tamir is in a unique situation where he will be influencing the way tens of thousands of people perceive Orthodox Jews." Still, Teichman's view was that, in the end, a Torah institution had to project scholars and not athletes as the consummate role models. In many ways it was a distant replay of sagas that had been previously played out at Chaim Berlin, RJJ, and even at Yeshiva University. Only none of those long-standing schools had confronted the dilemmas of sports' incursions into their lives under the light of such media attention.

Interestingly enough, early on, *Sports Illustrated* picked up on that tension in its own piece when it observed that Teichman and his associates were not

> pleased with the way the younger kids view Tamir as an idol, for idolatry is antithetical to Judaism's most basic tenet. They are happy for Tamir and are proud of him, but athletic success in the secular world is meaningless to them. Raising strictly observant Jews, learned in their own traditions, who will work towards *Tikun Olam,* the repair of the world, that is the school's purpose.[21]

Besides which, the Baltimore Talmudical Academy had a reputation to protect and competitors to oppose within its own local right-wing Orthodox community. One perceptive Jewish journalist observed that "many of the rabbis are worried that their school will not be thought of as the serious yeshiva it seeks to be" in a town where the "internationally respected Ner Israel Rabbinical College a couple of miles up the road" held sway. And now "comes Tamir, attracting scouts, not scholars to campus."[22]

So conflicted, "concerned that the Talmud and Torah image of the school was being replaced by basketball," just a few weeks after Goodman "wowed" crowds in the Big Apple, school officials moved to downgrade the sports program. Teichman announced a "cut back [in] the number of TA's post season tournaments." He declared, "I want a season, but I [am] taking a minimalist view of the season. This current season may have served Tamir's needs, but it was not good for everyone." Though the rabbi and his school's president asserted that the yeshiva "wasn't showing the door" to either the athlete nor his sports mentor, Goodman was effectively told that "the Talmudical Academy [could] not facilitate the goals of a future Division I basketball player." Taking stock of the situation at this early moment of truth, Chaim Katz's assessment was that "TA is a Torah institution. The emphasis is the teaching of Torah to its students. Tamir will continue to learn Torah. But the bottom line is he's a basketball player."[23]

Initially, this coach and player's search for a more "competitive" environment led them in the spring and summer of 1999 to check out a number of local independent schools with academically rich and athletically strong programs. Beth T'filoh, a more modern Jewish day school in Baltimore, put its bid in for the ever-rising star. They certainly would accede to Goodman's non-negotiable demand that he not be pressured to play on the Sabbath. Ultimately, however, the young man cast his lot with the Takoma Academy, a Seventh-Day Adventist institution.[24]

Goodman's choice of a Christian school as the arena where he would now further refine his basketball skills had no discernible effect on his ever-growing legend. Though one Jewish journalist reported that "eyebrows were raised when the yeshiva star announced that he would spend his senior year at a Seventh–Day Adventist School," no one within that community of scribes took Goodman's move to task. The only national organ to pass critical comment on his enrollment was the decidedly irreligious *Village Voice*, which reported that "apparently, the hoops schedule at his old Talmudical Academy was stunting his growth. So . . . the skull-capped slasher will attend Takoma Academy . . . but Takoma is a Seventh Day Adventists School. Oy Vey!"[25]

It was Goodman's erstwhile yeshiva that took some significant hits for not having tailored its program to meet the youngster's prodigious abilities and worth to the Jewish community. At this stage of the game, Tamir Goodman now came to symbolize many of the toughest tensions and fissures within his own community's life. Chaim Katz led the chorus of boos against the Talmudical Academy. He argued "Tamir had to find a place to go to school because his high level of achievement in an area abnormal in our [really, the yeshiva's] little world was not appropriate and we could 'no longer accommodate his needs.' " And "all this because a 16-year-old boy dared to achieve more than he was supposed to all the while telling the world that to him ha-Shem [God] was above all else in his life." Katz also had more than a choice word or two for those within Baltimore's TA or elsewhere who "will ask how will this look for a religious boy to attend a non-Jewish school." First, he declared, let those who judged the young man, his family, and his coach look at "why he was put in this position to begin with." Secondly, and more angrily, the Goodman family spokesman told opponents to "realize that with our precious children, it's not about what they are supposed to look like — it's about teaching them that being a servant of ha-Shem with a pure heart is more important than a $1,500 watch or a human hair sheitel [wig] for our sons and daughters in law." With a further nasty swipe at the lifestyle of his supposed religiously narrow critics, Katz concluded, "Ha-Shem wants our service, dedication and repentance far more than he wants our big weddings and lavish bar mitzvahs." In response, all Rabbi Teichman would say was that his so-called "little world" was not to be measured by "the number of fans and the size of stadiums." Rather "the world of Torah and mitzvot is a much 'larger' world and of eternal value." Moreover, despite Goodman's unquestionable and commendable commitment to the Torah, in the end, sports with its "origins in Greek culture and the empty value it places on physical performance and fame disallow[ed]" Teichman from "encouraging" it among his disciples.[26]

A week after Katz's attack, Baltimore letter writer Irwin Kramer pilloried the yeshiva further for missing the lessons Goodman's dedication to faith was teaching "members of all races and religions nationwide." And he warned that "having chosen to isolate itself in a confined space where outsiders are unwanted, Talmudical Academy can hardly expect these same persons to support a school that would not even support one of its own."[27]

For Philadelphia Jewish newspaper columnist Ami Eden, who more calmly echoed Katz's sentiments, the reason for Goodman's leaving the Baltimore yeshiva "strikes at the heart of what might be the most controversial theological dilemma currently facing the Orthodox community . . . its rightward shift." As he saw it, when Goodman's teachers denigrated his "athletic exploits" as "nothing to take pride in [and as] . . . a distraction from his own studies and the religious mission of the school," they were "building up walls between themselves and a world that they believe is rotting." Eden implied that a more fitting response would be to embrace "Goodman's quest" as a "model for many committed Jews who wish to engage the world around them without compromising their religion."[28]

While Katz and the others took on the yeshiva and its world, Tamir's father, Karl, speaking in a more positive vein, also got out in front of any possible criticism when he reassured the legion of followers that "we're not shipping our son off to the Vatican. . . . He's got to go to minyan in the morning and learn Torah before he even steps foot in the school, each day." His boy would also "have access to rabbis in the area [and] there's kosher food in the area. We didn't do this without rabbinic consultation."[29]

A few months later, Tamir would tell all that he had adjusted well to his new environment. No one was forcing Christian religious beliefs on him. Indeed, he had the opportunity at Takoma to teach Judaism to his teammates and classmates as he was learning about other traditions. And, of course, he continued to pray three times a day, always ate kosher food, home and away, while averaging twenty-three points, seven assists, and nine to ten rebounds a game for the Tigers. For his many backers, who flocked now to Takoma games with their own yarmulkes proudly perched on their heads, Tamir continued to be the consummate Orthodox role model even if before Academy home games commenced, Goodman's coach offered a prayer, within the young man's and his fans' earshot, for "a safe, injury free game . . . in Jesus' name."[30]

Arguably, these game-day salutes to Christianity were totally of no account to Goodman's followers because by the time their hero first suited up for the home team, he had already elevated his own public affirmation of Judaism to yet another, stratospheric level. *Kiddush ha-Shem* was again on people's lips in September 1999, when it was reported that rather than "bend over the issue of Shabbat," the ballplayer had turned down the Maryland offer. The Goodman saga had taken a new and unexpected turn.[31]

The way Tamir's camp told it, their star had backed away from signing a letter of intent essentially because Coach Williams was found wanting on the all-important issue of religious tolerance. Katz and his ballplayer told both the general and the Jewish media that Maryland had reneged on its offer "to try and accommodate his observance of the Jewish Sabbath." Instead, they put undue pressure on the high school senior, figuring that the "lure of big time college basketball" would entice him away from his faith. Here's how Chaim Katz fervently related the showdown between Goodman and Williams:

> They told him that Shabbos was a problem. He told them Shabbos was a blessing. They told him if he didn't play it would affect his "career." He told them if he did play it would affect his "life." They drew a line in the sand. He planted his feet firmly and told them who he was and what he believed in.[32]

Chava Goodman reset the scene in its bottom-line terms. Williams, she said, told her and her son that, notwithstanding his unquestionable basketball abilities, if Goodman missed practices and games, he would forfeit his spot in the lineup to a kid who was always ready to compete. There would be no scheduling appeals to the NCAA and the ACC. Her son had been betrayed, but he would stand foursquare for his faith. "If it comes to playing basketball or the Sabbath," Tamir declared, "I'm going with the Sabbath."[33]

At the time, NCAA rules prohibited Gary Williams from publicly discussing negotiations with a potential scholar-athlete. And in subsequent years, he continued to take a low profile on an encounter that stirred the Jewish community and brought unfavorable publicity to his university.[34] However, almost a year after the controversy over Goodman began, Williams did briefly offer his side of the story to the *New York Times*. There his implicit defense was that Maryland certainly had not failed any tolerance test. After all, Goodman was still eligible for a free education at the university and could be a member of the team, notwithstanding his Sabbath needs. For the coach, the issue was whether he and his team had to go the extra yard, to turn over the way the Terrapins and their league did business, for a fellow who was, ultimately, a mediocre player. Admitting that he and his staff had initially misjudged Goodman's talent, Williams explained, "The whole story is that if he's a star, you might make more concessions. But if you're an eighth or ninth man, you take your chances. If you can't play, and the other guy does the job in your absence, he should play. Every once in a while you make a mistake. We made a mistake." The Goodman camp's retort was that Williams's second thoughts were based on seeing their star when he was injured in off-season pickup games and summer camp. For them, the religious insult began with a basket-ball scouting failure to do all due diligence.[35]

Where Williams erred, as I see it, was in his lack of comprehension of what this "folk hero" — as one journalist called Goodman — meant to so many Jews in Baltimore and beyond. But then again, how could he understand? Williams only saw a basketball player, not the fulfillment of Jewish dreams of American tolerance and religious commitment. *USA Today* sports reporter Jeff Zillgitt explained the social situation very well when he said that "people bought into the idea of a great Orthodox Jewish basketball player before they determined Goodman was a great basketball player period."[36]

Subsequent to the Maryland imbroglio, Goodman found himself caught up in a twisting basketball-Judaism odyssey as he searched for just the right situation for himself. But through it all, his story continued to show just how tolerant the American sports world — and later on, even the secular Israeli sports scene — might be of a twenty-first-century Jew's religious require-ments. So long, that is, if his abilities meshed harmoniously with a college's or club's athletic needs and priorities.

In October 1999, a month after parting ways with Maryland, Goodman signed on with the Towson State Tigers, a local "mid-major" Division I club. Coach Mike Jaskulski readily accepted the Sabbath restriction. The school's admissions director, public affairs officer, and fund-raisers also loved having the Baltimore attraction at their place. And America East conference mem-bers were ready to accommodate all of Towson's scheduling needs. Con-ference Commissioner Chris Monasch would say, sometime later, that "in an educational setting, we're not about to create anything that would be an obstacle to someone's religious beliefs." Coach Jay Wright of Hofstra Uni-versity was particularly sensitive to Goodman's religious values since he had a Mormon ballplayer on his own team who was then struggling with the question of whether to play on his Sunday day of rest. Ultimately, Lance Dunkley decided that he would play on his holy day, but sit out practices. In retrospect, the tolerant Wright would recall that "I sort of felt bad for my guy that I did not request" help from the league.[37]

However, Goodman was destined to play but one full campaign for Towson State. At the end of the 2000–2001 season and after compiling only a 12-17 record, Goodman's new mentor, Jaskulski, was fired and was replaced by the hard-nosed Michael Hunt. While the new coach did not question Towson's peculiar game schedule, he did have problems with the Orthodox point guard's playing ability. He did not see him as a man who might lead the Tigers to the Colonial Athletic Association championship, let alone national, ACC-like prominence. (Towson switched its sports affiliation beginning in 2001. The coaches in the Colonial Athletic Association too, like William and Mary's Rick Boyages, acted with "a genuine respect and sensitivity for Goodman's beliefs."[38]) Hunt's negative evaluation resulted in limited minutes for the now second-string point guard. He scored but thirteen points and garnered only four rebounds and ten assists during Towson's first seven games. Then, in December 2001, Goodman alleged that his coach had menaced him with a chair held over his head and "later kicked a stool that hit [Goodman's] leg"[39] during a locker-room incident.

According to the Goodman camp, Hunt's tirade was sparked by Tamir's innocuous "smiling after the coach told him to back away from a team huddle." Initially, Tamir and his parents threatened legal action against their new enemy. But they soon dropped the assault charges, preferring to have the school investigate the matter. After a quick — maybe a perfunctory look — at the circumstances, Towson officials determined that Hunt had not engaged in "abusive behavior" and would not be suspended. All Hunt would concede is that he had "stepped out of character . . . yelled at every player in the room . . . about technical errors" even as he did admit that he would "definitely have to watch my tone in the future." But it was clear that for Hunt, Goodman was not a talent worth saving.[40]

As Goodman checked out a number of Division I schools in New York, some members of the general media started to take another, harder, look at the entire Goodman phenomena. Now, after further review, some scribes offered interpretations and advice that largely comported with Gary Williams's evaluation. As one uncharitable critic saw it, Goodman lived "in a world with high expectations and a very unrealistic nickname" all because of "the little hat that he wears during games and his superior play against lower level high school competition."[41]

At this very moment, there was some talk around town about Goodman coming to Yeshiva University. Coach Halpert and I felt that Goodman certainly would have been a very useful addition to our Division III club. And if he could help elevate our team's standing at our level of competition, it would be great for the kid, for the school and, yes, for us too. We also thought Yeshiva would be the best place for such a devoted Jewish youngster to grow as a member of the community and as a student. But no one from the Goodman camp really inquired of our opinion. Had he come to us, he would have started practice as our second-best guard. We already had Eli Hami on our team, a member of the 2001 United States Maccabiah Team.

In the summer of 2002, Goodman took his hoop dreams and Jewish commitments off to Israel. He then signed a three-year professional contract with Maccabi Tel Aviv. But he did not stay long with that top Israeli club. In due course, it determined that Goodman was not yet—or might never be—a prime-time player, and his owners decided to loan him to Givat Shmuel, a lower-level outfit. When that temporary demotion took place, a red-faced *Sports Illustrated* finally admitted that "in retrospect, maybe we went a little too far with the whole 'Jewish Jordan' thing." Experience had shown that "Goodman wasn't built for college basketball." His tale at Towson had confirmed "any doubts the Terps might have had about him." Now they predicted that when the Givat Shmuel season started, the yarmulke-wearing twenty-year-old would "likely be regarded as more curiosity than contributor as he's expected to come off the bench."[42]

The 2002–2003 Givat Shmuel season proved this particular *Sports Illustrated* prediction correct. The former phenom averaged but two points and less than one rebound and one assist per game as Goodman played less than ten minutes each night. As far as his new hope of playing top-flight pro ball in Israel was concerned, his Givat Shmuel coach weighed in with the following estimation: "I hope for him that he can make it. To be honest, I don't think he can be at that level in the next two years. Maybe as a 12th man," the last man off the bench.[43]

Still, Tamir Goodman became not only a drawing card for Orthodox fans and others wherever he went, but he emerged as a symbol of the possibilities for the end of Judaism's face-off with secular *Israeli* sports. As one adoring fan said as part of a five-page spread in a May 2003 edition of the *Jerusalem Post:*

> Tamir opened the gate. You can be religious, you can be Shomer Shabbat [a Sabbath observer]; and you can be in professional sports. He's a pioneer. There is no doubt about it.

Goodman did little to distance himself from that role. Describing himself as an avowed, dedicated follower of the Lubavitch movement, he said that he is "on a special *shilihut* (mission) from Hashem." Basketball, he continued, "brings me closer to Hashem [who] wants me to represent him and represent Judaism and spread Judaism throughout the world as much as possible and show everyone that you can be Jewish and compete in anything you want and still be proud of being Jewish."[44]

Though Goodman remains fired up to prove that a love of sports and devotion to Judaism can today go hand in hand, relatively few twenty-first-century Jews share his—or, for that matter, Golshirazian's and Salita's—religious values. The numbers on "the scorecard in the running battle between Jewish assimilation and Jewish survival," to borrow a sports metaphor from grandstand sitter Michael Freund, do not point in favor of this country's "loyal and faithful" Jews. Rather, at this stage of the game, disaffection may be grounds for—with another rhetorical assist from Freund—a "seventh inning *kvetch* [complaint]." And one of the most undeniable specific problems, to revisit Rabbi David Rosen's lament, is that "after-school sports" lure too many Jewish kids, with their parents' acquiescence, away from Jewish life.[45]

Other American rabbis have lodged similar complaints against their communities' priorities. Once, for example, possibly in a moment of elevated exasperation, Rabbi Harold Kushner went so far as to publicly link this endemic dilemma with sports' earliest challenge to Judaism's future. It was "Hanukkah" when he "suggested that maybe the Maccabees lost the war, that the gymnasium had triumphed over the synagogue and our children were opting for Little League and youth soccer over junior congregation." To his dismay, Kushner has admitted, "it did not change many minds or hearts."[46]

Rabbi Stuart Weinblatt of Potomac, Maryland, understood that kids naturally would "desire to play soccer on Saturday." But for Judaism to survive, he unabashedly told his B'nai Tzedek congregants on Rosh Hashanah 2001, parents had to stop "capitulating" to their youngsters. Pulling no punches, Weinblatt said, "[I]n the large scheme of things, ask yourself—is little league or soccer or even an exam really more important than an eternal binding covenant for which many of our ancestors gave their lives to preserve?"[47]

As it turned out, a year later, the rabbi would be made keenly aware of how difficult parenting was when it came to controlling sports' constant incursions into present-day children's lives. On Yom Kippur morning 2002, he revealed to his congregants that his own son, Noam, had asked him "on our way to shul for Rosh HaShanah services . . . [whether] he could play football on Rosh HaShanah afternoon with the neighbors." And this was a kid, Weinblatt honestly reminded all, who had studied in Israel, had attended a day school, and was "the son of a rabbi." And yet his young man persisted—sports was clearly in his blood—until his father absolutely prohibited him from turning out for the gridiron on the Jewish new year. After making that definitive call, Weinblatt reported, "there was no reaction, just silence. I assumed what I said was sinking in. After a few minutes, he punctuated the quiet by asking me, 'How about basketball?' " It is not known whether Noam slipped away that afternoon to join his friends.[48]

Of course, for the rabbi, the older generation had to do more than merely follow his lead and just say no to their indulged kids. They had to mend their own religious ways. Telling his listeners to devote themselves as much to the future of their Judaism as they do to the fortunes of their home team, he asserted that "parents who would never dream of missing kickoff or the final seconds of a Redskins game, don't give a second thought to coming to services late, or leaving early." Even worse, "parents who would never dream of missing a kid's soccer practice don't give a second thought to dropping their kids off at Saturday morning services," and then go on their merry ways. Generations ago, kids slipped away from their elders on holy days to play their informal street games. Today's parents carpool their youngsters to events and constitute the largest parts of the cheering sections.[49]

Brookline rabbi Moshe Waldoks has also challenged congregants "as to the heavy investment they make on sports in their kids lives." In an only partially ironic way, he has asked parents "how many want their kids to be professional soccer players." When confronted this way, generally a few listeners raise their hands, "usually in a kidding way." If so, the preacher has advised, they had best move "to Brazil or Romania" to pursue that unrealizable dream. He then has inquired of the assembled "how many want their kids to be Jews?" To this call for affirmation, there is always majority assent. Then why, Waldoks has continued, do parents "invest in a project whose return is not desired." To this interrogatory have come honest responses that really explain what Judaism ultimately is up against in an integrated, accepting America. Blessed with the opportunity to witness their youngsters truly chosen in — a reality that eluded their own parents and grandparents, and maybe even themselves — present-day parents say, "I don't want my kid to feel left out!"[50]

When he occupied a pulpit position, Jewish outreach professional Rabbi Kerry Olitzky decided that a good way of tackling this issue among Jewish parents and children was to "show up in the afternoon of some of their [Saturday] games." Non-judgmental in approach and demeanor, Olitzky showed the kids that he was "not just interested in them when they were in synagogue (same with their parents) but in them in general." Although he believed that his going out to the fields "won a lot of them over," his ultimate faith was in "build[ing] institutions of meaning." Sounding much like Rabbis Goldstein, Kaplan, and Levinthal of three generations earlier, Olitzky has asserted that "currently, people make the choice between an uninspiring synagogue and forms of entertainment. So the choice is made for them."[51]

Olitzky might have had some additional success had he lived in a town that possessed a "never on Saturday" or a "kosher" Little League. Over the past quarter-century, a number of predominantly Orthodox or intensely committed Conservative communities have created their own athletic loops that have schedules which do not challenge youngsters to choose between Jewish commitments and team allegiances. When run well, these associations have many of the accoutrements of those other leagues, starting with regular uniforms and trained coaches and officials. In Newton, Massachusetts, not far from Moshe Waldoks' town, for example, the Schechter Soccer League has been in operation since the early 1990s and, at last count (2003), offers 150 boys and girls the opportunity to play structured youth games. Similar operations have existed since the 1970s for observant baseball and softball players in six sections of the metropolitan New York area and Los Angeles.[52]

Riverdale, in the Bronx, New York, has also been home since 1994 to "A League of Our Own," a girls-only softball league run under the auspices of the Women's Tefillah of the Hebrew Institute of Riverdale. Applying their Orthodox feminist sensibilities toward creating a level playing field, league founders Ronnie Becher and Mary Pilossoph wanted their daughters to have equal opportunities for success in sports. Until then, all but the very best girl players in the coed league were stuck at catcher or shunted to right field and made to feel left out. Now, in the new athletic incarnation, girls could shine on Sundays, even as some of their mothers worked to have females take an active part in Orthodox ritual on Saturdays. From an initial group of forty girls, the league grew over the succeeding ten years to more than 150 participants.[53]

On balance, however, none of these leagues has ever come close to capturing the allegiances of the majority of any community's Jewish youths. Though these leagues are often constituted as all-inclusive, most of their kosher athletes already come from observant homes, not the type of families with whom rabbis Waldoks and Olitzky have typically worked. Essentially, these leagues are more preventive than palliative when it comes to the Jewish sports problems. In some cases, they keep a new generation of youngsters from slipping away from their family traditions. More generally, they simply give observant kids the chance to look and play like all others, even if the level of play is not up to neighborhood par. However, none of these athletic associations really have had much to say to the Jewish parent and kid who are comfortable with Saturday game days and who might harbor dreams of future excellence in sports.

It is precisely these hopes that motivated Zohar Azoulay, in the spring of 2003, to show off his pitching talents within the North Riverdale Little League and not to be part of a kosher squad. However, in this somewhat unusual case, the decision to play on the Sabbath day was not so much a dismissal as it was a redefinition, with a challenge to tradition, of a core message of the faith. This story merits consideration as a reminder that the boundary lines are not always so clear in Judaism's present-day encounter with American sports.

During the week, the then twelve-year-old hurler was a student at the SAR Academy, a local Orthodox day school. His family valued highly the importance of Zohar's receiving a quality Jewish education. But the young man disdained the Sunday games, with his mother's approval, in order for him to have the chance to compete against a better type of player. For Zohar and Julie Azoulay have been told, and they fervently believe, that he is "very talented, that he has an extraordinary degree of focus for a kid his age, with a natural curve [and being] a lefty doesn't hurt either."

But what is most instructive about that decision — at least as a mature Julie expressed it — is that Zohar's playing on the Sabbath is their way of keeping the holy day special. Julie explained all of this to me one Saturday afternoon as we stood together behind a batting cage watching her pride and joy work on the mound: "I am a single mom," she said, "Saturday is the only time I have to be with my son. Watching him play is a source of great joy for both of us. It turns Shabbat into a fun, joyful experience. This is the way I have decided to have an *oneg shabbat* [enjoyment of the Sabbath day]." Besides which, she would argue some time later, "I'm not entirely sure that had baseball existed back then [in ancient times], it would have been on the list of forbidden activities." For Julie Azoulay, the diamond can be a very Jewish place, especially on a Saturday.[54]

What about more conventional "Jewish places," like Ys and JCCs, as sites that address Judaism-athleticism face-offs less idiosyncratic than the Azoulay case? In the late 1940s, so many of its affiliates were still just "common meeting grounds" for Jewish people, and Jewish programming, as always, received short shrift. Moreover, these institutions often conducted events "in direct violation of Jewish tradition and ritual" because their "Jewishly illiterate" workers and officials were only concerned with athletic and social programs. And powerful elements remained within the Jewish social work world that bore their non-sectarian commitments with pride, if not arrogance. With so many facilities narrowly focused on "gyms, swimming pools and dancing Jews," the movement's harshest critics could still contend that JCC venues were inhospitable to the inculcation of religious values and commitments among Jewish athletes.

As late as 1963, it seemed that, notwithstanding two decades of pressure from the Synagogue Council of America (SCA), those JCCs that cared little about "Jewish content" were not about to change their ways. And the National Jewish Welfare Board was not about to force their hands. When the Board then rejected the Council's call "for a moratorium on further openings of Jewish Community Centers on the Sabbath," because the national leaders would not dictate terms to its local agencies, it might have appeared as if the "assimilationists" continued to hold the upper hand over the "preservationists" within the Center community. From some SCA vantage points, it looked like the labors of the several Joint Consultative Committees that had come and gone over the years — not to mention the recommendations of the by-then-legendary Janowsky report — had come to naught.[55]

A year later, the situation looked like it was getting even worse when the Central Conference of American Rabbis (CCAR) broke ranks with the SCA on this issue. At its 1964 convention, Reform rabbinical delegates decided not to endorse the Synagogue Council's moratorium resolution. From that point on, there would be no external Jewish communal pressure on the many fiercely independent JCCs to Judaize themselves. And yet, over the last four decades and largely on their own accord, most Jewish Community Centers dedicated themselves to the goal of creating viable Jewish religious environments that could be attractive to the many youngsters who really have no interest in synagogue "play and pray" formula.

What the Ys and JCCs have done, in a remarkable historical twist, is to adopt as their own the essence of the rank-splitting stance which the Reform Conference took, back in 1964, when it broke with the SCA's position. Why, the CCAR then argued, did a Jewish institution have to keep its doors closed and its lights off in keeping with strict halachic strictures — values that they as Reform rabbis did not own — if it could remain open and do good Jewish work? As Rabbi Ferdinand M. Isserman told his colleagues, "We have reinterpreted the Sabbath concept and we should reflect that interpretation." So the liberal rabbinical body advocated that Jewish Centers be closed only "from sundown Friday through 1:00 or 1:30 Saturday, so as not to violate the time for Sabbath worship in temple and synagogue." And, they continued, when Centers did open their doors, their facilities should be used "in the fullest way to satisfy athletic and recreational needs, and to sponsor programs and activities which are not offensive to the spirit of the Sabbath as we understand it." Janowsky the sociologist had pushed that point years earlier. Now a group of rabbis bought into that line of action.

At that 1960s turning point, the CCAR made that move largely to assert its independence from "subservience to Orthodoxy in religious decisions." Clearly that position — which, a cynic might say, protected the integrity only of the time of Reform services — did little to maintain good relations among American Jewry's several competing religious forces. However, the CCAR stance did, in its wake, offer a model for shul-pool cooperation which, over the long haul, many communities came to live by.[56]

In fact, today, in keeping with that CCAR recommendation, seven out of ten JCCs that responded to a 2002 internal national survey reported that their facilities were open on Sabbath afternoon after being closed on Friday night before sundown. Only 10 percent of such affiliates open their portals on Saturday morning. When the doors of these JCCs do swing open, the athletic programs are usually restricted to informal swims or shoot-arounds. For example, league sports are generally not held on Saturday. It is far more likely that special Shabbat programming will complement non-structured sports activity. In deference to the restrictions of Sabbath traditions, no smoking is permitted and no money changes hands in the precincts of most JCCs. Moreover, at more than half of the JCCs that answered the survey, their Shabbat ended with a *havdalah* [concluding ceremony] service. For "preservation," or today's by-word "continuity," is on the lips of the overwhelming majority of JCC workers, most especially the ninety or more Jewish education specialists who serve communities coast to coast.[57]

During the week, that highly skilled team of Jewish pros runs a myriad of classes for those who want them, designed to "fortify those who are already Jewishly affiliated," "attracting and involving the unaffiliated," "developing future Jewish leadership," "stimulating interest . . . in Judaic studies," etc. You name the Jewish objective, the JCCs have operatives on the case of Jewish survival.[58]

Without a question, the JCCs Jewish mission is on display most graphically every summer, where now up to 6,000 Jewish teenagers, boys and girls, participate in its regional Maccabiah games. Here a conscious effort is made to "infuse . . . Jewish meaning [into] the athletic experience." Everywhere players turn they are exposed to "Jewish values." The no "trash talking rule" is pitched as a violation of the Torah's teachings against *lashon hara* (gossip). Kids are involved in community social service projects to remind them of their ancestral obligation to *tikun olam,* to improve the world. And in many informal educational modes, young athletes are instilled with a love for Israel and the Jewish state.[59]

Though the era of "[Jewish] value–free social work" is over within the Centers movement, nevertheless, "Sabbath issues" still arise sometimes as localities debate whether a particular activity is truly appropriate for their "Jewish Place" on a holy day.[60] And more often than not, arguments break out over a Center's gym practices. Just this type of episode occurred in December 2002 in Newton, Massachusetts, when the Leventhal-Sidman JCC announced "that to enhance participation in the Jewish community by continuing to bring Jews together in a Jewish environment," classes in "tai chi, swimming and yoga would be offered between noon and 7 p.m. on Saturday." Non-structured athletic activities had been part of the Sabbath scene since the Center opened in 1983. Vocal supporters of the initiative — beginning with the JCC's leadership but also including a local Reform rabbi and Orthodox letter writers — agreed that here "families can exercise their mind, body and spirit on Saturday in a Jewish space." They projected that ideally such classes could be "entry point[s] into the Jewish community . . . in a safe, non-threatening way [for] families who were not yet ready to join a synagogue or perform Jewish rituals at home." For them, evoking their own "from play to stay" scenario, "if a secular Jew who is not observant chooses to spend their time with other Jews, hopefully it will lead to other Jewish activities." Opponents, most notably the head of the local Orthodox rabbinical council, asserted that the move was a clear violation of the original concordat between Newton's synagogues and the Center that prohibited activities that "would encroach on congregations" or "compromise the spirit of the Sabbath." On this particular issue, a different local Reform rabbi joined Orthodox colleague Rabbi Abraham Halbfinger's brief when he publicly admitted to "mixed feelings" about the classes. "It's not the first I've heard of a JCC offering programs on Shabbat," said Rabbi Eric Gurvis. "I would wish the activities would be more related to Shabbat than athletics."[61]

Ultimately, however, these squabbles are of little moment to those with the largest vision of the JCCs' "serv[ing] as a laboratory for shaping Jewish identity." For them, and not unlike all other Jewish outreach, survivalist, or continuity outfits of the contemporary era, the more daunting task is to recruit more young Jews to their Judaism-athleticism message. Though today, a JCC gym can be a place for a Jewish athlete who cares about his or her religious identity, other voices and venues vie competitively and successfully for their allegiances.

If "continuity" is the primal *kvetch* of the contemporary American Jewish community, "delegitimization" runs a close second in the lexicon of present-day laments. And occasionally, the sore feelings that arise out of these inter-denominational struggles find their way into Judaism's sports arena. When they do, they not only show how and why today's Conservative and Orthodox Jews stand their ground against one another, but they also reveal that neither denomination is of one mind over whether to get along with or differ on points of principle with the other.

Though other Jewish cities have experienced some spates of such sports tensions, the metropolitan New York area in 2001 was the venue for the most publicized and intriguing intra-Jewish face off. Actually, the issue of "who is a point guard," a takeoff for one pundit on the "hot question on the religious pluralism front" of "who is a Jew?" dates back to the early 1970s. It was then that the Orthodox rabbis who controlled the Metropolitan Jewish High School League first rejected appeals from local Solomon Schechter schools for admission into their "yeshiva league." The restrictionists' argument then was, and long remained, that according formal "recognition" through athletics to Conservative schools was tantamount to granting a degree of religious legitimacy to their theological opponents. Exhibition games could and did take place between rival schools, even if some of the yeshivas did not list these athletic encounters on official school calendars. And no one said anything about kids from different backgrounds fraternizing with one another at these non-league games. But only Orthodox schools could be in the loop.[62]

The issue was rejoined in 1996 when the Metropolitan *Yeshiva* High School League turned down the latest Schechter school request for membership. Note the name change from "Jewish" to "Yeshiva." Schechter supporters have felt that the shift in nomenclature was for "the purposes of excluding the Schechter schools."[63] One official of the Board of Jewish Education (BJE) — whose Principals Council ran the league — tried to soften the blow. He helped organize an alternate league linking the three Conservative schools in the region — Hicksville, Long Island, West Orange, New Jersey, and the Solomon Schechter School of [Manhattan] New York — with those Orthodox schools that were comfortable associating on the hardwood with the Schechterites. This move revealed that the Orthodox community was not of one mind on the issue. Ramaz's principal, Rabbi Haskel Lookstein, said, "we have enough things that divide us ideologically without being divided athletically." So his school and Flatbush and the Torah Academy of Bergen County signed up with the rump association.

But that initiative did not last long. For the Orthodox youngsters, the game-day burdens of playing in two leagues were just too much. For a Ramaz athlete, that meant playing in as many as thirty games a season. What were they, a Division I ballclub? For the Schechter group, this sports construct was not the league membership they sought.[64]

Several months later, in the fall of 1997, when the next Schechter petition was turned down, with "one [unnamed] yeshiva principal" reporting that "the feeling was that allowing [the Schechter schools] into the yeshiva league would be recognizing their values in a way that went beyond basketball," some Schechter people decided to counterattack. They took their case to pluralism-leaning elements within the United Jewish Appeal–Federation of Greater New York (UJA), which funded the BJE, asking them to push open the doors to the league. This was not the first time such deputations were made to the funding agency. It was, however, the first time Conservative moves were publicized. But to the dismay of Schechter forces, the UJA did not take on their cause.[65]

The crucial encounter began early in 2001 when the Schechter schools once again renewed their applications and UJA backers now made significant noises about withholding portions of BJE funding. That more-than-implied threat had the telling effect of moving the restrictionists within the Principals Council toward officially severing the league from the educational board at the very moment they turned down the latest Schechter request. With that surgical strike in place, some league leaders reasoned, the UJA could have no future call on their prerogatives.[66]

That action, voted on one snowy night in February with nary a quorum in sight, infuriated those Orthodox schools that did not share the restrictionists' viewpoint. Convinced that it was just the wrong call for Orthodoxy, and maybe fearful that the bad press that was coming out would tar them too, Ramaz and the Hebrew Academy of Nassau County (HANC) let all concerned know that they had not been at that controversial meeting. Inclusion advocates like HANC board chairman Isaac Blachor told a Jewish newspaper that his community had, years earlier, approved a policy of inclusion and had "continuously practiced that policy to this day." Moreover, as he understood it, what his school stood for was totally in line with the BJE's own policies. Rabbi Lookstein informed his own Ramaz parent body — and the Jewish media — that "it is an outrage that our school cannot engage in interscholastic sports activities with other Jewish schools." For him, the restrictionists' "policy [was] inconsistent with Judaism and Jewishness" and was a veritable *hilul ha-Shem* (desecration of God's name). Rabbi Lookstein and his compatriots threatened that if the policy were not reversed Ramaz and other like-minded schools would establish their own new league, surely with Schechter schools as full members.[67]

Now, with Schechter people largely on the sidelines, except for their students, who cried out for the right to "compete against fellow Jews rather than resorting to non-Jewish leagues,"[68] two factions within the metropolitan area's modern Orthodox community had it out against each other. Fearing what "right to play" concessions might ultimately lead to, Rabbi

Saul Zucker of the Mesifta of New Jersey sounded the warning that "it would be seen by some as a natural step to go from athletic competition to having the various schools get together to discuss curriculum. But we have fundamental disagreements [with non-Orthodox schools] and are concerned about efforts to blur the line." While sure to assert that his position was not "anti-Conservative," Rabbi Teitz reportedly raised the specter of "possible religious conflicts at games, for instance, if a prayer service was held prior to a game and the Schechter students insisted on an egalitarian service." For the JEC principal, there was indeed a nightmare scenario, where the Conservatives might end up pushing a "value system that does not adhere to the legitimacy of the Torah."[69]

Convinced of the wisdom of the Teitz position, a Yeshiva College student op-ed contributor went one step further and expressed an even deeper Orthodox worry. Yehuda Kraut questioned the very "sagacity of placing yeshiva high-schoolers — who are likely still forming their religious personalities — into situations that will almost certainly lead to friendships or personal relationships with members of a community who maintain doctrinal belief antithetical to halachic Judaism." For him, even non-league games were a problem. While Kraut admitted that "the union would almost certainly generate some beneficial elements, not least of which [would be] the banishment of the perception that Orthodox Jewry regards other forms of Judaic practice with an air of condescension" for him, making "the Orthodox community appear more tolerant," would be "scant consolation . . . for the parents of an Orthodox child who befriends a Schechter student and decides that Conservative Judaism conforms more to his personal taste than does strait-laced [sic] halachic practice."[70]

Poised in a different corner, inclusion advocates like Rabbi Yosef Adler of the Torah Academy of Bergen County and Daniel Vitow of the soon-to-open North Shore (Long Island) Hebrew Academy High School feared that unnecessary Jewish divisiveness was the last thing the community needed. As Vitow put it, "[I]f we do not stick together as one people, we send a terrible message to our parents and students. Ultimately, this will cause our destruction." Also foursquare in this camp, Rabbi Zev Meir Friedman of the Rambam Mesivta in Lawrence, Long Island, made clear that for him, this religious communal issue was hardly "frivolous." Rather, it was "all about Jews being part of one people." Like Rabbi Lookstein, he told his parent body that "if nothing changes . . . for next year we will consider every alternative which will allow us to balance the desire to play competitive sports with doing the 'right thing.'" Meanwhile, another Yeshiva College op-ed writer, Yehuda Shmidman, had no sympathy whatsoever for his schoolmate's angst. For him, "because the opponents of Schechter have battled so fiercely, it has now resulted in an even sharper divide within the Jewish people. Is that what we need now . . . ?"[71]

It would take several months of "behind-the-scenes movement" as "the matter [was] rethought and reinvestigated" before cooler heads prevailed, or maybe better said, until these Orthodox combatants found a way of ending their self-destructive head butting. (It has been suggested that the rapprochement was due in part to pressure placed upon some of the restrictionists from non-Orthodox benefactors of their schools who were less than enamored of exclusionary stances. BJE officials have reportedly asserted that a "key reason for the change of heart was that several prominent Orthodox rabbis let it quietly be known that they were in favor of allowing Schechter schools to participate.") In all events, finally, in May 2001, Rabbi Zucker announced, as head of the league, that the principals agreed unanimously to grant the Schechter schools "full athletic participation," but with the key, essential proviso that the "status quo would apply on matters of halacha." The Orthodox principals would alone have a say-so in the religious arenas that might surround the matches. This stipulation evidently reassured the erstwhile restrictionists against any future "invasion into non-purely athletic activities." Orthodoxy would thus be protected from the possible "blurring of ideological lines." Still, when Rabbi Zucker officially "welcom[ed] Jewish youngsters to play ball together" and deemed the inclusion as a *kiddush ha-Shem*, it did constitute a step back from his brand of Orthodoxy's stance against "recognition" of Conservatives.[72]

But would the wording of this sport concordat—with its explicit bow to Orthodox practice and religious hegemony—sit well with the Conservative schools? While the question of services at games was purely hypothetical because no one had forced anyone to pray, egalitarian-style or otherwise, throughout the many years of non-league competition, acceptance of the Orthodox "status quo" meant that Schechter schools had to conform to yeshiva league game-day strictures regarding no cheerleaders and sweat pants and long shirts for female athletes. Even more troubling for Schechter officials was the stipulation that accorded the Orthodox schools sole authority and authenticity on religious matters. Now a different sort of "recognition" clash began. Would the Conservatives implicitly concede that Orthodoxy's way of doing things was the way to go? The Schechter group's answers showed that they too were of several minds on a right-to-play principle.

For Marc Medwed and his Long Island Schechter school, "not having a vote was an issue." But in the end, "the baseline agenda for us is to play ball with other Jewish kids, not to be recognized by Orthodox day schools." Besides which, "it was unlikely that religious issues would come up." That position was fully in line with what his board chair Beth Ostrow had said several years earlier when the league's doors were closed to her school. For her, membership was "not an attempt to link this issue to the greater pluralism debate. This is about Jewish youngsters playing other Jewish youngsters. . . . Why should we have to play in a league with Catholic schools when there is an active yeshiva league?" So disposed, this school stayed clear of larger ideological postures and quickly joined up.

Scheduling problems ultimately precluded the West Orange Schechter school from joining the league. But before turning down the invitation, its principal Elaine Cohen made it clear that she and her constituency had some problems with the so-called "ideological" issue. Reportedly, she let it be known that a much better and pluralistic-minded system would see the determination of "league rules — religious and otherwise . . . on a collaborative basis." For example, she was not certain that her school could go along with the league's present strictures regarding cheerleading and girls' athletic attire. "What is acceptable to her school as an occasional accommodation" (like when they played exhibition games), she was quoted as saying, "might not be acceptable as a general rule." Now the games counted more than just on the scoreboard. Rabbi Teitz would have agreed. As league members, keeping the pom-pommers home and putting the gym shorts away would be a statement of principle, a tacit recognition that the Orthodox way of doing things possessed greater legitimacy than their own.[73]

Many leaders of the board of the Solomon Schechter School of New York harbored similar principled apprehensions. There was much talk in its meeting room that the yeshiva league offer was "demeaning," that it "did not accept Schechter as an equal" and that the Orthodox "have to recognize that they are not the only game in town. We also uphold halacha; this is not a case of winner take all." Speaking in a similar vein, another school trustee wondered out loud what this "invitation" would do to "the self-image of the kids that they should play in an atmosphere where they would be classified officially or otherwise as second-class citizens." For this contingent too, it was a point of principle, not just basketball.

Others who governed that school felt as strongly that whatever the rules were, for the sake of *k'lal Yisrael,* the unity of the Jewish people, their Schechter school should be in a Jewish league. Seconding the sentiments of their sister school in Hicksville, they reportedly argued that "it is better . . . to play in a Jewish high school league . . . than in a more diversified [private school] league." As divided, as so many other Conservative and Orthodox Jews were on this right-to-play issue, Schechter of New York backed away from joining the league.[74]

While today's modern Orthodox schools are often at loggerheads with each other in determining whom to include in, and whom to exclude from, the religious sports world they have created, in a different corner of the Orthodox world stand their yeshiva world counterparts, who are well along in their own efforts to minimize the impact most forms of athleticism make within their increasingly cloistered world. And yet, victory for old-line Judaism over sports remains both inconclusive and incomplete.

Interscholastic competition ended as part of mesifta student life as early as the 1970s. From that time on, boys at the Chofetz Chaim Yeshiva of Queens, New York, the Kamenetz or Mirer Yeshivas of Brooklyn, and other like-minded schools would not play against each other in any official way. Moreover, by the close of that decade — again as a sign of the times that were unfolding — those students who listened closely to decisive rabbinic admonitions were less likely than ever before to show up at ballparks or arenas. Rabbi Moses Feinstein went on record as prohibiting yeshiva students — to be more precise, all Jews who might listen to him — from attending professional stadium sporting events. The same renowned decisor, who some thirty years earlier had tacitly approved of his disciples' playing in the MJHSL, now decreed that while modern stadiums were not *ipso facto* places of idolatry — as they were in ancient times — believing Jews were still admonished to avoid attending such events because they were homes to "frivolousness, profanity and possibly licentiousness."[75]

Nonetheless, as any attendee at a contemporary ballpark can immediately attest to, Rabbi Feinstein's formal interdiction has failed to inhibit many very Orthodox fans from cheering on their home teams. Ball-capped Abraham Genauers are not the only black-hatted Orthodox Jews at today's major league ballparks. Jewish men in black also frequent basketball games, hockey matches, and even wrestling "contests" at America's most famous indoor arenas. There is also some proof, from a study of the inner life of yeshiva world schools of the late 1970s and early 1980s, that students then still liked to recreate among themselves and to keep close tabs on the sports around them. Indeed, in some such circles, a "source of status [was] a reputation of the student as an 'all-around guy.' This [was] usually synonymous with ability in sports." The rebbe that had played sports as a youth and who knew who led the major leagues also acquired a positive reputation among students for being in tune with their interests. These teachers had to make sure, simultaneously, "that this [sports] interest does not result in a loss of respect on the part of the students."[76]

By the late 1980s, such a well-attuned rebbe might even use "Rebbe" or "Torah Trading Cards" to turn the interests of student sports aficionados in their right direction. These "glossy pictures of smiling rabbis" with their Torah pedigrees and achievements on the flip side — their Jewish batting averages — then became "the rage among Orthodox Jewish youngsters . . . even without bubble gum" as entrepreneurs, and ultimately educators, attempted to redirect yeshiva youths' evident interest in sports heroes and memorabilia. "Be in the First in Your Yeshiva," it was trumpeted in 1989, to own the original set of thirty-six cards (two times the Jewish lucky number of eighteen) complete with the religious superstars' most vital statistics. Kids were encouraged to set aside their Topps or Upper-Deck sports cards and begin trading these new collectibles after memorizing "the facts and pictures that are held dear to the Jewish people." It is not clear whether the flipping of Rebbe Cards onto the ground was an approved collateral pastime. What is certain is that by 1997, one on-line religious outfit offered customers a massive "checklist" that included not only cards on rabbis, but also on Bible stories, Biblical animals, and ancient Jewish coins and synagogues. For all involved with this enterprise, there might be no better way for a yeshiva teacher to appropriate a piece of sports' irresistible culture in the service of religious instruction.[77]

Notwithstanding this evidence of sports' persistence, by the 1990s there were also signs that in some of these same Orthodox circles, the athletically attuned rebbe and his "all-around guy" counterparts no longer possessed the admired status they once had within their community. The following remarkable exchange that appeared in 1991 in *The Jewish Observer,* a publication of the stridently Orthodox Agudath Israel in America, suggests that some of the oldest Orthodox opinions, not even about sports but toward physical training itself, have some resonance within today's American yeshiva community.

At that moment, two physicians, "Dr. Susan K. Schulman, a pediatrician and Dr. Robert H. Schulman, an endocrinologist, [who] maintain their medical practice in the Boro Park section of Brooklyn," published "A Plea for Exercise in Yeshiva Programs." Speaking to "their patients . . . primarily of the yeshiva and orthodox population," and evoking the authority of Maimonides, who affirmed the value of active exercise, the Schulmans called attention to a "health hazard," the many incidences of "yeshiva *bachur* back" — "the terrible posture and chronic back problems in our yeshiva children." The root cause was the lack of "recognition" among "our Roshei Yeshiva . . . that exercise is important and . . . to give their talmidim [students] every opportunity for a wholesome life." They declared, "it is incumbent upon them to designate some structured time every week for this purpose." Their clear message was that "proper health habits learned from childhood are our best means of helping *ha-Shem* to give us health and longevity."[78]

Their plea evoked the following angry — and instructive — response from a *Jewish Observer* reader. This exercised interlocutor from Lakewood, New Jersey — the home of the Beis Medrash Govoha of the late Rabbi Aharon Kotler — took the magazine to task for printing the doctors' call. In her view, "for the past 2,000 years no such idea was ever proposed. Exercise may be important but to make it part of the curriculum?" Linking herself further to her sense of the transplanted European past, she continued, "It is well known that Rabbi Moshe Feinstein z"tl [may the memory of this saint be a blessing] did not sit on a chair with a back until he was 40 years old (and he lived to a ripe old age), and they propose a desk with a '*shtender*-like [lectern-like] top' so students should not have to bend towards their *Gemoras* [tractates of the Talmud]. . . . One should bend over towards *Gemora* and toil in his learning. The whole proposition is alien to *ruach ha-Torah* [the spirit of the Torah]." She was also quick to emphasize that those schools "which do have regular gym or swimming classes have them only to fill state regulations." Otherwise, the American-based rabbis that she reveres, like the leaders of the lamented yeshiva world of the past, would not have acceded to

Rabbi Elya Svei and Rabbi Moshe Heinemann's "Torah
Personalities" trading cards (1993). Courtesy of Torah
Personalities, Inc.

such wastes of valuable study time. "Again," she concluded, "there is nothing inherently wrong with exercise — but to make it part of a yeshiva curriculum is not the way to raise true *b'nei Torah*" [lit. boys or students who are
truly committed to Torah study].[79]

However, it does not seem so many others within Rochel Shapiro's Lakewood community feel the same way about the value of physical education
and fitness in their lives and in the lives of their contemporary *b'not Torah,*
their own daughters. In that New Jersey Torah enclave, there were reportedly, as of 2003, at least "one secular (women's only) gym, and three basement gyms (ten ladies pay to use ten machines.) There is also Curves, for
frum [punctiliously observant] women in a storefront (painted over, of
course)," not to mention "a pool in Bais Kalla H.S." And if a woman wants
to work out at home, she can do her "reps" to the beat of a specially recorded "Jewish Aerobics" tape. The athlete has only to pop in the cassette
and follow a woman's voice-over instructions to the sounds of the best-
known wedding and other religious tunes. To one observer of her own local

הרב משה היינעמאן, שליט"א
רב אגודת ישראל דבאלטימאר
והרב אליהו שוויי, שליט"א
ר"מ ישיבת דפילאדעלפיא

Rav Elya Svei, shlita, and Rav Moshe Heinemann, shlita, were
both close talmidim of Rav Aharon Kotler, zt"l. Rav Svei, the
elder of the two, is a member of the Moetzes Gedolei HaTorah
of Agudath Israel of America, while Rav Heinemann is a senior
member of the Conference of Rabbonim of Agudath Israel. Rav
Svei is consulted on many national and international matters, and
Rav Heinemann, especially known for his expertise on kashrus,
is consulted on many halachic matters.

Rav Aharon Kotler, zt"l

Front Photo by C. Shugarman
כל הזכויות שמורות
Sold on condition not to copy.
© 1993 Torah Personalities, Inc.

אחדות

5 - #17
U.S.A.

Rabbi Elya Suei & Rabbi Mosle Heinemann's "Torah
Personalities" trading cards (1993). Courtesy of Torah
Personalities, Inc.

scene, it was a given that "in communities where people have a baby every
year or two, getting fit, staying fit during pregnancy and nursing, is a top
priority." Once these women condition themselves to routinized physical
training—in faith with Maimonides' teachings—they might take to the
gym's regimens with the same regularity and dedication that they normally
apply to prayer and study, the most honored values of their community.[80]

But even as the yeshiva world group is deciding how far it wishes to move its sons, much more than its daughters, to the athletic sidelines, its by now long-standing attitudes on how sports should be played — if Orthodox Jews must take part in these unnecessary games — has deepened its impact on the more modern Orthodox community. The latest yeshiva league adoption of social protocols that they did not originate began in the early 1990s when the Principals Council acceded to requests from all-girls' schools and yeshivas with female-only divisions for assistance in starting leagues of their own. As constituted, all players, coaches, and officials would be females. And no men — even the fathers and brothers of players — would be allowed to observe girls in sweats at play. Those familiar old-line Orthodox concerns over gender separation and religious modesty in the sports milieu, issues that first began at Chaim Berlin in the mid-1950s, were now extended to limiting who might be permitted to sit in the stands at modern Orthodox contests.[81]

With this policy in place, the lineup of schools, league by league, has come to reflect changes in religious sensitivities and the extent of the fissures within the present-day modern Orthodox community. Here, once again, sports tell the tale of Judaism's larger and divided contemporary state of affairs. The solidly coeducational schools like Ramaz and Flatbush have stuck with the old system. But they now have no athletic-based relationship with girls-only operations like a Bat Torah of Rockland Country or a Queens Sevach Academy. For a while, Yeshiva University's Central High School for Girls, oscillating left and right to meet its community's centrist proclivities, fielded teams in both leagues. Its better players, and/or girls from families who were not overly concerned about dads in the stands, suited up against the coed schools. Meanwhile, Central's Junior Varsity did battle against the Bat Torahs in half-empty gyms. As of 2002–2003, this school is comfortable in the so-called "A League." Male relatives can attend games. No one stands at the door to check lineages. Still, an active effort is made to discourage fraternization among unattached males and females before and after action takes place on the court.[82]

And then there is Elizabeth, New Jersey. Rabbi Teitz's community has demonstrated that it too is of several minds over whether to conform to strict gender separations. JEC's girls' school, Bruriah, has found an enduring comfort zone playing in both leagues. For the record, if Bruriah principal Chaya Newman had her druthers, she would have only "all-girl teams," even as her school is staunchly vigilant against a "social scene" at her games Still, Bruriah remains responsive to its "demographics" and accommodates both families that are soundly in tune with the sirens of separatists as well as those who are aligned with a different set of Orthodox social values.[83]

In sum, as these sports encounters underscore, the first decade of the new millennium found American Jews safely at home within American society, They were truly chosen in, and very often on their own terms. But there is tension in Judaism's own clubhouse. There are so many that do not want to remain part of their faith's contingent. And those who occupy the increasingly separate and partitioned off corners of their religion's locker room have definite and competing ideas about who can really be a Jewish teammate. Judaism's battles of the early twenty-first century take place within, and not without, their community's arena.

EPILOGUE: A CLEAR PATH TO THE FINISH LINE

This epilogue gives me a final chance to really prove George Baron's locker room prediction wrong. Though never a champion performer on the field, court, or road, here I am, as this book ends, primed and ready to be profiled within a Jewish sports book, and a reliable one at that. This is my story of American and Jewish values and personal encounter within the universe of sports.

I am an American Jewish male athlete who has "run New York" a dozen times and has mentored a generation of Yeshiva's ballplayers. Like most highly dedicated sports people of my generation, I value competition to the core of my being and am blessed, as a middle-aged man, to be battling still for playing position. The possibility of victory, however remote, or at least to rate the public recognition that sports hold out, captivates me. As an American, I would have made Theodore Roosevelt proud. Maybe this desire has something to do with the fact that as a youth I never achieved sports stardom. So motivated, as an adult, I have done what is necessary—within the rules—to reach my goals. For the record, I have yet to trip a fellow runner as we dash toward a finish line.

My running marathons had, thus, nothing to do with Maimonides' Jewish call to maintain physical health and vigor. Rather, it was a chance to be special, particularly at that incredible moment when upon exiting the 59th Street Bridge, fifteen miles into the race, half a million people lined up along First Avenue called out my name. Having my name written on my uniform shirt helped. Anxious to be noticed, I often took one additional step to stand out in the crowd. One of my former students was host to a daily Jewish-content radio show. For many years, I was his "official runner." In that guise, I appeared on the air on the Friday before the event to discuss my "chances" —just like the pros. And I called in on Monday, as my healing process began, to recap my performance. The world-class athletes had the networks to profile their achievement. I created my own momentary celebrity status.

As a twenty-first-century Jewish athlete, I have made it in America. I am a teammate with all other competitors in this tolerant country. One of my father's prized "possessions" was a purloined towel that he helped himself to when he wrestled against the New York Athletic Club. That was as close as a Jew, like him, could get to membership in that then-exclusive sports preserve. My parents were also once turned away from a New Hampshire hotel whose unwelcome sign read "No Jews, Dogs or Consumptives." Like most baby-boomer Jews, I have never experienced discrimination within or without the American sports world. During my marathons, I bonded with runners of all backgrounds. I once sang a few bars of "La Marseillaise" with some French distance men as we awaited the gun at the Verrazano Bridge. Also symbolic of my people's position in America was the presence at a designated place for a prerace minyan at the marathon staging area — readily available, if I chose to attend. This Jewish place rested comfortably next to the Catholic Mass tent and the Protestant prayer area. I have wondered, did the cultural pluralistic values of that proud Jew, the late Fred Lebow, inform that example of religious tolerance?

Growing up in a third-generation American Jewish household, I also had no conflicts with my athletically oriented parents over my passion for sports. They also had it in their blood. My father Jack — Jacob the wrestler — was my first coach. My mother was proud of her claim that as a girl in the Bronx, she played handball with Hank Greenberg. And games were always on in my home. Most kids of my generation, those who had American-born parents, were at least sports fans, if not players. Fancier types in my parents' friendship group wore their madras Bermuda shorts on the golf links. Blue-collar guys like my father liked softball or paddleball. My only sports battle with my Dad was when, as a teenager, I coached against him in a men's softball league. Where we spent our summers, it was a puberty rite for boys when they were allowed to compete with, or against, their elders. My father was more than annoyed with me when, in our first contest, my club — made up of my swift-footed contemporaries — scored nine runs in the top of the first inning against his contingent of old-timers. And, nasty kid that I was, I implored my troops to pour it on. That move was an act of adolescent separation.

But if my personal story until now resembles that of so many of my fellow Jewish competitors, I also differ from most Jewish athletes of my time — and from most American Jews — in my elevated sense of group identification. That gravitational pull toward my people and its traditions came through those times when I attended that premarathon minyan. I showed up both to implore God to "give strength to the weary" and to seek out those who share my ancestral heritage. One of the forces that has kept me close to the basketball program at Yeshiva University is my faith in Sarachek's teaching that as "American Jewry's team," we represent our people on the athletic field of honor. I feel that pride most profoundly before every game at the Max Stern Athletic Center as "Hatikvah" is played along with "The Star Spangled Banner." Here, as a postmodern Jew, I do not subscribe to an athletic version of the modern Jewish question of "what will the Gentiles say." Instead, I am very comfortable with the playing of a Jewish anthem as a way of expressing American Jewish love for the State of Israel. Not incidentally, how have visiting teams and refs taken to the Israeli anthem? Some opposing coaches have told me that their kids "love the scene." Far from feeling offended, the international musical mood "reminds their players of the Olympics." Their tolerant reaction is another measure of our acceptance among our non-Jewish neighbors.

Does my passion for sports ever face off against Judaism's religious teachings? Rather than conflicting with faith, athletic participation enhances me spiritually. The prophet Isaiah's runners' creed always moves me:

> Even the youths shall faint and be weary, and the young men shall utterly fall. But they who wait for the Lord shall renew their strength. They shall mount up with wings as eagles. They shall run and not be weary. They shall walk and not faint.

It is fitting that this particular prophetic portion is read in synagogues the week before or after the New York City Marathon. Here, Judaism and sports' calendars surely intersect. I also encounter the Almighty up close and personally at the starting line of an arduous race when I confidently "entrust my spirit . . . as long as my soul is with my body. The Lord is with me, I am not afraid." A staunchly religious Christian colleague has chided me for failing to immediately thank God, with equal prayerful reverence, when the race is over and I am swept up in the euphoria of meeting a personal challenge. It is a weakness of character and of faith that I have to work on. Nonetheless, I still believe that even if sports has not necessarily made me a more observant Jew, my deep devotion to athleticism has certainly bonded me closer to my Creator.

So, if in the end I am not challenged religiously, do I ever confront conflicts between my Jewish and sports identities? As a player in the Jewish

Studies world, I am still engaged in professional battles in search of full acceptance as an unusual scholar who has merged skills in two very different realms, academics and athletics. When I have been asked, over the past few years, about my current research projects, I have found myself obliged to emphasize that I am writing a *serious* book about Judaism and sports, as if there were really a question about the legitimacy of my topic. I also was put off, beyond words, when some people in a conference audience giggled when they heard me say that a Judaism-sports book could "accord with the canons of our academic industry."

I have to keep my eyes on the prize and react, as a good teacher of American Jewish history should always do. I must explain that the American culture of sports requires study because of its challenge to millennia-old Jewish images and values. How Jews in this country dealt with the ideas, symbols, and circumstances that were largely foreign to their prior historical experience demands scholarly exploration. And for anyone who still might raise his or her eyebrows, I will only say that such a comprehensive examination is neither meretricious nor self-indulgent. I trust that through this book, I have won this crucial encounter.

NOTES

PROLOGUE

1. For George Baron's listing, see Bernard Postal, Jesse Silver, and Roy Silver, *Encyclopedia of Jews in Sports* (New York: Bloch Publishing Co., 1965), 359.

2. Jeffrey S. Gurock, "'Different Streams into a River Yet to Be': Movement towards an All-Inclusive American Judaism, 1920–1945," in *The Margins of Jewish History*, ed. Marc Lee Raphael (Williamsburg, Va.: College of William and Mary, 2000), 34. Significantly, I should note that I toned down my use of sports metaphors, at Professor Raphael's suggestion, in the final written version of the paper.

3. Robert Slater, *Great Jews in Sports* (Middle Village, N.Y.: Jonathan David Publishers, 1983).

4. This point was first made in an early work on America, America's Jews, and the Holocaust. See the chapter entitled "The Olympic Spirit" in Arthur D. Morse, *While Six Million Died: A Chronicle of American Apathy* (New York: Random House, 1968). See also Peter Levine, "'My Father and I, We Didn't Get Our Medals': Marty Glickman's American Jewish Odyssey," *American Jewish History*, (March 1989) 399–424.

5. William M. Simons, "Hank Greenberg: The Jewish American Sports Hero," in *Sports and the American Jew,* ed. Steven A. Riess (Syracuse, N.Y.: Syracuse University Press, 1998), 192–200.

6. "Yankees, Behind Murphy, Defeat Tigers," *New York Times,* September 19, 1934, 30.

7. For a recent recounting of Koufax's absence on Yom Kippur and the positive reaction to it, see Jane Leavey, "The Chosen One," *Sports Illustrated,* September 6, 2002, 64–65.

8. George Vecsey, "Sports of the Times: Mets Forecast, A Deluge," *New York Times,* October 1, 1986, B13.

9. A few weeks later, the cardinal spoke out against parents who chose Little League over Sunday church services. See, on both statements, David W. Chen, "O'Connor Assails Sunday Little League," *New York Times,* May 15, 1998, B3.

10. Jeffrey S. Gurock, *The Men and Women of Yeshiva: Orthodoxy, Higher Education and American Judaism* (New York: Columbia University Press, 1988), 173–179.

11. Peter Levine, *Ellis Island to Ebbets Field: Sport and the American Jewish Experience* (New York: Oxford University Press, 1992), 257.

12. Jeffrey S. Gurock, "Training Chaya for the Run," *Amit,* Fall 1999, 48–51.

INTRODUCTION

1. M. E. Ravage, *An American in the Making: The Life Story of an Immigrant* (New York: Harper and Brothers Publishers, 1917), 216–217.

2. Ludwig Deubner, quoted by Ludwig Drees, *Olympia: God's, Artists, and Athletes,* trans. Gerald Onn (New York: Praeger, 1968), 24, noted in Allen Guttmann, *From Ritual to Record: The Nature of Modern Sports* (New York: Columbia University Press, 1978), 21.

3. Nessa Rapoport, "Chametz: The Bread of Externals," *The Jewish Week,* April 13, 2001, online edition, 16.

1. FROM ANCIENT STRUGGLES THROUGH A MEDIEVAL TIME-OUT

1. On Moses' exploits, see Exod. 2:11, 2:17. On Samson, see Judg. 15:15–16. For a description of Saul and his election as king, see, I Judg. 9:12, 10:1.

2. For the talmudic source on swimming and life saving, see *Kiddushin* 29a, 30b. I am grateful to Professor Steven Fine for reminding me of the physical nature of the agricultural work that premedieval Jews engaged in. For a listing and some analysis of talmudic sources that relate to varying forms of athletic activity, see Jehosua Alouf, "Physical Culture in the Period of the Talmud" [Hebrew], in *Physical Education and Sports in Jewish History and Culture: Proceedings of an International Seminar,* ed. Uri Simri (Natanya, Israel: Wingate Institute for Physical Education and Sport, 1973), 5–11, 39. For Maimonides' statements about physical health, see *Mishneh Torah, Hilchot Deot,* 4:1ff., 4:14–15. See also on Maimonides' attitude toward physical activity, Meir Baskhi, "Physical Culture in the Writings of Maimonides" [Hebrew], in Simri, *Physical Education and Sports in Jewish History and Culture,* 11–18, 50.

3. For a description of Jacob at Laban's well, see Gen. 29:2–3. For Rabbi Hama bar Haninah's midrashic statement, see *Genesis Rabbah* 77. For rabbinic discourses on the difference between Jacob and Esau, see *Genesis Rabbah* 63:10ff., Gen. 25:27. See also Louis Ginzberg, *Legends of the Jews* I (Philadelphia: Jewish Publication Society, 1909), 316. On the primordial yeshiva, see Steven Fine, " 'Their Faces Shine with the Brightness of the Firmament': Study Houses and Synagogues in the *Targumim* of the Pentateuch," in *Biblical Translation in Context,* ed. F. W. Knobloch (Bethesda: University Press of Maryland, 2002), 79.

4. See 1 Maccabees 1:14–15 and 2 4:14–17 for Hasmonean castigations of their opponents.

5. For the account of the "road trip" to Tyre, see 2 Maccabees 4:18–20. For a useful view that suggests that those sent by Jason did not share his assimilationist values and the opinion that few Jewish athletes reversed their circumcisions, see Jonathan Goldstein, "Jewish Acceptance and Rejection of Hellenism," in *Jewish and Christian Self-Definition,* vol. 2: *Aspects of Judaism in the Graeco-Roman Period,* ed. E. P. Sanders, A. I. Baumgarten, and Alan Mendelson (London: SCM Press, 1981), 78–79.

6. For the record, there is a reference, in the writings of a second-century C.E. author named Pausanias, that women competed in their own separate mini-sports gathering at Olympia, called Heraea. But there was but one event on the calendar, a short race through the stadium. There is no source extant that suggests that a Jewish female runner participated in those meets. By the way, this source also indicates that married women were barred from attending the men's events. Virgin girls could be spectators. Maybe there they might meet their future husbands. See on these topics.

Oxford Classical Dictionary, ed. Simon Hornblower and Anthony Spawforth (Oxford and New York: Oxford University Press, 1996), 207, 1129.

7. Louis H. Feldman, *Jew and Gentile in the Ancient World: Attitudes and Interactions from Alexander to Justinian* (Princeton, N.J.: Princeton University Press, 1993), 57–59.

8. See ibid., 58 for Feldman's critique of Harry Austryn Wolfson's supposition that Jews of Alexandria did not join Greek gymnasia and established their own sports associations. For Wolfson's opinion, see his *Philo: Foundations of Religious Philosophy in Judaism, Christianity and Islam,* vol. I (Cambridge, Mass.: Harvard University Press, 1962), 80–81.

9. Feldman, *Jew and Gentile in the Ancient World,* 58–59.

10. Victor Tcherikover, *Hellenistic Civilization and the Jews* (Philadelphia: Jewish Publication Society, 1959), 350.

11. David Gordon Mitten, "A New Look at Ancient Sardis," *The Biblical Archaeologist* XXIX (1966): 63–65.

12. On Resh Laqish's athletic background, see the Jerusalem Talmud, *Avodah Zorah* 2:3 (41b), *Terumot* 8:10 (40b) Babylonian Talmud, *Gittin* 47a. See also Michael Poliakoff, "Jacob, Job, and Other Wrestlers: Reception of Greek Athletics by Jews and Christians in Antiquity," *Journal of Sports History* 11, no. 2 (Summer 1984): 62.

13. See *Tosefta Avodah Zarah* 2:4–2:7 and Babylonian Talmud *Avodah Zarah* 18a. See also Goldstein, "Jewish Acceptance and Rejection of Hellenism," 84.

14. Poliakoff, "Jacob, Job, and Other Wrestlers," 60–61; On Mishnaic references to wrestling activities and the Sabbath, see Saul Lieberman, *Greek in Jewish Palestine: Studies in the Life and Manners of Jewish Palestine in the II–IV Centuries C.E.* (New York: Feldheim, 1942), 92–97

15. On Jews engaging in a variety of informal sports within Jewish boundaries, see the very instructive work of Joshua Schwartz, " 'Ball-Playing' in Jewish Society and in the Greco-Roman World," *Proceedings of the Eleventh World Congress of Jewish Studies* (Division B) I (1993): 17–24, "Ball-Play in Jewish Society in the Second Temple, Mishnah and Talmud Periods" [Hebrew], *Zion* (1995), 247–276. See also on talmudic and later sources dealing with prohibitions and permissions for Jews to play ball on the Sabbath, see Saul J. Berman, "Playing Ball on *Shabbat* and *Yom Tov,*" *The Edah Journal* 1, no. 1 (2001): 1–3.

16. On the nature of the medieval tournament, see Marc Bloch, *Feudal Society* (Chicago: University of Chicago Press, 1961), 304–305; Alan Young, *Tudor and Jacobean Tournaments* (Dobbs Ferry, N. Y.: Sheridan House, 1987), 1; Urban Tigner Holmes, *Daily Living in the Twelfth Century: Based on the Observations of Alexander Neckam in London and Paris* (Madison: University of Wisconsin Press, 1952), 180–181. On the Jews' "right to bear arms" in the Middle Ages and the withdrawal of that right, see Guido Kisch, *The Jews in Medieval Germany: A Study of Their Legal and Social Status,* 2nd ed. (New York: KTAV Publishing House, 1970), 111–128, and the more recent Christine Magin, "Armed Jews in Legal Sources from the High and Late Middle Ages," *Jewish Studies* 41 (2002): 67–82.

17. On the paramilitary nature of medieval sports under Islam with particular reference to the Mamluks, see David Ayalon, "Furusiyya," in *The Encyclopaedia of Islam,* vol. II, ed. B. Lewis, Ch. Pellat, and J. Schacht (Leiden and London: E. J. Brill and Lazac & Co., 1965). On Jewish minority status as *dhimmis,* see Bernard Lewis, *The Jews of Islam* (Princeton, N.J.: Princeton University Press, 1984), 21–29 and passim. See also *Jewish Prince in Moslem Spain: Selected Poems of Samuel Ibn Nagrela,* introduction, translation, and notes by Leon J. Weinberger (University: University of Alabama Press, 1973), 1–7 for a discussion of Shmuel ha-Nagid's exceptional life and times.

18. Cecil Roth, *The History of the Jews in Italy* (Philadelphia: Jewish Publication Society, 1946), 140, 236, 386–387.

19. On the mimic tournaments in conjunction with weddings, see L. Rabinowitz, *The Social Life of the Jews of Northern France in the XII–XIV Centuries as Reflected in the Rabbinical Literature of the Period* (New York: Hermon Press, 1972), 145–146. See also Israel Abrahams, *Jewish Life in the Middle Ages* (New York and London: Macmillan, 1896), 193. My projected description of the mimic event is derived from Abrahams, 378, which quotes a somewhat later source on Jewish cavaliers, and from the *Jewish Encyclopedia* (New York and London: Funk and Wagnall's, 1905), vol. II, 372, which also sets the scene for such a mimic tournament.

20. For the account of the German Jewish tournament I have written up as a possible occurrence, see Emanuel Hecht, "Miscellaneen aus der Geschichte der Juden in Deutschland," *Wertheimer's Jahrbuch fur Israelitschen Kultur* III (1856–1857): 169–170. Israel Abrahams, based on references which he quotes from the works of Leopold Zunz and Abraham Berliner, questions whether a "real tournament" actually took place. His equally obscure remark is that "it would seem that the fight was not in sport, but in earnest, and that the Jews merely defended themselves against the attack of a party of armed bandits." See Abrahams, *Jewish Life in the Middle Ages*, 378.

21. Ibid., 376–379.

22. Markus J. Wenninger, "Bearing and Use of Weapons by Jews in the (Late) Middle Ages," *Jewish Studies* 41 (2002): 83–92. See also Wenninger, e-mails to and from the author, August 8, 2003.

23. Irving A. Agus, *Rabbi Meir of Rothenburg: His Life and His Works as Sources for the Religious, Legal, and Social History of the Jews of Germany in the Thirteenth Century*, vol. II (Philadelphia: Dropsie College, 1947), 659.

24. Historian Salo W. Baron has asserted that as boys were socialized and educated within their traditional society, little time was allocated within the school experience for leisure-time activities. Indeed, for Baron, "sporadic voices in favor of recreational pauses [from study] were as ineffective as those which advocated physical exercises. Northern European Jewry, especially had little use for physical education or sports, and paid little heed even to the demand that a father give his son instruction in swimming as a life-saving precaution." In this regard, he seconded and expanded upon Israel Abrahams' observation that "intellectual pastimes were far more common than physical as the middle ages advanced." See Abrahams, *Jewish Life in the Middle Ages*, 379. But no one really knows whether the best, or even most, students of that time always stood by their books as their rabbis would have wanted and did not sneak outside for "recess." Besides which, clearly the schools of the Tosaphists — for example — did not provide education for all. Thus, even in the best of situations in twelfth- or thirteenth-century France or Germany, there had to have been masses of hardscrabble youngsters who occupied themselves with tossing a pelota — a "jai alai" ball — around, while their most erudite contemporaries pined away in the halls of the yeshiva. The problem with Baron's evaluation, which has been generally accepted as approximating reality, is that the sources he quotes to back his assertion are not from the specific High Middle Ages time and places we are discussing. See Salo Wittmayer Baron, *The Jewish Community: Its History and Structure to the American Revolution*, vol. I (Philadelphia: Jewish Publication Society, 1948), 197–198.

25. Isaac of Corbeil, *Sefer Mitzvot Katan [Amudai Golah]*, no. 280. See also Rabinowitz, *The Social Life of the Jews of Northern France*, 228.

26. S. D. Gotein, *A Mediterranean Society: The Jewish Communities of the Arab World as Portrayed in the Documents of the Cairo Geniza*, vol. V (Berkeley: University of California Press, 1988), 12–13.

27. Berman, "Playing Ball on *Shabbat* and *Yom Tov*," 3–4.

28. Robert W. Henderson, "Moses Provençal on Tennis," *Jewish Quarterly Review*, New Series 26 (1935–1936): 3. Roth, *The History of the Jews in Italy*, 130–131, 173;

see also idem, *The Jews of the Renaissance* (Philadelphia: Jewish Publication Society, 1959), 12.

29. For a full discussion of this oft-referenced responsum, see Henderson, "Moses Provençal on Tennis," 1–6. See also Roth, *The Jews of the Renaissance,* 28–30.

30. Roth, *The History of the Jews in Italy,* 328.

31. Baron, *The Jewish Community,* vol. 14, 154–156. See also Josef Fraenkel, ed., *The Jews of Austria* (London: Valentine-Mitchell, 1967), 3–5.

32. Felix Pinczower, "Jews as Teachers of Sport in the Middle Ages" [Hebrew], *Atidot* (1946), 261–64.

33. On Jewish status and rights in pre-1648 Poland, despite church pressures, see Edward Fram, *Ideals Face Reality: Jewish Law and Life in Poland 1550–1655* (Cincinnati: Hebrew Union College Press, 1997), 17–18, and Bernard D. Weinryb, *The Jews of Poland: A Social and Economic History of the Jewish Community in Poland from 1100 to 1800* (Philadelphia: Jewish Publication Society, 1973), 37–40. On relations between Poles and Jewish elites during this era, see Gershon Hundert, "An Advantage to Peculiarity: The Case of the Polish Commonwealth," *AJS Review* 6 (1981): 36–37.

34. Joseph Trachtenberg, "Jewish Education in Eastern Europe," *Jewish Education* 11 (1939): 126–127.

2. JUDAISM'S FIRST MODERN SPORTS SKIRMISHES

1. Todd M. Endelman, *The Jews of Georgian England 1714–1820: Tradition and Change in a Liberal Society* (Philadelphia: Jewish Publication Society, 1979), 218–223.

2. Keith H. Pickus, *Constructing Modern Identities: Jewish University Students in Germany, 1815–1914* (Detroit: Wayne State University Press, 1979), 50–51; for a critique of fraternity life, see Philipp Lowenfeld's memoir in *Jewish Life in Germany: Memoirs from Three Centuries,* ed. Monika Richarz (Bloomington: Indiana University Press, 1991), 239.

3. Patricia Vertinsky, "Body Matters: Race, Gender, and Perceptions of Physical Ability from Goethe to Weininger," in *Identity and Intolerance: Nationalism, Racism, and Xenophobia in Germany and the United States,* ed. Norbert Finzsch and Dietmar Schirmer (Washington, D.C.: German Historical Institute and Cambridge University Press, 1998), 354–356, 360; Allen Guttmann, *Games and Empires: Modern Sports and Cultural Imperialism* (New York: Columbia University Press, 1994), 141–143; Alfred D. Low, *Jews in the Eyes of the Germans: From Enlightenment to Imperial Germany* (Philadelphia: Institute for the Study of Human Issues, 1979), 164.

4. Richarz, *Jewish Life in Germany,* 238–239; Guttmann, *Games and Empires,* 142; Low, *Jews in the Eyes of the Germans,* 164–165.

5. Richarz, *Jewish Life in Germany,* 239.

6. Pickus, *Constructing Modern Identities,* 55.

7. Adolph Asch and Johanna Philippson, "Self-Defense at the Turn of the Century: The Emergence of the K.C.," *Leo Baeck Institute Yearbook* III (1958): 123; Deborah Hertz, "Why Did the Christian Gentleman Assault the Judischer Elegant? Four Conversion Stories from Berlin, 1816–1825," ibid. XL (1995): 99–101.

8. Ludwig Philippson, "Das Duell vom Standpunkte des Judenthums," *Allgemeine Zeitung des Judenthums* 20, no. 28 (July 7, 1856): 1–2.

9. For a useful summary statement on the abundant historiography on non-observance and dissociation that plagued nineteenth-century German Jewish life in so many economic, social, and cultural spheres, see Michael A. Meyer, ed., *German-Jewish History in Modern Times,* vol. 2 (New York: Columbia University Press, 1997), 102–105, 151–152. In my view, the experience of these Jewish athletes should be added to the general theme of patterns of falling away from Judaism.

10. It has been suggested that in dealing with the decline in observance among German Jews, both liberal and traditional rabbis were not aggressive in addressing the private behavior of deviating Jews. See Meyer, *German-Jewish History in Modern Times*, 103, 152. Further research is required to explain whether this proclivity may explain the lack of rabbinic involvement offering alternatives to assimilation within the athletic-university setting.

11. Asch and Philippson, "Self-Defense at the Turn of the Century," 123.

12. Ibid., 124; Pickus, *Constructing Modern Identities*, 97.

13. Ute Frevert, *Men of Honour: A Social and Cultural History of the Duel* (London: Polity Press, 1995), 113–114; Asch and Philippson, "Self-Defense at the Turn of the Century," 132.

14. Pickus, *Constructing Modern Identities*, 97–98.

15. Meyer, *German-Jewish History in Modern Times*, vol. 3, 146; Asch and Philippson, "Self-Defense at the Turn of the Century," 124–125.

16. Pickus, *Constructing Modern Identities*, 98–99.

17. Ibid., 99–103.

18. Arthur Hanak, "The Historical Background of the Creation of the Maccabi World Union," in *Physical Education and Sports in the Jewish History and Culture*, ed. Uriel Simri (Netanya, Israel: International Seminar on Physical Education, 1973), 149–152; Pickus, *Constructing Modern Identities*, 107.

19. Hanak, "The Historical Background of the Creation of the Maccabi World Union," 151. On opposition within German Jewish society to these various youth groups, see Ismar Schorsch, *Organized Jewish Reactions to German Anti-Semitism* (New York: Columbia University Press, 1972), 72, 97.

20. See Samson Raphael Hirsch, *Horeb: A Philosophy of Jewish Laws and Observances*, vol. II, trans. Dayan Dr. I. Grunfeld (London: Soncino Press, 1962), 408. I am indebted to Professor Mordecai Breuer for his insights on physical training within Hirsch schools in the nineteenth century that he shared with me through Professor Kimmy Caplan on July 29, 2000. See also Aaron Ahrend, "Physical Culture in Rabbinical Literature in Modern Times," *Korot: The Israel Journal of the History of Medicine and Science* 15 (2001): 64. Ahrend notes that in the 1920s, Rabbi Yosef Zvi Carlebach, a Hirschian, expanded the sports program in his Hamburg Reali Talmud Torah.

21. David Henry Ellenson, "Continuity and Innovation: Esriel Hildesheimer and the Creation of Modern Orthodoxy" (dissertation, Columbia University, 1982), 297; see also *The Responsa of Rabbi Esriel, Orah Hayim* [Hebrew], no. 48 (1882), and Professor Kimmy Caplan communication with Professor Breuer, August 15, 2000.

22. Richard Davis, *The English Rothschilds* (Chapel Hill: University of North Carolina Press, 1983), 92–95.

23. Raphael Loewe, "Cambridge Jewry: The First Hundred Years," in *Gown and Talith: In Commemoration of the Fiftieth Anniversary of the Founding of the Cambridge University Jewish Society* (London: Harvey Miller Publishers, 1989), 15–18, 21, 29. On Abrahams' experiences, see Norris McWhirter, "Abrahams, Harold Maurice," in *Dictionary of National Biography* (1971–1980), 2–3.

24. Loewe, "Cambridge Jewry," 29. On criticism of sports's prevalence at British public schools, see Leonard Woolf, *An Autobiography*, vol. 1 (New York: Oxford University Press, 1980), 55.

25. Rudolf Glanz, "Jews in Relation to the Cultural Milieu of the Germans in America Up to the Eighteen Eighties," in *Studies in Judaica Americana* (New York: KTAV Publishing House, 1970), 203–55, esp. 256–257. On the ideology and behavior of the liberal Turnerites in America, see Robert Knight Barnet, "Knights of Cause and Exercise: German Forty-Eighters and Turnvereine in the United States during the Antebellum Period," *Canadian Journal of History of Sport* 13, no. 2 (1982): 62–89.

26. Stanley Nadel, *Little Germany: Ethnicity, Religion, and Class in New York City, 1845–1880* (Urbana and Chicago: University of Illinois Press), 102–103; William M. Kramer and Norton B. Stern, "The Turnerverein: A German Experience for Western Jewry," *Western States Jewish History*, April 1984, 227–228.

27. Nadel, *Little Germany*, 102–103; Norton B. Stern and William M. Kramer, "The Major Role of Polish Jews in the Pioneer West," *Western States Jewish Historical Quarterly*, (July 1976) 333.

28. For a brief discussion of German Jewish immigrant disinterest in American sports, see Glanz, "Jews in Relation to the Cultural Milieu," 237. On the early growth of sports options in America circa 1850, see John Rickards Betts, "The Technological Revolution and the Rise of Sport, 1850–1900," *Mississippi Valley Historical Review* XL (September 1953): 231–233. See also on different ethnic groups' interests in different sports, Benjamin G. Rader, *American Sports: From the Age of Folk Games to the Age of Televised Sports* (Englewood, N.J.: Prentice Hall, 1996), 30–31, 64–69.

29. Irving Katz, *August Belmont: A Political Biography* (New York and London: Columbia University Press, 1968), 1–8.

30. Ibid., 2; Glanz, "The Rise of the Jewish Club in America," in *Studies in Judaica Americana*, 178–179, 183; Naomi W. Cohen, *Encounter with Emancipation: The German Jews in the United States, 1830–1914* (Philadelphia: Jewish Publication Society of America, 1984), 51.

31. Glanz, "The Rise," 180–183.

32. On the founding and mission of the YMHA, see Benjamin Rabinowitz, *The Young Men's Hebrew Associations (1854–1913)* (New York: National Jewish Welfare Board, 1948), 2–37, and *A Documentary Story of a Century of the Jewish Community Center, 1854–1954* (New York: Jewish Community Center Centennial Committee, 1954), 13. See also Cohen, *Encounter with Emancipation*, 53.

33. Rabinowitz, *The Young Men's Hebrew Associations*, 8–9, 13–14, 18, 51–52, 55, 60, 63.

34. Oscar S. Straus, *Under Four Administrations* (Boston: Houghton Mifflin, 1922), 32–33.

35. Rabinowitz, *The Young Men's Hebrew Associations*, 52.

36. The story of the 1877 split decision appeared in the short-lived *Association Review* (October 1877), as quoted by Rabinowitz, *The Young Men's Hebrew Associations*, 51. Unfortunately, this journal is no longer extant—Rabinowitz had it in 1948—making it impossible to know the cause of this decision. Interestingly enough, Y minutes for 1877 do not mention this decision although its board did decide on October 30, 1877, that "rooms will be opened . . . Saturdays from 10 a.m. to 10 p.m." On the 1878 decision noted in my text, see Board Minutes of the Y.M.H.A, June 3, 1878. My thanks to Steven Siegel, Y archivist, for these sources. On the "Jewish ministers'" views, see *Jewish Messenger*, November 18, 1888, quoted in David Kaufman, *Shul with a Pool: The "Synagogue-Center" in American Jewish History* (Hanover, N.H., and London: Brandeis University Press, 1999), 54.

37. Frank J. Adler, *Roots in a Moving Stream: The Centennial History of Congregation B'nai Jehudah of Kansas City, 1870–1970* (Kansas City: Congregation B'nai Jehudah, 1972), 84–85.

38. Ibid., 83; *American Hebrew*, November 9, 1888, 2.

39. Henry Berkowitz, *Intimate Glimpses of the Rabbi's Career* (Cincinnati: The Hebrew Union College Press, 1921), 70–71. See also Max E. Berkowitz, *The Beloved Rabbi: An Account of the Life and Works of Henry Berkowitz, D.D.* (New York: Macmillan, 1932), 8.

40. Kaufman, *Shul with a Pool*, 35–37. Moses J. Gries, "Conference Lecture," *Yearbook of the Central Conference of American Rabbis* [hereinafter *CCAR*] XI (1901): 147–148.

41. "Report of Gymnasium Committee," *The Temple Year Book* 1 (1902): 48–49, 70. See also Ruth Dancyger to Jeffrey S. Gurock, December 5, 2001, which contains excerpts from the synagogue minute books from 1902 related to the gymnasium issue.

42. See Kaufman, *Shul with a Pool*, 44, for a sense that rabbis still characterized gyms as "pagan." See also Leo M. Franklin, "Congregational Activities outside the Pulpit and Sabbath School," *CCAR* XII (1902): 210, 213.

43. *1900–1910: Congregation Beth El, Detroit, Mich.* (Detroit: Winn and Hammond, 1910), 44–45.

3. THE CHALLENGE AND OPPORTUNITY OF
A NEW WORLD OF AMERICAN SPORTS

1. For retrospective studies of the socialization and education of children in the shtetl, with emphases on idealizing the scholar, see Mark Zborowski and Elizabeth Herzog, *Life Is with People: The Culture of the Shtetl* (New York: Schocken Books, 1952), 74–77, 341–343, 353, 391, and Emanuel Gamoran, *Changing Conceptions in Jewish Education* (New York: Macmillan, 1924), 112–113. Diane K. Roskies and David G. Roskies, *The Shtetl Book* (New York: KTAV Publishing House, 1975), 150, 158, 211, and passim, notes that the games children played during their heder years were of the non-physical type, like tic-tac-toe, memorization games, "it" etc. They do however note, 150, that sometimes in a heder, youngsters "yelled or fought with each other," we imagine outside the purview of their teachers. For another vision of Jews as non-sportsmen in eastern Europe, see Chaim Bermant, *The Jews* (New York: New York Times Books, 1977), 180. See also Cary Goodman, "(Re)Creating Americans at the Educational Alliance," *Journal of Ethnic Studies*, (Winter 1979) 19–20.

2. For a discussion of truly unromanticized views of the heder experience, see Steven J. Zipperstein, *Imagining Russian Jewry: Memory, History, Identity* (Seattle and London: University of Washington Press, 1999), 42–45.

3. See Zborowski and Herzog, *Life Is with People*, 124–128. For Antin's comment, see her *The Promised Land* (Boston: Houghton Mifflin, 1908), 111, quoted in Sydney Stahl Weinberg, *The World of Our Mothers: The Lives of Immigrant Jewish Women* (New York: Schocken Books, 1988), 44.

4. David G. Roskies, *Against the Apocalypse: Responses to Catastrophe in Modern Jewish Culture* (Cambridge, Mass., and London: Harvard University Press, 1984), 141–149.

5. On Jewish defense efforts against pogroms in the early 1880s, see Jonathan Frankel, *Prophecy and Politics: Socialism, Nationalism, and the Russian Jews, 1862–1917* (Cambridge: Cambridge University Press), 54–55.

6. My reference to Jewish students returning to "their people" from periods of estrangement is derived from Frankel's conceptualization. See Frankel, *Prophecy and Politics*, 49–53.

7. Ibid., 155, 335–336.

8. "Sports in Poland," in *Nowa Encyklopedia Powszechna*, vol. 5 (Warsaw: PWN, 1998).

9. For an analysis of the transformation of Russian Jewish masses in the nineteenth century and their acquisition of industrial skills as well as an incipient labor consciousness, see Ezra Mendelsohn, *Class Struggle in the Pale: The Formative Years of the Jewish Workers' Movement in Tsarist Russia* (Cambridge: Cambridge University Press, 1970).

10. Frankel, *Prophecy and Politics*, 335–336.

11. On the periodization of the arrival of more activist Bundist types and Socialist

Zionists, see Will Herberg, "The Jewish Labor Movement in the United States," in *American Jewish Year Book* (1952), 695–696, and Gerald Sorin, *Tradition Transformed: The Jewish Experience in America* (Baltimore: Johns Hopkins University Press, 1997), 44. For a look at what transpired when Jewish "rioters" took to streets, particularly the evidence that most of the violence emanated not from the Jewish protestors but from the cops who broke up the protest, see Paula E. Hyman, "Immigrant Women and Consumer Protest: The New York City Kosher Meat Boycott of 1902," *American Jewish History*, (September 1980) 92–94. Hyman's article suggests that Jewish violence consisted of breaking windows, not breaking heads.

12. For the quotations on Roosevelt's attitudes toward sports, see the citation in Benjamin G. Rader, *American Sports: From the Age of Folk Games to the Age of Televised Sports* (Englewood Cliffs, N.J.: Prentice Hall, 1996), 100. For a sense of Jewish affection for Roosevelt, see "Roosevelt and I," *American Hebrew* [hereafter *AH*], January 17, 1919, 260.

13. Henry Smith Williams, "The Educational and Health Giving Value of Athletics," *Harper's Weekly*, February 16, 1895, 166. See also, for comments about Jewish lack of physicality by both friends and foes of immigrants, Hutchins Hapgood, *The Spirit of the Ghetto: Studies of the Jewish Quarter of New York* (New York: Funk and Wagnalls, 1902), 76; Madison Grant, *The Passing of the Great Race* (New York: Charles Scribner's Sons, 1916), 14; Edward A. Ross, *The Old World in the New: The Significance of Past and Present Immigration to the American People* (New York, 1914), 189–190, noted in Riess, "Sport, Race and Ethnicity in the American City, 1870–1950," in *Immigration and Ethnicity: American Society— "Melting Pot" or "Salad Bowl*, ed. Michael D'Innocenzo and Josef P. Sirefman (Westport, Conn.: Greenwood Press, 1992), 215, n.15; Charles S. Bernheimer, *Half a Century in Community Service* (New York: Association Press, 1948), 44.

14. Cary Goodman, *Choosing Sides: Playground and Street Life on the Lower East Side* (New York: Schocken Books, 1979), 38–39; Edmund J. James, ed., *The Immigrant Jew in America*, (New York: B. F. Buck and Co., 1907), 298, 316. See also Goodman, "(Re) Creating Americans," 19.

15. Goodman, *Choosing Sides*, 112; Williams, "The Educational and Health Giving Value of Athletics," 166; "Adjusting to the New World," in *Readings in Modern Jewish History*, ed. Eliezer L. Ehrmann (New York: KTAV Publishing House, 1977), 371.

16. Irving Howe, *The World of Our Fathers: The Journey of the East European Jews to America and the Life They Found and Made* (New York: Harcourt, Brace, Jovanovich, 1976), 182.

17. Stephan F. Brumberg, *Going to America Going to School: The Jewish Immigrant Public School Encounter in Turn-of-the-Century New York City* (New York: Praeger, 1986), 73–75; see also J. Thomas Jable, "The Public Schools Athletic League of New York City: Organized Athletics for City Schoolchildren, 1903–1914," reprinted in Steven Riess, *The American Sporting Experience: A Historical Anthology of Sport in America* (New York: Leisure Press, 1984), 234.

18. Roy Lubove, *The Progressives and the Slums: Tenement House Reform in New York City, 1890–1917* (Pittsburgh: University of Pittsburgh Press, 1962), 189; Robert A. Woods and Albert J. Kennedy, *The Settlement Horizon: A National Estimate* (New York: Russell Sage Foundation, 1922); *Philanthropy and Social Progress* (College Park, Md.: McGrath Publishing Company, 1893), 83; Irene Kaufmann Settlement *Neighbors* 1 (October 25, 1923): 4, "Good, Clean Sport,' Motto of C.H.I.," Philip L. Seman Collection, Scrapbook, I (1910–1916), Chicago Hebrew Institute, "News Letter #11," all quoted from Linda J. Borish, "The Place of Physical Culture and Sport for Women in Jewish Americanization Organizations" (unpublished conference paper, 2001); George Eisen, "Sport, Recreation and Gender: Jewish Immigrant Women

in Turn-of-the-Century America (1880–1920)," *Journal of Sport History* 18, no. 1 (Spring 1991): 112; Steven Riess, *City Games: The Evolution of American Urban Society and the Rise of Sports* (Urbana and Chicago: University of Illinois Press, 1989), 165.

19. For more comments on Jewish youngsters in informal play or swimming, see Bernard MacFadden quoted in Goodman, *Choosing Sides,* 20, and Eisen, "Sport, Recreation and Gender," 108; see also "The Jewish Athlete," *AH,* December 11, 1908, 171, for an account of the success of young Freedman and other Public School Athletic League Jewish athletes.

20. *AH,* January 1, 1915, 249.

21. *AH,* June 23, 1916, 206.

22. *AH,* June 6, 1919, 96.

23. Howe, *The World of Our Fathers,* 182; "Adjusting to the New World," 371; Riess, "Tough Jews: The Jewish American Boxing Experience," in *Sports and the American Jew,* ed. Steven A. Riess (Syracuse, N.Y.: Syracuse University Press, 1998), 67–68, 77.

24. Sid Gerchik, interview, February 24, 2003 [rough cut of "The First Basket"].

25. Sol "Butch" Schwartz, interview, February 24, 2003 [rough cut of "The First Basket"].

26. Abraham Cahan, "The New Writers of the Ghetto," *The Bookman* 39 (August 1914): 633. This source is an account by Cahan of an untitled Yiddish story written by Aaron Weitzman.

27. Peter Levine, *Ellis Island to Ebbets Field: Sport and the American Jewish Experience* (New York: Oxford University Press, 1992), 36.

28. For references to problems fathers had with sons, see the observations of Arthur H. Gleason in "Religion for the Jew" that appeared in *Harper's Weekly,* reprinted in *AH,* January 29, 1915, 340. For comments on so-called "half-baked" youngsters and their parents, see Isaac B. Berkson, *Theories of Americanization: A Critical Study with Special Reference to the Jewish Group* (New York: Columbia University Teachers College, 1920), 185–186. See also, on youthful disinterest in synagogue life, "The Weakness of the Synagogue," *AH,* January 8, 1915, 276.

29. For a translation of this piece from its original Yiddish, see *Hebrew Standard* [hereafter *HS*], August 14, 1914, 12–13.

30. Julius H. Greenstone, "The Talmud Torah in America: A Problem of Adjustment," *The Jewish Teacher,* January 1916, 30.

31. There is, to be sure, a massive literature on the evolution of the modern talmud torah in the early twentieth century, with specific reference to New York. The works range from the contemporaneous survey volume by Alexander M. Dushkin, *Jewish Education in New York City* (New York: Bureau of Jewish Education, 1918), to Arthur A. Goren's *New York Jews and the Quest for Community: The Kehillah Experiment, 1908–1922* (New York: Columbia University Press, 1970), to Jeffrey S. Gurock, *When Harlem Was Jewish, 1870–1930* (New York: Columbia University Press, 1979). All of these reference the complex role such new elite leaders like Fischel and Hyman played in the backing of these educational initiatives. For specific references to the need for play and health facilities in these schools, see Dushkin, *Jewish Education in New York City,* 214–215 and passim; "Modern Orthodoxy," *AH,* April 7, 1916, 630; "Dedication of the Central Jewish Institute," *AH,* May 26, 1916, 78–9.

32. On the history and facilities offered at these several model institutions, see *AH,* November 3, 1911, 9; March 8, 1912, 574; March 22, 1911, 609; *HS,* March 5, 1909, 4; *AH,* September 9, 1913, 570; March 5, 1915, 469.

33. Truth be told, these new elite leaders of the eastern European community — especially the hard-driving Fischel — had plenty of problems with their fellow immigrants over other aspects of their educational modernization plans. See Gurock, *When Harlem Was Jewish,* 107–109.

34. On the mission of the Seminary during Solomon Schechter's era, see Jack

Wertheimer, ed., *Tradition Renewed: A History of the Jewish Theological Seminary of America*, 2 vols. (New York: Jewish Theological Seminary of America, 1997), especially articles by Mel Scult, "Schechter's Seminary," vol. 1, 43–102 and David Weinberg, "JTS and the 'Downtown' Jews of New York at the Turn of the Century," vol. 2, 1–52.

35. For the legendary Schechter-Finkelstein "sports" remark, see "A Trumpet for All Israel," *Time*, October 15, 1951, 54; Rabbi Ezra Finkelstein, e-mail to and from the author, June 17, 2002.

36. "A Trumpet for All Israel," 54, and Finkelstein, e-mail.

37. Herbert S. Goldstein, "The Younger Orthodox Rabbis in America," *HS*, June 18, 1915, 1–2.

38. Ibid., 2.

39. Aaron I. Reichel, *The Maverick Rabbi: Rabbi Herbert S. Goldstein and the Institutional Synagogue—"A New Organizational Form"* (Norfolk and Virginia Beach, Va.: Donning, 1984), 31, 274.

40. Goldstein, "The Younger Orthodox Rabbis in America," 2.

41. "The New Y.M.H.A. Building," *AH*, June 5, 1900, 65–8.

42. For Goldstein's remark, see "The Institutional Synagogue," *HS*, September 15, 1916, 2; for praise of the Y, see "Editorial Notes," *AH*, November 9, 1900, 1095.

43. For a discussion of, and statistics on, YMHA activities, see David Kaufman, *Shul with a Pool: The "Synagogue-Center" in American Jewish History* (Hanover, N.H., and London: Brandeis University Press, 1999), 70–72; on the Y's mission, see "Y.M.H.A. Meeting," *AH*, January 26, 1917, 382; For Goldstein's staunch upbraiding of the Ys, see "What Ails American Judaism," *Jewish Forum* (hereafter *JF*), June 1918, 278–279.

44. Goldstein, "Institutional Synagogue," 2.

45. On the founding of the Central Jewish Institute, the role Goldstein played there, and some sense of its range of activities, see "Dedication of the Central Jewish Institute," *AH*, May 26, 1916, 78; Reichel, *The Maverick Rabbi*, 64–68; and Joseph Epstein, "The Early History of the Central Jewish Institute: The Emergence of a Jewish Community School Center" (M.A. thesis, Bernard Revel Graduate School, Yeshiva University, 1978).

46. "The Institutional Synagogue," *AH*, January 18, 1918, 322. For a fuller discussion of this synagogue innovation, see Gurock, *When Harlem Was Jewish*, 122–130.

47. "Ideal Jewish Manhood," *AH*, January 8, 1915.

48. On the founding and activities of the Brooklyn Jewish Center, see Deborah Dash Moore, "A Synagogue Center Grows in Brooklyn," in *The American Synagogue: A Sanctuary Transformed*, ed. Jack Wertheimer (Cambridge: Cambridge University Press, 1987), 297–326.

49. Israel Herbert Levinthal, "The Value of the Center to the Synagogue," *United Synagogue Recorder* [hereafter *USR*], June 1926, 19. See also Levinthal, *Steering or Drifting—Which: Sermons and Discourses* (New York: Funk and Wagnalls, 1928), 11–12, and idem, *A New World Is Born: Sermons and Addresses* (New York: Funk and Wagnalls, 1943), 213–214.

50. *The Jewish Center Bulletin*, April 20, 1923, 4.

51. On the Brooklyn-Levinthal crowd's ready acknowledgment of a relationship to Kaplan and his Manhattan-based model, see Kaufman, *Shul with a Pool*, 249. On Goldstein's sometimes tumultuous relationship with his erstwhile professor, see Reichel, *The Maverick Rabbi*, 45, 48–52, and passim. On Kaplan's negative attitudes toward Goldstein, see Jeffrey S. Gurock and Jacob J. Schacter, *A Modern Heretic and a Traditional Community: Mordecai M. Kaplan, Orthodoxy and American Judaism* (New York: Columbia University Press, 1997), 99.

52. On Kaplan's involvement with Kehilath Jeshurun, where Fischel was his congregant, see Gurock and Schacter, *A Modern Heretic*, 51–54. See also Gurock, *When*

Harlem Was Jewish, 103–104, 124–129, for a discussion of Kaplan's involvement with the UTT and the CJI.

53. See Gurock and Schacter, *A Modern Heretic,* 25, for an account of Kaplan's sports interests.

54. For Kaplan's public and private views on the Y and the need for a Jewish Center alternative, see Moshe Davis, "Jewish Religious Life and Institutions in America (A Historical Study)," in *The Jews: Their History, Culture and Religion,* ed. Louis Finkelstein, vol. 1 (New York: Harper, 1949), 331; Mordecai M. Kaplan, "At the Crossing of the Roads," *Yiddishes Tageblatt,* July 19, 1915, 8, and July 21, 1915, 8; Minutes of "Sabbath Afternoon Group, April 8, 1916," found in the Kaplan Archive, Reconstructionist Rabbinical College. For more on Kaplan's activities at the Y during these years, see Mel Scult, *Judaism Faces the Twentieth Century: A Biography of Mordecai M. Kaplan* (Detroit: Wayne State University Press, 1993), 131–135.

55. See Gurock and Schacter, *A Modern Heretic,* 91–92, for a discussion of how witnessing kids playing ball in the streets on the Sabbath motivated Kaplan and his supporters to move forward with their Jewish Center plans.

56. On the Kaplan version of the "seven day a week synagogue" metaphor and the sources from the Jewish Center newsletter, see Schacter, "A Rich Man's Club'? The Founding of the Jewish Center," in *Hazon Nahum: Studies in Jewish Law, Thought and History Presented to Dr. Norman Lamm on the Occasion of His Seventieth Birthday,* ed. Yaakov Elman and Jeffrey S. Gurock (New York: Michael Scharf Publications Trust of Yeshiva University Press, 1997), 693, 716.

57. On the efforts and the rhetoric of United Synagogue congregations to create their own "happy combinations," see, for example, *USR,* July 1921, 4; October 1921, 8; October 1922, 11–12; January 1923, 4; October 1923, 23; June/July 1924, 28; April 1925, 19; April 1926, 19, 27; April 1927, 24.

58. On sports in early Young Israel plans and activities, see *HS,* September 30, 1916, 6; *USR,* April 23, 1923, 24.

59. Louise Schneider, "The Boy Who Didn't Want to Go to Temple," *USR,* October 1922, 16.

60. On Kehilath Israel's building plans for a "community center" that did not include sports facilities, see *USR,* October 1922, 11; January 1925, 30; October 1925, 25. On Louis Finkelstein's views on other synagogues' building sports facilities, see Finkelstein, e-mail.

61. On complaints about the "secularization" of the synagogue, see *USR,* April 1928, 2; on opposition within the CJI, see Berkson, *Theories of Americanization,* 188; on Fischel's problems with opponents of modernization, see Gurock, *When Harlem Was Jewish,* 107–109.

62. Solomon Schechter, "Lovingkindness and Truth," in *Seminary Addresses and other Papers* (Cincinnati: Ark Publishing Co, 1915), 251–252.

63. Quote from the *American Israelite* that appeared in *HS,* May 28, 1915, 3.

64. "To Re-unite the Synagogue and Jewish Life," *USR,* April 1928, 2.

65. For evidence that athletic facilities were part of B'nai Jeshurun's life, see *USR,* April 1922, 15. For Israel Goldstein's comments, see "Inadequacies in the Status of the Synagogue To-day," *Proceedings of the Twenty-Eighth Annual Conference of the Rabbinical Assembly of the Jewish Theological Seminary of America* (1928), 33–34, and "The Menace of Secularism in the Synagogue," *Proceedings of the Twenty-Ninth Annual Conference of the Rabbinical Assembly of the Jewish Theological Seminary of America* (1929), 94–95.

66. Joel Blau, "Lapses of Taste," *AH,* January 7, 1916, 249. For similar sentiments, see J. H. Hadad, "Letters to the Editor," *AH,* February 19, 1915, 422.

67. Blau's remarks and Levinthal's response that appeared in the [Brooklyn] *Jewish Center Annual* (1925) are quoted from Leon Spitz, "The Synagogue Center

Marches On: The History of the Synagogue Center Movement in the United States," *Brooklyn Jewish Center Jubilee Book,* April 1946, 61. For Freedman's remarks, see his "Observations on the American Rabbinate," *Proceedings of the Twenty-Eighth Annual,* 136.

68. M. A. Stavitsky, "The Functions of the Y.M.H.A.," *AH,* April 6, 1917, 23.

69. Norman Salit, "Young Folks' Activities," *USR,* July 1921, 16.

70. Harry Weiss, "The Synagogue Center," *Problems of the Jewish Ministry* (New York: New York Board of Rabbis, 1927), 131–133.

71. Samuel M. Cohen, "The Synagogue Center," in *Problems,* 110, 113–114. For a biographical sketch of Cohen, who was a traveling executive for the United Synagogue, see Pamela S. Nadell, *Conservative Judaism: A Biographical Dictionary and Sourcebook* (Westport, Conn.: Greenwood Press, 1988), 61–62.

72. Alter F. Landesman, "Synagogue Attendance (A Statistical Survey)," *Proceedings of the Twenty-Eighth Annual,* 49; Abraham J. Levy, "The Status of the Synagogue in Jewish Life," ibid., 32.

73. Philip David Bookstaber, "The Place and Function of the Temple Center in Congregational Life," *Yearbook of the Central Conference of American Rabbis* [hereafter *CCAR*] (1925), 280–283; *Proceedings of the Thirty-Sixth Annual Convention of the Central Conference of American Rabbis, October 20th–23rd, 1925* (typescript transcript of remarks), 183.

74. S. D. Schwartz, "The Place and Function of the Temple Center," *CCAR,* 291–292.

75. There is a lack of clarity in the source as to the identity of Rabbi Schwartz. The typescript transcript of the discussion at the CCAR convention quotes a Rabbi Schwartz's remarks, but offers no first name. The listing of conference members in the printed report of the convention notes two rabbis with the surname "Schwartz," Samuel of Chicago and William of Alabama. Moreover, the printed report does not list a "Rabbi Schwartz" as one of the speakers in that discussion. On the mysterious Rabbi Schwartz, see *CCAR,* 124, 150, 395, 399; *Proceedings of the Thirty-Sixth Annual,* 193–194; see also Louis M. Gross, "Comment," in *Problems,* 138–139.

76. Marc Lee Raphael, *Abba Hillel Silver: A Profile in American Judaism* (New York: Holmes and Meier, 1989), 52–53. See also Kaufman, *Shul with a Pool,* 277.

77. Raphael, *Abba Hillel Silver,* 53.

78. Horace J. Wolf, "The Rabbi and the Community," *AH,* April 10, 1914, 686–687.

79. Raphael, *Abba Hillel Silver,* 53, and Ruth Dancyger to the author, December 5, 2001.

4. THE TRAINING OF "ALL-AMERICAN" YESHIVA BOYS

1. On the early history of Etz Chaim and its curriculum, see Jeffrey S. Gurock, *The Men and Women of Yeshiva: Higher Education, Orthodoxy and American Judaism* (New York: Columbia University Press, 1988), 14–17.

2. Ibid., 18–19.

3. On the Kaplan family's experiences with Etz Chaim, see Jeffrey S. Gurock and Jacob J. Schacter, *A Modern Heretic and a Traditional Community: Mordecai M. Kaplan, Orthodoxy and American Judaism* (New York: Columbia University Press, 1997), 13–14. On the amount of time allocated to general education, including physical education as opposed to religious study in Etz Chaim and its sister schools the Rabbi Jacob Joseph Yeshiva, Yeshiva of Harlem, and Yeshiva Chaim Berlin that came into existence after 1900, see Alexander Dushkin, *Jewish Education in New York City* (New York: Bureau of Jewish Education, 1918), 326–328.

4. For the noted quotation and a sense of student attitudes toward being Americanized rabbis, see Gurock, *The Men and Women of Yeshiva*, 28–29.

5. For a discussion of the student strikes and Harry Fischel's backing of student ideals, see ibid., 32–33.

6. Ibid., 52–54. See also Seth Taylor, *Between Tradition and Modernity: A History of the Marsha Stern Talmudical Academy* (New York: Yeshiva University High School, 1991), 9–10 and passim.

7. For a supporter's views of Revel's plans, see Isaac Rosengarten, "Order Out of Chaos in Jewish Education," *Jewish Forum* [hereafter *JF*], November 1920, 520.

8. The Academy's first principal, Solomon Hurwitz, died in 1919, after only three years in his position. Safir served from 1919 to 1963. On Safir's goals for the school and its students, see Shelley R. Safir, "Our Next Step," *The Elchanite*, June 1925, 13–14. On the qualifications of M. Schoenbrun, see "Annual Report of the Board of Trustees of Talmudical Academy for the School Year Ending July 31, 1919 to the University of the State of New York" (Norman Abrams Collection, Yeshiva University Archives). For a report on the faculty-student ballgame, see *The Annual Elchanite* (1923), 86. On Safir's interest in tennis, see *The Commentator*, March 18, 1935, 4.

9. For the remark about "physique," see *The Elchanite* (1925), 40. For the comment on an "athletic stronghold" at the yeshiva, see *The Elchanite Jr.* (January 1926), 9. See Berman's and Grilihas's brief biographical sketches in *The Elchanite* (1923), 15, 17.

10. For student reports that Yager was playing college basketball, see *The Elchanite* (1926), 54. For the schedule, results, and highlights of the CCNY Main Branch team in the 1925–1926 season, see *The 1926 Bulletin* (New York: CCNY Evening School, 1926), 48, 81–82.

11. Undated taped reminiscences of Louis J. Yager in the possession of Mary Yager Jaffe; phone conversation with the author, July 23, 2002.

12. Undated taped reminiscences of Rabbi Ascher M. Yager in the possession of Mary Yager Jaffe, April 20, 1997.

13. For Louis J. Yager's yearbook biography, see *The Elchanite* (1925), 26. For information on his life after CCNY, see Louis Yager tape.

14. See Louis Yager tape. See also undated letter of Mary Yager Jaffe to the author (July 2002).

15. See *The Elchanite Jr.* (January 1925), 43, for students' pride in their scholastic and athletic balances. For Safir's report on athletic facilities, see his "[Report to] The University of the State of New York, The State Department of Education, Albany" (May 1921) (Norman Abrams Collection).

16. *The Elchanite* (1928), 88.

17. See Bernard Revel, "Jewish Education," *JF* (March 1926), 10–11. For more on Revel's views of "harmonization" or "synthesis" as a goal of education at his modern yeshiva, see Gurock, *The Men and Women of Yeshiva*, 90–91 and passim.

18. On the Berlin-Polachek relationship, see Meir Bar Ilan Berlin, *M'Volozhin ad Yerushalayim*, vol. I, New Edition (Tel Aviv: Foundation for the Publication of the Writings of Rabbi Mayer Bar Ilan, 1971). On Polachek's experiences at Revel's institution, see Aaron Rothkoff, *Bernard Revel: Builder of American Jewish Orthodoxy* (Philadelphia: Jewish Publication Society, 1972), 65–73.

19. See R. P. Mankin in *Shaarei Tziyon* (Tammuz-Elul, 5694 [1934]) quoted in Aaron Ahrend, "Physical Culture in Rabbinical Literature in Modern Times," *Korot: The Israel Journal of the History of Science and Medicine* 15 (2001): 63.

20. See above, chapter 2, for a discussion of Nordau's statement and its impact upon the evolution of Zionist sports clubs in Germany and Great Britain.

21. Zvi Yaron, *The Philosophy of Rabbi Kook* (Jerusalem: Department for Torah

Education and Culture in the Diaspora of the World Zionist Organization, 1991), 104–107.

22. For a discussion of ideological and political opposition to Rabbi Kook's views on sports, see Ahrend, "Physical Culture," 73–77. See Gurock, *The Men and Women of Yeshiva*, 67–81, for the history of the integration of a Mizrachi-initiated Teachers Institute within Revel's American yeshiva community.

23. On the problems Orthodox students of the 1920s had in balancing religious values and college educational polices, see Gurock, *The Men and Women of Yeshiva*, 85–88.

24. See *The Yeshiva College: What It Is and What It Stands For—A Challenge and a Promise to American Jewry* [1927?] (pamphlet on file at the Yeshiva University Archives) for discussions and artist's rendering of the proposed eight-building campus. See also Gurock, *The Men and Women of Yeshiva*, 82–89, on the founding of Yeshiva College.

25. Yeshiva College was established in 1928 and was housed in temporary quarters until the opening of the campus in 1929. For information on courses offered in physical education at the college and where the courses were given, see *Yeshiva College Catalogue* (1928–1929), 9, 31; (1933–1934), 36.

26. *The Elchanite* (1938), 82.

27. Basketball, then generally the most popular sport played by Jews in America, was, likewise, the flagship sport at the Talmudical Academy and Yeshiva College. Periodically, baseball teams were organized. And at times there was talk on campus of establishing swimming and tennis teams. Of course, those teams would have to meet away from Washington Heights; Yeshiva had no pool or tennis facility. See, on these "minor" sports, *The Elchanite*, June 1938, 82; *The Commentator*, April 8, 1935, 3.

28. For college basketball schedules, results, and the highlights noted, see *Masmid* (1931), 35; (1933), 64; (1934), 62; (1938), 66–67; and *The Commentator*, March 1, 1935, 3.

29. See *The Commentator*, December 19, 1935, 2, for editorial support for the importance of the basketball team. See Abe Novick, "On the Sidelines," *The Commentator*, April 7, 1937, 3. See also Jack Goldman, "On the Sidelines," *The Commentator*, September 24, 1938, 3.

30. See Rothkoff, *Bernard Revel*, 137, for the fanciful report about a yeshiva football team. See *The Commentator*, December 19, 1935, 2, for the *Advocate*'s quotation about sports at Yeshiva.

31. *The Commentator*, September 1, 1939, 4; January 4, 1939, 4.

32. On Yeshiva teams showing how their school was so similar to other colleges, see *The Commentator*, November 11, 1936, 3. On the founding of a Yeshiva cheering squad, see *Masmid* (1940), 64. On the alleged use of "ringers," see *The Commentator*, February 19, 1942, 5.

5. SHUL VS. POOL

1. See chapter 2, 39–40.

2. See chapter 3, 60, 65–66.

3. Samuel A. Goldsmith, "The YMHA and the Synagogue," *American Hebrew* [hereafter *AH*], September 7, 1917, 432.

4. Irving Lehman, "The Jewish Center and the Community," *The Jewish Center* [hereafter *JC*], October 1922, 7; see also Goldsmith, "The YMHA and the Synagogue," for the comment praising the JCC as "a great agency."

5. Oscar Leonard, "The Jewish Settlement," *AH*, June 4, 1915, 110.

6. For a presentation and analysis of these student surveys, see Nathan Goldberg,

"Religious and Social Attitudes of Jewish Youth in the U. S. A.," *Jewish Review* (1943), 146–149.

7. Nettie Pauline McGill, "Some Characteristics of Jewish Youth in New York City," *Jewish Social Service Quarterly*, (December 1937) 251–272. See also McGill and Ellen Nathalie Matthews, *The Youth of New York City* (New York: Macmillan, 1940), 241–242.

8. For a portrait of this form of three-day-a-year synagogue attendance in an overwhelmingly Jewish neighborhood, see Jeffrey S. Gurock, "Jewish Commitment and Continuity in Interwar Brooklyn," in *Jews of Brooklyn*, ed. Ilana Abramovitch and Sean Galvin (Hanover, N.H., and London: University Press of New England, 2001), 231–232.

9. For a discussion of the growth of school sports and their implications for American patriotism during the 1920s, see Elliott Gorn and Warren Goldstein, *A Brief History of American Sports* (New York: Hill and Wang, 1993), 177–182.

10. For discussions of how reporting and technology changed the nature of sports participation, see Peter R. Shergold, "The Growth of American Spectator Sport: A Technological Perspective," in *Sport in History: The Making of a Modern Sporting History*, ed. Richard Cashman and Michael McKernan (Queensland: University of Queensland Press, 1979), 31–34. See also Benjamin G. Rader, *American Sports: From the Age of Folk Games to the Age of Televised Sports* (Englewood Cliffs, N.J.: Prentice Hall, 1996), 117–118.

11. For documentation and discussion of what I am calling the Semitic pantheon of 1920s and 1930s Jewish sports heroes, see Steven A. Riess, ed., *Sports and the American Jew* (Syracuse, N.Y.: Syracuse University Press, 1998), 24, 36, 75, 77, 84. For the *Harper's* comment on college football constituting a national religion, see William J. Baker, *Sports in the Western World* (Totowa, N.J.: Rowman and Littlefield, 1982), 217.

12. For a rabbi's complaint during the 1930s that congregants would prefer sitting at home listening to the radio than attending services Friday night, see Louis M. Levitsky, "The Story of an Awakened Community," *The Reconstructionist*, February 7, 1936, 9. Levitsky did not specify what shows — sports or otherwise — were favored by delinquent congregants.

13. On Kraft's vision of the JCC movement's mission, see his *A Century of the Jewish Community Center (1854–1954)* (New York: Jewish Community Center Centennial Committee, 1954), 20–21, and Philip Goodman, comp., *A Documentary Story of a Century of the Jewish Community Center 1854–1954* (New York: Jewish Community Center Centennial Committee, 1953), 57. On the great growth of JCCs in the 1920s and 1930s, see *JC*, February 1923, 38, 47; June 1923, 52–53; June 1924, 2–20; March 1930, 40; March 1934, 30; December 1935, 29–30; September 1942, 6.

14. Tobias Roth, "Jewish and Religious Elements," *JC*, October 1922, 29; William Pinsker, "Physical Education in the Jewish Community Center," *JC*, June 1926, 48.

15. Jacob S. Golub, "The Curriculum of the Jewish School," *JC*, February 1923, 22–23; Mordecai Soltes, "A Program of Jewish Activities for Jewish Community Centers," *JC*, September 1925, 42–45.

16. Alter F. Landesman, "Jewish Activities in Community Centers," *JC*, September 1925, 48–50. See also idem, "The Technique of the Jewish Program of the Jewish Center," *JC*, June 1926, 27.

17. Abraham W. Rosenthal, "Physical Education in the Jewish Community Center," *JC*, June 1926, 44–45.

18. Aaron G. Robison, "Physical Education in the Jewish Community Center (Discussion)," *JC*, June 1926, 48–49.

19. Samuel Leff, "Health and Physical Education in Jewish Community Centers," *JC*, September 1930, 14, 18.

20. Bernard Sarachek, interview with the author, February 23, 2003; Sid Gerchik and Herman Romash, interviews with the author, February 24, 2003.

21. Harry Lebau, "Self Expression the Major Function of the 'Y,'" *JC*. June 1929, 54–55.

22. Frank S. Lloyd, "The Place of Physical Education in the Jewish Center Program," *JC*, December 1931, 6–10.

23. Louis I. Newman, "The Organization of American Jewry," *Yearbook of the Central Conference of American Rabbis* [hereafter *CCAR*] (1936), 242; Simon Greenberg, "President's Message," *Proceedings of the Rabbinical Assembly of the Jewish Theological Seminary of America* (1939), 33; B. Benedict Glazer, "Spirit of American Jewish Community," *CCAR* (1940), 320; Nachman Arnoff, "The Rabbi and the Jewish Center," *Proceedings of the Rabbinical Assembly of the Jewish Theological Seminary of America* (1940), 136.

24. Armand E. Cohen, "The Rabbi and the Jewish Center," *Proceedings of the Rabbinical Assembly of the Jewish Theological Seminary of America* (1940), 127–129.

25. Ibid., 128. See also Ludwig Lewisohn, "Centers and Ys," *The Institutional*, January 7, 1938, 2.

26. Harry L. Glucksman, "The Synagogue Center," *Proceedings of the Rabbinical Assembly of the Jewish Theological Seminary of America* (1930–1932), 273. On the subject of Jewish Welfare Board unhappiness with Synagogue Centers "that are ready to accept all the services we are in the position to render them, but are very uncooperative," see Minutes of Staff Meeting, Jewish Center Division, December 15, 1943 (National Jewish Welfare Board Archives, Library of the American Jewish Historical Society [hereafter NJWB]), 1–2.

27. Philip R. Goldstein, *Centers in My Life: A Personal Profile of the Jewish Center Movement* (New York: Bloch Publishing Co., 1964), 87. See also "The Relations of the Synagogue to National Jewish Organizations," *Proceedings of the Rabbinical Assembly of the Jewish Theological Seminary of America* (1945), 100.

28. Jacob B. Agus to Rabbi Goldstein, November 1, 1944, Center Movement Committee files (Synagogue Council of America Archives, Library of the American Jewish Historical Society [hereafter SCA]).

29. For an example of a call for committee membership, see Rabbi Ahron Opher to Rabbi Moses J. Abels, November 7, 1944, Jewish Center Movement files [SCA]; Robert Gordis, "Annual Report of the President, July 1, 1944–July 1, 1945," *Proceedings of the Rabbinical Assembly of the Jewish Theological Seminary of America* (1945), 38–39, and "The Relations of the Synagogue to National Jewish Organizations," 98.

30. For an internal evaluation of what went wrong with the initial Joint Consultative Committee, see the minutes of "Conference on Center Movement—February 4th, 1948, Sharon Hotel" [SCA]; see also Rabbi Abraham Simon, "Report on Synagogue-Center Relations," *Proceedings of the Rabbinical Assembly of the Jewish Theological Seminary of America* (1947), 315.

31. "Our Expansion Program-A Revaluation," *Proceedings of the Rabbinical Assembly of the Jewish Theological Seminary of America* (1946), 208.

32. "On the Furtherance of the Synagogue-Center Movement," *Proceedings of the Rabbinical Assembly of the Jewish Theological Seminary of America* (1947), 349.

33. Simon, "Report on Synagogue-Center Relations," 318–319.

34. Oscar I. Janowsky, *The JWB Survey* (New York: Dial Press, 1948), 259–261, 263–265, 319–331.

35. Ibid., 274–275.

36. Ibid., 7, 33.

37. Israel M. Goldman, "Presidential Message," *Proceedings of the Rabbinical Assembly of the Jewish Theological Seminary of America* (1948), 89–90; Hyman R. Rabinowitz, "The Future of the American Jewish Community," ibid., 216–217; David Aronson,

"The Demands of the New Diaspora," *Proceedings of the Rabbinical Assembly of the Jewish Theological Seminary of America* (1949), 134.

38. On the origins and rationale for this survey, see Rabbi Ahron Opher to Colleague, November 3, 1947, and Rabbi Ahron Opher to Rabbi William F. Rosenblum, November 18, 1947. See also a compilation of the questionnaire results submitted to the "Synagogue Council Conference on Center Movement, February 4, 1948." See also the manuscript responses to the questionnaire. All of these documents are part of the Center Movement Committee [SCA] files.

39. Kraft, *A Century of the Jewish Community Center*, 40–41; Mrs. Leonard H. Bernheim et al., Sponsors of an Independent Study of the NJWB Survey Commission Report to "Friend," May 1, 1948, 1 [NJWB].

40. "Report of the NACJW Committee on the Janowsky Survey, Presented at the National Executive Committee Meeting, April 9, 1948," 2 [NJWB].

41. "Address of Professor Oscar I. Janowsky in Response to the Report of the 'Independent Group' Presented by Professor Louis Wirth Delivered at the meeting of the Jewish Center Division Committee, Saturday evening, April 17, 1948" [NJWB].

42. Rabbi Ahron Opher to Frank Weil, April 25, 1948. See also "Resolution on the Synagogue and the Center Movement adopted by the Executive Committee of the Synagogue Council of America, May 5, 1948" [SCA].

6. THE MISSION OF AMERICAN JEWRY'S TEAM

1. On the general nature of suburban living, see Herbert J. Gans, *The Levittowners: Ways of Life and Politics in a New Suburban Community* (New York: Pantheon Books, 1967), and Kenneth T. Jackson's *The Crabgrass Frontier: The Suburbanization of the United States* (New York: Oxford University Press, 1985). On the decline of social anti-Semitism in the immediate post–World War II period, see Nathan C. Belth, Harold Braverman, and Morton Puner, eds., *Barriers: Patterns of Discrimination against Jews* (New York: Friendly House, 1958), which charts the decline in such prejudice.

2. Herbert J. Gans, "Park Forest: Birth of a Jewish Community," *Commentary*, April 1951, 331.

3. On patterns of Jewish behavior in a community where Jews were generally accepted, see Benjamin B. Ringer, *The Edge of Friendliness: A Study of Jewish-Gentile Relations* (New York: Basic Books, 1967), 114–115, 213–215, and passim. See also on this subject Marshall Sklare and Mark Vosk, *The Riverton Study: How Jews Look at Themselves and Their Neighbors* (New York: American Jewish Committee, 1957), 28.

4. On the social significance of Jewish recreational choices in suburbia, see Ringer, *The Edge of Friendliness*, 107–114. On this pattern, see also Judith R. Kramer and Seymour Leventman, *Children of the Gilded Ghetto: Conflict Resolutions of Three Generations of American Jews* (New Haven, Conn., and London: Yale University Press, 1961), 64–65, 91, 188.

5. On Jewish youngsters' attitudes toward Gentiles in suburbia, especially their "discovery" of Protestants, see Simon Glustrom, "Some Aspects of a Suburban Jewish Community," *Conservative Judaism*, (Winter 1957) 28, and Nathan Glazer, *American Judaism* (Chicago and London: University of Chicago Press, 1957), 118–119.

6. Glustrom, "Some Aspects," 29; Gans, "Park Forest," 333. The palpable desire of most suburban parents to transmit a sense of Jewish identity to their children permeates the classic study of a Chicago suburb. See Marshall Sklare and Joseph Greenblum, *Jewish Identity on the Suburban Frontier: A Study of Group Survival in the Open Society* (New York: Basic Books, 1967).

7. For examples of suburban Jewish attitudes toward intermarriage and their

fears of this yet-unrealized problem, see Sklare and Greenblum, *Jewish Identity on the Suburban Frontier,* 306–313, 315–320, and passim. See also Glazer, *American Judaism,* chapter VII, for the characterization of this period as a Jewish revival.

8. Herbert Gersh, "The New Suburbanites of the 1950s," *Commentary,* March 1954, 220–221. Similar sentiments were expressed in a synagogue flyer that appears in Albert I. Gordon, *Jews in Suburbia* (Boston: Beacon Press, 1959). The flyer says that "the community needs a place for our children and we adults need some place to carry out our social lives." It is also noted in Jack Wertheimer, "The Conservative Synagogue," in *The American Synagogue: A Sanctuary Transformed* ed. Wertheiner (Cambridge: Cambridge University Press, 1987), 126.

9. For studies and comments on the multiple roles, functions, and demands imposed on the postwar suburban rabbi, see Jerome E. Carlin and Saul H. Mendlovits, "The American Rabbi: A Religious Specialist Responds to Loss of Authority," in *The Jews: Social Patterns of an American Group,* ed. Marshall Sklare (New York: The Free Press, 1958), 377–414, and Rabbi Albert I. Gordon, "The Problems and Promises of Suburban Life," *Proceedings of the Rabbinical Assembly of America* 24 (1960): 49–55.

10. For a description of a Conservative rabbi saying and doing what was necessary to attract a constituency and to build a large commodious institution, see Morris Freedman, "New Jewish Community in Formation: A Conservative Center Catering to Present-Day Needs," *Commentary,* January 1955, 43–45.

11. Rabbi J. Leonard Azneer, "Blueprinting Your Congregation of Tomorrow," *Proceedings of the 1952 Biennial Convention of the United Synagogue of America* (1952), 163.

12. Rabbi Hyman Chanover, "Discussion," *Proceedings of the Rabbinical Assembly of America* 13 (1949): 176–177.

13. On the founding and mission of Camp Ramah, see Shuly Rubin Schwartz, "Camp Ramah: The Early Years, 1947–1952," *Conservative Judaism,* Fall 1987, 12–25. See p. 23 for Cohen's remark about the importance of sports at the camp.

14. For Gerson Cohen's memoir of his error, see Gerson D. Cohen, "Introduction," in *The Ramah Experience: Community and Commitment,* ed. Sylvia C. Ettenberg and Geraldine Rosenfield (New York: The Jewish Theological Seminary in cooperation with The National Ramah Commission, 1989), 41. See also Riv-Ellen Prell, "Post-War American Jewish Youth and the Redemption of Judaism" (unpublished typescript article, 2003), 12, for more information on Ramah's Judaism and sports synthesis. I am grateful to Professor Prell for sharing sources with me.

15. On Davis's sports metaphor, see Michael Brown, "It's Off to Camp We Go: Ramah, LTF and the Seminary," in *Tradition Renewed: A History of the Jewish Theological Seminary,* ed. Jack Wertheimer, vol. I (New York: The Jewish Theological Seminary, 1997), 829–830.

16. Max L. Forman, "The Relationship of the Rabbi to the Men's Club," *The Torch,* Fall 1951, 20–22; Albert Kaufman, "A Men's Club Bowling League," *The Torch,* Fall 1950, 39–40.

17. For Rabbi Karp's remarks, see a discussion on Synagogue Center life in *Proceedings of the Rabbinical Assembly of America* (1955), 219. On synagogue attendance among Conservative lay leaders, see Dr. Emil Lehman, "The National Survey on Synagogue Leadership," *Proceedings of the 1953 Biennial Convention of the United Synagogue of America* (1953), 36–37.

18. On the phenomenon of "Debate Night," see Gans, *The Levittowners,* 73–76, which sets the scene for these activities within that town. It also notes parental concerns over Jewish education and their fears of intermarriage. See also Victor B. Geller, *Orthodoxy Awakens: The Belkin Era and Yeshiva University* (Jerusalem and New York: Urim Publication, 2003), 115–116, which describes such a meeting from an

Orthodox perspective. See also Jeffrey S. Gurock, *The Men and Women of Yeshiva: Higher Education, Orthodoxy and American Judaism* (New York: Columbia University Press, 1988), 146, which contains the reference to herring and spittoons.

19. Between 1948 and the mid-1950s, the leadership of Orthodox efforts to stem the tide of Conservatism went back and forth between Yeshiva University and the Union of Orthodox Jewish Congregations. Yeshiva's bureau spearheaded efforts from 1948 to 1950, The Union's Community Activities Department led the activities from 1950 until 1954. And from 1954 on, the work was under Yeshiva's Community Service Division. Still, the message articulated remained fundamentally the same since key operatives like Victor Geller and Irwin Gordon served both organizations. These men had close personal and family relations with the YUAA people. On these organizations and their messages, see Gurock, *The Men and Women of Yeshiva*, 147–148, and Geller, *Orthodoxy Awakens*, 101–104, 149–152, 192–194.

20. Bernard Weisberg, "As a Means to an End," *The Commentator,* January 2, 1944, 5.

21. Myron M. Fenster, "Athletics Promote Synthesis," *The Commentator,* September 9, 1946, 3.

22. Lewis N. Ginsburg, "Is Physical Ed. Possible Without a Gymnasium?" *The Commentator,* December 13, 1945, 4.

23. On the early history of students running the sports program and themselves engaging coaches, see Bernie Hoenig, "Yeshiva Sports Celebrates Silver Jubilee as Past History Culminates Bright Era," *The Commentator,* May 18, 1953, 14. See "Bernard Sarachek to Coach Revamped College Varsity," *The Commentator,* November 5, 1942, 3, for a report on his hiring. For examples of complaints about the sports facilities, see "Renovate the Gym!" *The Commentator,* May 23, 1946, 2, and Fenster, "Student Body Heartened by Gym Repairs," *The Commentator,* November 7, 1946, 2. For student criticism of the omission of sports from the college catalogue see "Rabbis in Training," *The Commentator,* December 19, 1935, 3, and "Time Marches On," *The Commentator,* April 16, 1951, 2.

24. On Belkin's educational background, see Gurock, *The Men and Women of Yeshiva,* 137. For a student's sense that Belkin and his administration were unaware of the importance sports played in their lives, see Fenster, "Student Body," 2. For Belkin's plan to expand Yeshiva's purview, see Gurock, *The Men and Women of Yeshiva,* 142–162.

25. For background information on Avrech, see "Abraham Avrech" (Biographical Record Form, September 1, 1948, Yeshiva University Department of Public Relations).

26. See Samuel Hartstein, interview with the author, August 2, 2000, on his role in influencing Belkin. See also the myriad of 1950s press releases and brochures on sports from the public relations files of Yeshiva University. On the role and functions the YUAA played in its early years, see "YUAA Plans for the Coming Year Disclosed by Rabbi Abraham Avrech," *The Commentator,* September 30, 1948, 3, and Sheldon Rudoff, "Progress and Plans of YUAA Lauded; New Ideas Presented," *The Commentator,* September 27, 1951, 3. On the history of the recruitment of additional coaches for Yeshiva's teams, see the retrospective article by Josh Muss, "The Professors," *The Commentator,* September 20, 1960, 12.

27. Julie Landwirth, "Sound Mind—Sound Body: Everybody Preaches it, Who Believes It?" *The Commentator,* May 10, 1956, 3, for an account of Lookstein's Kookian message.

28. See Sheldon Rudoff, "Shabbos and Basketball Invade Williamsport, Pennsylvania" (Yeshiva University press release, February 1952), and Seymour Essrog, "They Can Pray and Play" (Yeshiva University press release, November 19, 1954), for examples of YUAA "invasions" of Jewish communities. See also "A Win Despite the Loss," *The Commentator,* February 11, 1952, 2; Aaron Freiman, "Dual Purpose of Road

Trip," *The Commentator,* December 15, 1954, 5; and Wally Fingerer, "Invitational Tournament," *The Commentator,* December 11, 1954, 10, for student newspaper accounts of the YUAA on the road.

29. Seymour Essrog, "On the Sidelines," *The Commentator,* March 16, 1953, 3.

30. For an analysis of the commonality of non-observance among Orthodox, Conservative, and Reform Jews in postwar suburbia and for statements of lament about this situation by spokesmen for Orthodoxy, see Jeffrey S. Gurock, *From Fluidity to Rigidity: The Religious Worlds of Conservative and Orthodox Jews in Twentieth Century America,* David W. Belin Lecture on American Jewish Affairs (Ann Arbor: Jean and Samuel Frankel Center for Judaic Studies, University of Michigan, 1998), 12–14. For an on-the-scene report from the 1960s, see Gershon Jacobson, "Inside Jewish Suburbia, U.S.A.," *Jewish Forum,* December 1961, 32.

31. For background on Sarachek as a player and as a coach, and his attitude toward sports at Yeshiva, see "Sports-Minded Youth Leaders Is Recipe for Yeshiva University Athletic Director" (Yeshiva University press release, November 15, 1954).

32. Marvin Hershkowitz, interview with the author, August 1, 2000.

33. On Sarachek's attitude toward Hershkowitz, see Seymour Essrog, "Student Attitudes, Hershko's Last game," *The Commentator,* March 25, 1953, 3. See Hershkowitz interview; see also Aaron Freiman, "Dual Purpose," 5, for Hershkowitz's combining with Avrech in outreach work.

34. For more on Sarachek's attitudes toward the importance of sports at Yeshiva, see *The Commentator,* March 25, 1954, 3; May 25, 1955, 5; October 19, 1956, 3; October 24, 1960, 5. See Hartstein, interview.

35. See "Dr. Belkin Discloses New Admissions Plan," *The Commentator,* February 8, 1956, 1, for the announcement of the founding of the Jewish Studies Program. For statistics on the record of Yeshiva's basketball team and the composition of the squad during those glory years, see the annual basketball brochures produced by the university's Public Relations Office for the years 1953–1954 through 1959–1960.

36. On opposition to the founding of JSP, see Joseph Walter Eichenbaum, ed., *James Striar School of General Jewish Studies Bar-Mitzvah Journal* (New York: Yeshiva University, 1969), 9.

37. See Isaac Gottlieb, "Unmitigated Villain Corners Rabbi Besdin," *Hamevaser* (Sivan, 5724 [1964]), for a reminiscence of how the first students were considered by some to be "non-Jews." See also Gurock, *The Men and Women of Yeshiva,* 177–178, on the behavior of JSP ballplayers and campus attitudes.

38. Artie Eidelman, "What Price Glory?" *The Commentator,* March 24, 1958, 4.

39. Artie Eidelman, "Reciprocal Trade," *The Commentator,* March 19, 1959, 4. The historical record is of several views on how supportive Rabbi Morris Besdin, the JSP director, was of the ballplayers. Hershkowitz, who studied with Besdin in the days before the JSP was a formal program, perceived him as extraordinarily supportive. Some early JSP men viewed him similarly, as one who "stuck out his neck on our behalf." Sarachek, on the other hand, has recalled a more ambivalent director, who loved the boys who were admitted and punctuated his affection by attending some games. At the same time, there were tensions between the two men when Besdin, who openly subscribed to the notion that "only those who are committed shall be admitted," took in "some boys . . . while others were kept out because they did not have (in the rabbi's eyes) the right background or were not ready for Yeshiva." It has also been suggested that when Besdin was more restrictive, his approach had a chilling effect both on the numbers of students from public school who applied to the school as well as on the morale of those already on campus. See Hershkowitz, interview, and Gurock, *The Men and Women of Yeshiva,* 177.

40. On the educational background and religious orientation of JSP students as the program matured, see Gurock, *The Men and Women of Yeshiva,* 179–185.

41. On the problems the basketball program faced, see Jonathan J. Halpert, interview with the author, August 21, 2000; see also "Cumulative Basketball Statistics Survey," *The Commentator,* April 4, 1963, 11, and *Yeshiva College Basketball '88–'89* (Yeshiva University basketball program, 1988–89) for statistics on Sarachek's record during the 1960s.

42. Norman Lamm, "Letter to the Editor," *The Commentator,* November 7, 1946, 5; see also, for examples of the issue of the primacy of Torah study raised by students at Yeshiva, Charles Weinstein, "A Gym Grows in Brooklyn," *The Commentator,* March 16, 1944, 5; Sol Blumenthal, "On the Sidelines," *The Commentator,* June 5, 1947, 7; and Seymour Essrog, "On the Sidelines," *The Commentator,* March 2, 1953, 5.

43. For Neil Koslowe's views, see "How to Succeed in Public Relations — by Trying," *The Commentator,* October 21, 1964, 6; "This Will Be the Year That Will Be," *The Commentator,* November 5, 1964, 8; "Yeshiva College and the Student Athlete," *The Commentator,* November 15, 1964, 8; "The Homecoming Weekend Affair — Whither a Yeshiva Generation," *The Commentator,* December 10, 1964, 8.

44. Chaim Brovender, "Should Yeshiva Condescend to the Level of the Ivy League Colleges?" *Hamevaser* (Shevat, 5725 [1965]), 7; Richard Hochstein, "Letter to the Editor," *The Commentator,* December 31, 1964, 9.

45. For the debate over the social implications of the proposed weekend, including the allegation of libertine behavior and women at Yeshiva socials, see David Ebner, "Letter to the Editor," *The Commentator,* November 19, 1964, 2; Joseph Isaiah Berlin, "Letter to the Editor," *The Commentator,* December 31, 1964, 7, 8; Stern College Students, "Letter to the Editor," *The Commentator,* December 31, 1964, 2; Anonymous, "Letter to the Editor," *The Commentator,* February 18, 1965, 6. This debate continued until the end of the academic year; see "Should Yeshiva Sponsor Social Events? The YU Students Voice Their Opinions," *The Commentator,* May 5, 1964, 4.

46. Koslowe, "The Homecoming," *The Commentator,* 8. For an attack on Sarachek, see Ephraim Hecht, "Letter to the Editor," *The Commentator,* December 31, 1964, 2, 8.

47. For a defense of Sarachek, see Moses M. Berlin, "Letter to the Editor," *The Commentator,* April 8, 1965, 2.

48. Victor Geller, "Letter to the Editor, *The Commentator,* February 18, 1965, 6. For more on the history of the synagogue and this crucial turning point in its history, see Adam Dickter, "Present at the Creation," *The Jewish Week,* May 17, 2002, 20; Bernard Sarachek, interview with the author, February 24, 2003.

49. See Jeffrey S. Gurock, "Bernard Sarachek, Yeshiva 'Role Model,'" *Yeshiva Review,* Spring 1995, 36–37, for a discussion of Sarachek's career and reputation in sports circles outside of Yeshiva.

50. Halpert, interview.

51. Shai Barnea, "Op-Ed: Student Apathy," *The Commentator,* February 22, 2001, 30.

52. Lamm, "Letter to the Editor," 5.

7. AN IRRESISTIBLE FORCE

1. For the best introduction to the history and outlook at Mendlowitz's and the other separatist schools of the period between the First and Second World Wars, see William B. Helmreich, *The World of the Yeshiva: An Intimate Portrait of Orthodox Jewry* (New York: Free Press, 1982), 26–51. For discussions of Mendlowitz's agenda by his followers, see, for example, Yonoson Rosenblum, *Reb Shraga Feivel: The Life and Times*

of Rabbi Shraga Feivel Mendlowitz the Architect of Torah in America (New York: Mesorah Publications, 2001), 78, 90.

2. Rosenblum, *Reb Shraga Feivel,* 95, 125.

3. In addition to Helmreich, see Noah Nardi, "The Growth of Jewish Day Schools in America," *Jewish Education,* (November 1948) 24. See also Meir Kimmel, "The History of Yeshivat Rabbi Chaim Berlin," [Hebrew] *Sheviley Hahinuch,* (Fall 1948) 51–54.

4. In addition to Helmreich's scholarly introduction to the history of MTJ, see the hagiographic Rabbi Shimon Finkelman with Rabbi Nosson Scherman, *Reb Moshe: The Life and Ideals of HaGaon Rabbi Moshe Feinstein* (New York: Mesorah Publications, 1986), 54–74.

5. For a brief biography of Rabbi Shkop, see Aaron Rothkoff, *Bernard Revel: Builder of American Jewish Orthodoxy* (Philadelphia: Jewish Publication Society, 1972), 119. Rothkoff notes that Shkop was in America from 1928–1929 and lectured for a few months at RIETS. On the report on the eastern European rabbi's visit to TVD, see D. B. Schwartz, *Artzot HaHayim* (Brooklyn, 5752 [1992]), 16b, noted in Aaron Ahrend, "Physical Culture in Rabbinical Literature in Modern Times," *Korot: The Israel Journal of the History of Medicine and Science* 15 (2001): 61.

6. See Alexander S. Gross and Joseph Kaminetsky, "Shraga Feivel Mendlowitz," in *Men of the Spirit,* ed. Leo Jung (New York: Kymson Publishing Co., 1964), 553–561.

7. For student and administration recollections of Mendlowitz's attitude toward physical fitness and recreation, see Dr. Norman Lamm, interview with the author, August 31, 2000; David Kranzler, interview with the author, September 7, 2000; Roy Chavkin, interview with the author, September 8, 2000; Moshe Mendlowitz, interview with the author, September 8, 2000; Rabbi Nesanel Quinn, interview with the author, September 11, 2000; Rabbi Hyman Fulman, interview with the author, September 12, 2000. See Rabbi Yaakov Pollak, interview with the author, August 31, 2000; the latter recalled being part of the 1930s gymnastic troupe. See also George Kranzler, *Williamsburg: A Jewish Community in Transition* (New York: Philip Feldheim, 1961), 150, which makes reference to acrobatics as part of the culture of the old-line yeshiva.

8. Jack Tomer, interview with the author, September 15, 2000. See also Kranzler, *Williamsburg,* 148–149, on faculty joining in at informal sports events.

9. Rosenblum, *Reb Shraga Feivel,* 170.

10. On the availability of facilities for recreation at YCB and MTJ, see Abraham Sodden, interview with the author, September 5, 2000, Rabbi Sheldon Steinmetz, interview with the author, September 6, 2000, and Rabbi Daniel Mehlman, interview with the author, August 3, 2000. On Rabbi Moses Feinstein's fundamentally positive attitudes toward physical fitness, see *Igrot Moshe, Even Ha-Ezer,* vol. 3, 61, 1 (New York: Balshon, 1973), 119–120; *Orach Chaim,* vol. 5, 40, 26 (New York: Balshon 1996), 69. On handball at MTJ, see Hanoch Teller, *Sunset: Stories of our Contemporary Torah Luminaries zt"l, and Their Spiritual Heroism* (New York: New York City Publishing Company, 1987), 55.

11. Teller, *Sunset,* 51.

12. Moshe Mendlowitz, interview with the author, September 19, 2000; Moshe Mendlowitz, conversations with Rabbi Samuel Mendlowitz and other "MTV alumni," reported to the author, September 19, 2000; Chavkin, interview; Rabbi Nesanel Quinn, interview. See below for further discussions of these attitudes.

13. For a perspective on dating and matchmaking within the yeshiva world of a somewhat later date, see Helmreich, *The World of the Yeshiva,* 159.

14. On early rabbinic views on the issue of female modesty while engaged in sports, see chapter 1 of this book.

15. For a report on the 1937 game and dance, see "Seminary Loses to Yeshivaites at Noar Affair," *The Commentator*, January 13, 1937, 2. For another example of a Yeshiva College game-dance activity, see "Varsity to Meet Alumni in Game: Joint Affair to Feature Dance as Well," *The Commentator*, January 5, 1938, 1.

16. Moshe Mendlowitz, Rabbi Hyman Fulman, and Jack Tomer, interviews with the author.

17. Moshe Mendlowitz and Rabbi Hyman Fulman, interviews. See also Kranzler, *Williamsburg*, 142, 144, which notes the presence of "out of town" youngsters who lived in the dormitory, although his generally laudatory account does not suggest they were behaviorally problematic.

18. Although there are no newspaper or other literary or scholarly accounts of this game, players in the game and some spectators remember such a now legendary activity and have dated it to either 1944 or 1945. Interviews with Moshe Mendlowitz, Rabbi Hyman Fulman, and Jack Tomer all suggest that the event took place. Were the heads of the schools aware and supportive of this particular "benefit" game? Although a comprehensive study of the Vaad Ha-Hatzala does not mention this game, it does point out the extraordinary effort men like Rabbi Mendlowitz made to raise money for the cause. Accordingly, it is plausible that had Rabbis Mendlowitz and Hutner been aware of the game, they would have supported this particular activity. See Efraim Zuroff, *The Response of Orthodox Jewry in the United States to the Holocaust: The Activities of the Vaad ha-Hatzala Rescue Committee, 1939–1945* (New York: Michael Scharf Publication Trust of Yeshiva University Press, 2000), 134.

19. For results of Talmudical Academy games versus TVD, see *Elchanite* (1944), 59; (1948), 61.

20. On the founding of the MJHSL and its mission, see an untitled Yeshiva University press release, November 11, 1952; Avrech and Hyman Wettstein, interviews with the author, August 29, 2000. Although there is a reference in the *Elchanite* (1946), 71, to a "recently founded Yeshiva League," the founding of the permanent MJHSL dates from the spring of 1951 when Yeshiva University sponsored "the first Jewish High School Invitational Basketball Tournament" involving TA, BTA, YCB, TVD, and RJJ. See "Basketball Tourney Molded by Yeshiva," *The Commentator*, April 16, 1951, 3. Some months later, 1951–1952, the league played a full schedule with Ramaz included. Flatbush and HILI (also known as Far Rockaway Yeshiva) entered in the 1952–1953 season, giving the league five all-boys schools and three coeducational schools. See *The Commentator*, March 6, 1952, 3, for league standings. In 1953, MTJ entered the MJHSL. See *The Commentator*, October 26, 1953, 3.

21. It is unclear precisely when boy-girl doubleheaders came into vogue. Certainly they were the case by the late 1950s. It is nonetheless possible that the inaugural Central-Ramaz games were "prelims" to boys' varsity games. What is certain is that as early as 1952 the Ramaz yearbook mentions a "tremendous crowd" that attended the Ramaz-Central game and commented that "it could have been [due] to the novelty of the game . . . ?" Evidently, Ramaz boy fans attended this game. See *Pioneer* (1952), 40–42. In all events, there was a yeshiva league for girl players as early as 1956 and Central cheerleaders at boys' games as early as 1951. Their presence and performances, as we will presently see, would become a *cause célébre*. See *Elchanette* (1952), 41; (1957), 51.

22. On Ramaz's mission and how it defined itself differently from other schools, as well as the religious culture that Rabbi Lookstein acknowledged and worked with, see Jeffrey S. Gurock, "The Ramaz Version of American Orthodoxy," in *Ramaz: School, Community, Scholarship and Orthodoxy*, ed. Jeffrey S. Gurock (Hoboken, N.J.: KTAV Publishing House, 1989), 40–42, 62–68. On the religious values harbored by Ramaz students, see Nathalie Friedman, "The Graduates of Ramaz: Fifty Years of Jewish Day School Education," in Gurock, *Ramaz*, 83–123.

23. Moshe Mendlowitz, conversation with Ronald Greenwald reported to the author, September 25, 2000.

24. For evidence of YCB's early involvement in the MJHSL, see *The Commentator,* March 6, 1952, 4. On Rabbi Hutner's expressed approbation for the team, see Sheldon Steinmetz, interview with the author, September 6, 2000. For more on Rabbi Hutner's reputation for being an all-knowing leader of YCB, see Helmreich, *The World of the Yeshiva,* 34–36. Additional recollections of experiences as YCB basketball players in the early 1950s are contained in interviews with Abraham Sodden, September 6, 2000, and Leonard Polinsky, September 12, 2000.

25. Interviews with Polinsky, Sodden, and Steinmetz all take note of the lack of appropriate sports facilities at YCB; Label Green, one-time coach of YCB, interview with the author, September 12, 2000. Recollections of how YCB officials related to his opting for a college education at Yeshiva University are noted in the interview with Sodden, November 29, 2000. On Sodden's and his friends' careers on Yeshiva University's basketball team, see *Yeshiva University: The Mites Basketball Prospectus* (1952–1953), (1953–1954), (1954–1955), and (1955–1956), Yeshiva University Public Relations Office.

26. Rabbi David Hartman, interview with the author, February 6, 2003. On Hartman's short career as a Yeshiva University basketball player, see *Masmid* (1950), 111.

27. On the history of cheerleading at MJHSL games in the 1950s, see Gurock, "The Ramaz Version," 80–81, n. 42. See also *Elchanette* (1953), n.p., and (1955), 82, 84–85.

28. Honey Seelenfreund Myers, interview with the author, January 22, 2003. See also *Elchanette* (1953), n.p., and (1955), 82, 84–85.

29. Myers, interview.

30. The dating for the YCB resignation from the MJHSL is derived from *The Elchanite* (1957), which lists that opponent's participating in the league for the last time. It is unclear precisely when and how the decision was made at the Brooklyn school to exit the league because of cheerleaders. Leonard Polinsky has contended that while he was a student — before the end of 1953 — "one of the rebbeim got wind of the fact that the game that we played against MTA and BTA, the Central girls cheering squad came to the game and they were prancing around and jumping around in short skirts and they banned us from the league." He recalls being in the *beis medrash* — that hotbed of debate — when he heard that the team had been banned. However, Daniel Mehlman, who played at YCB through 1954, recalls that the team was still in the league during his time with the "implicit proviso that there would be no cheerleaders at the games." From these sources, it may be suggested that the cheerleading issue was "in play" at YCB until a final decision was made in 1957 to exit the MJHSL; Daniel Mehlman, interview with the author, August 3, 2000.

31. On the early history of Rabbi Jacob Joseph School, see Alvin Irwin Schiff, *The Jewish Day School in America* (New York: Jewish Education Committee Press, 1966), 58–59; Helmreich, *The World of the Yeshiva,* 46.

32. Wettstein, interview.

33. For the articulated career hopes of that class, see *Rabbi Jacob Joseph School Scroll* (1962), passim.

34. Benjamin Mandel, interview with the author, August 3, 2000; Ira Steinmetz, interview with the author, August 3, 2000.

35. Retrospective student impressions that Rabbi Ginsberg was influential in this attempted change of attitudes are contained in interviews with Eli Feit, November 13, 2000, and with Barry Schwartz, November 16, 2000. In an interview with Rabbi Ginsberg, January 15, 2001, he asserted that he had the support of the roshei yeshiva. For an in-house appreciation of RJJ's successful attempt at linkage with Rabbi Kotler and his institution, see Marvin Schick, *RJJ Dinner Journal* (n.d., n.p). For

characterizations of MJHSL schools as "Hebrew Culture Schools," see "Raider Report," *RJJ Journal,* December 1963, 2.

36. "Raider Report." See also the cartoon entitled "We Shall Overcome," *RJJ Journal,* December 1963, 2.

37. The players also agreed to a provision that students on "probation" would be barred from participation in sports. It is unclear, however, whether probation was due to unsatisfactory academic or religious behavior.

38. "Raider Report."

39. Interviews with Feit and Schwartz speak of Rabbi Kurzrock's position as a sort of "ombudsman." For a reference to Kurzrock having played basketball for RJJ as a youth, see Noah David Gurock, "Yeshiva Sportsman," *The Jewish Press,* December 24, 1965, 26. Regrettably, Rabbi Kurzrock was unwilling to discuss with me his role in these important issues in a very brief phone conversation on November 17, 2000. For a report on Kurzrock's involvement, see "Raider Report."

40. On the repeat of canards against participation in the MJHSL, see Noah David Gurock, "Yeshiva Sportsman," 26. See also *The Tablet: Rabbi Jacob Joseph School Yearbook* (1966–1967), 44.

41. On MTJ's early involvement with the MJHSL, see *The Commentator,* October 26, 1953, 3, which notes the school's entrance into the league, and untitled Yeshiva University press release, April 3, 1954, which notes the Berezons' presence in the inaugural all-star game. See also Rabbi David Feinstein, interview with the author, November 14, 2000; Robert Berezon, interview with the author, November 14, 2000; and Gershon Berezon, interview with the author, November 14, 2000.

42. Rabbi Moshe Snow, interview with the author, November 27, 2000.

43. Rabbi Ginsberg and Benjamin R. Gampel, a former RJJ student-fan, interviews with the author, January 15, 2001.

44. *The Tablet: Rabbi Jacob Joseph School Yearbook* (1964–1965), 50.

45. Noah David Gurock, "Yeshiva Sportsman," 26.

46. Ibid.; Michael Rhein, interview with the author, January 15, 2001. Rhein is identified in the 1966–67 *Tablet* as G.O. President of RJJ and as a leader in the battle for the return of the school to the MJHSL.

47. Ibid.

48. Ibid.

49. Barry Schwartz, interview.

50. Interestingly enough, back in the 1950s, Chaim Berlin had a school yearbook. By the 1960s, that type of American-style school publication was no longer part of that yeshiva's life. See *The Shofar* (1952). I am indebted to Abraham Sodden for making his copy of that publication available to me.

51. Rhein, interview. On the decline of RJJ as a downtown-based institution and its move to Staten Island and Edison, New Jersey, see Schick, *RJJ Dinner Journal.*

52. Rabbi Elazar Teitz, interview with the author, March 13, 2003. Mrs. Chaya Newman, interview with the author, March 13, 2003. Regrettably, due to the absence of records from the league's Principals Council, which ran the league beginning in the late 1970s, it is impossible to determine precisely when these strictures were implemented. But as we will immediately see, we can logically date these changes from the late 1970s and 1980s through an analysis of responses to the edicts by coed schools like Ramaz and Flatbush. For the record, Mrs. Ruth Ritterband, formerly an administrator at Ramaz, has said that there was no "official rule," at least not while she was at the Yorkville school. She worked at Ramaz from 1977 to 1988. However, Richard Hagler, who began serving as league director in 1979–1980, has recalled that as early as the 1983–1984 season there was a dress code for female athletes. See Ruth Ritterband, e-mails to and from the author, February 6, 2003, and Hagler, interview with the author, March 20, 2003.

53. For an authorized biography of Rabbi Pinchas Teitz, which includes notes on the rabbi's interest in sports and use of sports metaphorically to promote Orthodoxy, see Rivkah Blau, *Learn Torah Love Torah Live Torah: Harav Mordecai Pinchas Teitz, the Quintessential Rabbi* (Hoboken, N.J.: KTAV Publishing House, 2001), 138–139, 232–233.

54. An examination of the Flatbush yearbook, *Summit,* from 1970–1980 revealed that until the academic year 1978–1979, cheerleaders in athletic garb were part of the school scene. Information on when and how that contingent was disbanded was derived from interviews with female "Rabble Rouser" leaders, Risa Levine and Debbie Reichman Auerbacher. See Levine, interview with the author, March 18, 2003 and Auerbacher, interview with the author, March 19, 2003. The "Rabble Rousers" actually date back to 1974. However, *Summit* (1979) states, 134, that Debbie Reichman "transformed an once forgotten club into a popular and explosive commission." For more on the "Rabble Rousers' " impact see *Summit* (1985), 142.

55. *Ramifications* (1987), 81; (1989), 90; (1991), 75; Tael Mc Lean, interview with the author, March 20, 2003; Ritterband, e-mail.

56. Ramaz's patterns of defiance and conformity to the league rules can be traced through notes in *Ramifications.* See, for example, *Ramifications* (1986), 103; (1987), 81; (1988), 87; (1989), 90; (1991), 75; (1992–1993), 134–135; Howard Stahl, interview with the author, March 18, 2003; Hagler, interview; and Ritterband, e-mail.

8. SAFE AT HOME: TENSION IN JUDAISM'S CLUBHOUSE

1. On the decline of anti-Semitism in the contemporary era, see Edward S. Shapiro's chapter "The Decline of Anti-Semitism," in his *A Time for Healing: American Jewry since World War II* (Baltimore and London: Johns Hopkins University Press, 1992), 28–59. See also his chapter "A Tale of Two Shapiros," which speaks of Harold Shapiro's election as president of Princeton and Irving Shapiro's selection as head of Du Pont. See also Nathan Perlmutter and Ruth Ann Perlmutter, *The Real Anti-Semitism in America* (New York: Arbor House, 1982), 75, for data on acceptance of Jews as neighbors.

2. For a perspective on those who would maximize the threat of anti-Semitism — beginning with Jewish defense officials — see Spencer Blakeslee, *The Death of Anti-Semitism* (Westport, Conn., and London: Praeger, 2000). This work also suggests that some polls that register high levels of Jewish concern over anti-Semitism often fail to reflect grass-roots Jewish thinking and optimism. The Perlmutters' book is also a good exemplar of the opinion that would maximize anti-Semitism.

3. On Sen. Lieberman's candidacy, his acceptance as a Jew in the popular mind, and the respect his Orthodoxy was accorded by most Americans, see, for example, Charles Krauthammer, "Demystifying Judaism," *Time,* August 21, 2000, 38; Richard Lacayo, "Walking the Walk," *Time,* August 21, 2000, 32–34; Temazas Bentriz and Michael Precker, "From Antipathy to Acceptance," *Dallas Morning News,* August 13, 2000, online edition; "Uncharted Waters," ABCNews.Com, August 8, 2000, online edition. On American attitudes toward Jews in the aftermath of September 11, 2001, see "Anti-Defamation League, National Survey, Completed October 31, 2001," ms. report prepared for the Anti-Defamation League of B'nai B'rith by Marttila Associates, Boston, Mass.

4. Samuel G. Freedman, *Jew vs. Jew: The Struggle for the Soul of American Jewry* (New York: Simon and Schuster, 2000), 347; Nathan Glazer, "New Perspective in American Jewish Sociology," in *Facing the Future: Essays on Contemporary Jewish Life,* ed. Steven Bayme (New York: KTAV Publishing House and the American Jewish Committee, 1989), 14, 16.

5. For some statistics on intermarriage patterns, see Charles S. Liebman, "The Quality of American Jewish Life: A Grim Outlook," in Bayme, *Facing the Future*, 52–53. See also Glazer, in ibid., 13.

6. The point of reference here is the vital, ongoing scholarly debate among historians and sociologists over whether American Jewry is assimilating or transforming itself. For good expositions of the alternative views, see Steven Cohen, "The Quality of American Jewish Life: Better or Worse," in Bayme, *Facing the Future*, 23–49. Cohen speaks articulately for the "transformation" view. See Liebman in ibid., 50–71 for the opposing view. See also Jack Wertheimer, *A People Divided: Judaism in Contemporary America* (Hanover, N.H., and London: Brandeis University Press, 1997), 44–94, for important discussions of both the "drift toward minimalism" and the examples of renewal within the Jewish community.

7. See Wertheimer, *A People Divided*, xii–xiii. See also Freedman, *Jew vs. Jew*, 284–337, for an extensive discussion of a battle between liberal and traditional Jews over a town zoning issue that would have benefited the Orthodox community.

8. For a good summary statement on the impact this highly resistant form of Orthodoxy has made upon the American Orthodox community, including the modern Orthodox component, see Freedman, *Jew vs. Jew*, 217–225.

9. Abraham Genauer, "Yankee Stadium's a Two-Hat Sort of Place," *Forward*, May 24, 2002, 19.

10. Michael Freund, "Seventh Inning Kvetch," *Jewish Sentinel*, August 16–22, 2002, 4.

11. Steve Lipman, "Batting 1.000 for Shabbat," *The Jewish Week*, August 30, 2002, 3.

12. On the progress of Salita's sports-Judaism synthesis, see Alona Wartofsky, "The Ring and a Prayer," *Washington Post*, September 1, 2002, F1ff; "Saturday the Fighter Slept, Fought Late," *New York Times*, November 17, 2002; Doug Fisher, "The Kid Can Fight," www.max.boxing.com, December 13, 2002; Steve Springer, "Faithful Fans," *Los Angeles Times*, February 1, 2003.

13. For examples of reports on Goodman's oral commitment to Maryland in early 1999, see Tara Finnegan and Jeff Seidel, "An Unorthodox Recruit: Talmudical Academy's Goodman Slated to Play Basketball for U-Md.," *Washington Post*, February 19, 1999, A1; Eli Groner, "He Won't Play on Shabbat," *Jerusalem Post, New York Edition*, February 5, 1999; Robert Goldberg, "Is This Shooting Guard the Jewish Jordan?" *Forward*, February 19, 1999, 20; "A Yeshiva Student Shoots His Way to the Big Time," *Jewish Exponent*, February 4, 1999.

14. On Katz's statements, see Barry Baum, "Jewish Jordan Wows Big Apple," *New York Post*, March 19, 1999; see also Groner, "He Won't Play on Shabbat."

15. See Groner, "He Won't Play on Shabbat."

16. Michael Bamberger, "An Unorthodox Player," *Sports Illustrated*, February 1, 1999, online edition.

17. For quotes on Goodman's sentiments, see Baum, "Jewish Jordan Wows Big Apple"; Groner, "He Won't Play on Shabbat"; and Goldberg, "Is This Shooting Guard the Jewish Jordan?"

18. Lenny Solomon, e-mail to the author, June 3, 2003. See the lyrics to the rap song at www.jewishrapper.com/secrets.html; on Goodman's nicknames, see "Disorganized Religion," www.frabrengen.com.

19. Steve Lipman, "Tamir Fills the House," *The Jewish Week*, February 28, 1999, 3; Peter Ephross, "Under Glare of Media Spotlight, Yeshiva Star Pursues Hoop Dream," *Hebrew Watchman* [Memphis, Tenn.], April 8, 1999. This Jewish Telegraphic Agency release appeared in at least ten Jewish newspapers nationwide between March 24 and May 5, 1999. See also Brad Berfus, "The Jewish Jordan," *The Jewish Press*, April 2, 1999, 13, which reported on the Silver award.

20. For Goldman's remarks, see Ephross, "Under Glare"; Rabbi David Rosen, "A Most Unusual Basketball Player," sermon delivered at Congregation Beth Yeshurun, February 19, 1999. www.bethyeshurun.com.

21. See Bamberger, "An Unorthodox Player."

22. Gary Rosenblatt, "Goodman Makes For a Full-Court Stress," *New Jersey Jewish News*, April 8, 1999, 17, 19.

23. Phil Jacobs, "Fade Away Jumper," *Baltimore Jewish Times*, April 23, 1999, 12–13.

24. Phil Jacobs, "Tamir Transfers," *Baltimore Jewish Times*, August 13, 1999, 12. See also Jacobs, "Fade Away Jumper," 12. For more on his transfer, see "The Main Adventist," *Jewish Week*, August 20, 1999, 3.

25. Ami Eden, "Could Yeshiva Hoops Star Become a Quaker," *Jewish Exponent*, September 16, 1999; "Jockbeat," *Village Voice*, August 18–25, 1999, online edition.

26. Chaim Katz, "What's Best for Tamir: A Comment by His Coach and Friend, Chaim Katz," *Baltimore Jewish Times*, August 13, 1999, 14. For the yeshiva's response, see Zvi Teichman, "Whose Flaws," ibid., August 27, 1999, 36.

27. Irwin Kramer, "Letter to the Editor," *Baltimore Jewish Times*, August 20, 1999, 33.

28. Ami Eden, "Why Root for a Yeshiva Hoopster," *Jewish Exponent*, September 30, 1999.

29. Jacobs, "Tamir Transfers."

30. Jennifer Jacobson, "Different Court, Same Game," www.jrnl.net/news/oo/Feb.

31. Phil Jacobs, "Goodman: No to Terps: Player Didn't Bend over Issue of Shabbat," *Baltimore Jewish Times*, September 17, 1999, 13.

32. Gabrielle Burman, "Tarnished Terps: Public Relations Professionals Talk about Image Fall Out from Tamir Goodman's Split with College Park," *Baltimore Jewish Times*, September 24, 1999, 24; Chaim Katz, "Tamir Hasn't Changed," ibid., 13; Mike DeCourcy, "Terps Dropped the Ball on Goodman Move," *The Sporting News*, September 21, 1999.

33. "Goodman Won't Play for Terps," *The Diamondback On Line*, September 13, 1999.

34. An attempt was made to contact Coach Williams in 2003 for his view of what transpired in the Goodman case. Unfortunately, he chose not to reply to inquiries. See the author's [unanswered] e-mail communication with Gary Williams, June 12, 2003.

35. Ira Berkow, "When Basketball is a Matter of Faith," *New York Times*, August 25, 2000, D4. For criticism of Williams, see not only the articles in the *Baltimore Jewish Times*, but also, for further examples, see Rob Miech, "College Ball Awaits: Can Jewish Jordan Live Up to Nickname," *CBS Sports Line*, June 27, 2000. For early questioning of Goodman's abilities as a ballplayer, see Michael J. Kruse, "Goodman Good Enough," *ACC Basketball Handbook*, August 20, 1999, online edition; Dayna Jackson, "Tamir Goodman, Hype Just Isn't Warranted," *The Diamondback Online*, September 20, 1999.

36. Jeff Zillgitt, "Maryland, Media to Blame for Goodman's Situation," *USA Today*, December 19, 2001, online edition.

37. On Goodman's selection of Towson State and the good reception he received there and in his league, see Phil Jacobs, "Tobacco Road to York Road: Tamir Goodman Makes a Verbal Commitment to Play Basketball Next Season for Towson State University," *Baltimore Jewish Times*, October 22, 1999, 13; Berkow, "When Basketball is a Matter of Faith," D4; Steve Lipman, "Tamir Mania," *The Jewish Week*, February 9, 2000, 28–29; Jay Wright, telephone interview with the author, June 9, 2003.

38. Rick Boyages, e-mail to and from the author, June 4, 2003.

39. "Goodman Alleges Towson Coach Assaulted Him," *New York Times*, December 11, 2001, F5.

40. Phil Jacobs, "I Wouldn't Break Down," *Baltimore Jewish Times*, December 12, 2001; "Towson Guard Urges No Charges," *New York Times*, December 12, 2001, S6; Edward Wong, "No Penalties for Towson Coach," *New York Times*, December 15, 2001, S5.

41. For criticism of Goodman's game, see Adam Shandler, "Unsolicited Commentary," www.hoopville.net. See also Dan Hauptman, "Goodman in Search of a Good Home," www.hoppville.net, and Zillgitt, "Maryland, Media to Blame."

42. Chris Ballard, "Unorthodox," *Sports Illustrated*, September 16, 2002, 28.

43. Hilary Leila Krieger, "Hoop Dreams," *Jerusalem Post Magazine*, May 9, 2003, 13–15; Hillel Kuttler, "A Talented 'Guard' in G-d's Army," *Inside*, Spring 2003, 60, 65.

44. Krieger, "Hoop Dreams," 13.

45. Freund, "Seventh Inning Kvetch," 4.

46. Rabbi Harold Kushner, e-mail to and from the author, June 1, 2003.

47. Stuart Weinblatt, "What Lieberman's Nomination Means," sermon delivered at Congregation B'nai Tzedek, September 30, 2000, www.bnaitzedek.org.

48. Weinblatt, "Soccer Parents, Soccer Goals, and What Really Counts," sermon delivered at Congregation B'nai Tzedek, September 28, 2001, ww.bnaitzedek.org.

49. Weinblatt, "What Lieberman's Nomination Means."

50. Rabbi Moshe Waldoks, e-mail to and from the author, January 27, 2003.

51. Rabbi Kerry Olitzky, e-mail to and from the author, January 24, 2003.

52. Rabbi Joshua Elkin, telephone interview with the author, June 18, 2003; Andrew Offit, telephone interview with the author, June 20, 2003.

53. Ronnie Becher and Mary Pilossoph, telephone interviews with the author, June 16, 2003.

54. Julie Azoulay, telephone interview with the author, June 17, 2003.

55. On the pre-1950s history of the JCCs, see chapter 5 of this book. On the 1963 rejection of the SCA demands, see "Resolution Adopted 1963 Biennial Convention, United Synagogue of America" (November 1963) and "Discussion on Section on Sabbath Opening of Jewish Community Centers," *Yearbook of the Central Conference of American Rabbis* [hereafter *CCAR*] (1964), 25.

56. "Discussion on Section on Sabbath Opening of Jewish Community Centers," *CCAR* (1964), 25–31. See Rabbi Philip Hiat, interview with the author, January 31, 2003.

57. For statistics on JCC patterns with regard to Sabbath and holiday closing and opening, see www.fghjcca.org/ShabbatHoliday/results, results current as of July 22, 2002. Allan Mann, senior vice president of the Jewish Centers Association, interview with the author, February 20, 2003. I am grateful to Mr. Mann for making these statistics available for this study.

58. For reports and statements that illustrate the evolution of the mission of today's JCCs in the area of Jewish education and continuity, see, for example, *Maximizing Jewish Educational Effectiveness of Jewish Community Centers* (New York: National Jewish Welfare Board, September 1984), 1–6 and passim, and *COMJEE II: Task Force on Reinforcing the Effectiveness of Jewish Education in JCCs* (New York: JCC Association, 1995).

59. For a description of the mission and the range of Jewish activities at a typical JCC Maccabiah venue in 2003, see www.palisadesmaccabi.org/overview.

60. Although the national office of the Jewish Centers Association does not dictate local policies — that is probably the movement's most hallowed tradition — it does

publish a useful pamphlet for affiliates that lays out the issues involved in Sabbath openings and closing. See *Shabbat and Holiday Opening: A Discussion Guide for JCCs* (New York: JCC Association, n.d.)

61. On this Newton episode, see "JCC to Offer Programs on Shabbat," *The Jewish Advocate*, December 13–19, 2002, 1, 35. See also letters to the editor appearing in *The Jewish Advocate* in the December 27–January 2, 2003 edition, 16, and the January 3–9 edition, 17.

62. It is noteworthy that editor Gary Rosenblatt used the sports term "Who Is a Point Guard," in both his 1997 and 2001 editorials on this issue. See his "Hoop Schemes," *The Jewish Week*, December 12, 1997, 7, and "Net Worth," *The Jewish Week*, February 23, 2001, 6. See also Ruth Ritterband, e-mail to the author February 6, 2003, and Rabbi Elazar Teitz, interview with the author, March 13, 2002.

63. Meryl Wiener, telephone interview with the author, July 25, 2003.

64. "Catch March Madness Too," *The Jewish Week*, March 28, 1997, 14.

65. Rosenblatt, "Hoop Schemes," See also Wiener, telephone interview.

66. Gary Rosenblatt, "Orthodox Game Plan," *The Jewish Week*, February 23, 2001, 10. There is a disagreement in the sources as to whether in fact the league actually left the Board of Jewish Education and if so, when did that happen. *The Jewish Week*, noted above, suggests that the split took place as of 1997, arguably at the time the first word was heard about the UJA threat, although it also notes that "even the principals themselves were confused as to whether their Principals Council was formally affiliated with the BJE the last several years." Meanwhile, BJE officials then said that the board had not had an official relationship with the league for four years, while the principals said that "in practice, the links had been maintained." Rabbi Haskel Lookstein's letter to the Ramaz parent body of February 8, 2001, speaks of the split and the UJA-Federation pressure that engendered its taking place at that latter point. Richard Hagler, the league's commissioner, asserts that "the split never officially took place but was on the table and discussed by the principals at that point." See Richard Hagler, interview with the author, June 25, 2003. In all events, the threat or the reality of the split in the context of the denial of the Conservative schools' applications sparked that intense round of intra-Orthodox debate that we are following.

67. Isaac Blachor, "Letter to the Editor," *The Jewish Week*, March 9, 2001, 6. See also Rabbi Haskel Lookstein to "[Ramaz] Parents," February 8, 2001.

68. Josh Liebman and Jonathan Kotler, "Letter to the Editor," *The Jewish Week*, March 9, 2001, 6.

69. For reports on these types of views, see Rosenblatt, "Orthodox Game Plan," 11, and Mark Srulowitz, "Conservative School Excluded from Athletic League," *The Commentator*, February 22, 2001, 18, 52.

70. Yehuda Kraut, "Maintain Schechter but Equal," *The Commentator*, April 3, 2001, 5.

71. Rosenblatt, "Orthodox Game Plan"; Srulowitz, "Conservative School Excluded from Athletic League," 52; Yehuda Shmidman, "Intrafaith Dialogue," *The Commentator*, February 22, 2001, 4.

72. "Unity in Play," *The Jewish Week*, May 18, 2001, 3. The suggestion that the restrictionists' accommodation was due in part to pressure from outside of Orthodox forces was related to me by a source who wishes to remain anonymous. In this context, it is relevant to note that the original Rosenblatt article that played a role in sparking the debate did suggest that some of the schools that objected to the Schechter inclusion did have constituents who were "Schechter parents" and that these schools sought funding from "non-Orthodox families." See Rosenblatt, "Orthodox Game Plan," 10. For the BJE's statements on Orthodox rabbis approving Schechter

admission, see Eden, "Yeshiva Sports League Opens Door to Conservatives — with Conditions," *Forward,* May 25, 2001, online edition.

73. For this range of Conservative opinions, see Eden, "Yeshiva League." See also Beth Ostrow, "To the Editor," *The Jewish Week,* January 2, 1998.

74. Aryeh Davidson, telephone interview with the author, July 24, 2003; Michael Greenbaum, telephone interview with the author, July 18, 2003; and Wiener, telephone interview.

75. Moses Feinstein, *Igrot Moshe: Yoreh De'ah,* vol. 4 (Jerusalem: Moriyah, 1996), 168–169.

76. William B. Helmreich, *The World of the Yeshiva: An Intimate Portrait of Orthodox Jewry* (New York: Free Press, 1982), 64, 161–162, 172–173, 185.

77. For information on the phenomenon of "Torah Trading Cards," see, for example, a 1987 AP news item that appears in "SubGenius Digest #212," www.subgenius.com. See also "Torah Link Collecting Cards," www.toratots.com/cards, and "When Beard Length Makes a Difference (You're on a Torah Trading Card)," *Spirituality and Health,* Fall 2000, online edition.

78. Susan K. Schulman, M.D., and Robert H. Schulman, M.D., "A Plea for Exercise in Yeshiva Programs," *The Jewish Observer,* May 1991, 21–24.

79. Rochel Shapiro, "Questions Formal Exercise Programs in Yeshivos," *The Jewish Observer,* October 1991, 36.

80. http://groups.yahoo.com/group/ChozrimWomen/message 6341, April 25, 2003. For an example of one such workout tape, see "Jewish Aerobics/Instructions by Ella Adler/Neshomo Orchestra."

81. Richard Hagler, interview with the author, March 27, 2003.

82. Rochelle Brand, telephone interview with the author, July 2, 2003.

83. Chaya Newman, interview with the author, March 13, 2003.

INDEX

Numbers in *italics* refer to illustrations

Scholar-athlete

JEFFREY S. GUROCK,

Libby M. Klaperman Professor of Jewish History at Yeshiva University, is author or editor of thirteen books, including *A Modern Heretic and a Traditional Community: Mordecai M. Kaplan* and *Orthodoxy and American Judaism,* which received the Saul Viener Prize from the American Jewish Historical Society for the best book written in that field. Gurock has also served for the past quarter-century as assistant men's basketball coach at Yeshiva and has run the New York City Marathon twelve times.